BEYOND HOME OWNERSHIP

In the context of ongoing transformations in housing markets and socio-economic conditions, this book focuses on past, current and future roles of home ownership in social policies and welfare practices. It considers owner-occupied housing in terms of diverse meanings and manifestations, but in particular the part played by housing tenure in the political, socio-economic and demographic changes that have characterised the pre- and post-crisis era.

The intensified promotion of home ownership in recent decades helped stimulate an increasing orientation towards the private consumption of housing, not only as a home, but also as an asset – or possibly speculative vehicle – that enhances household economic capacity and can be transferred to children or other family, or even exchanged for other goods. The latest global financial crisis, however, has made it clear that owner-occupied housing markets and mortgage sectors have become deeply embedded in networks of socio-economic interdependency and risk.

This collection engages with numerous debates on housing and society in a range of developed societies from North America to Asia-Pacific to North, South, East and West Europe. Interdisciplinary contributors draw upon diverse empirical data to explore how housing and home ownership has become so embedded in polity, economy and household welfare conditions in various social and cultural contexts. Another concern is what lies beyond home ownership, considering that the integration of housing systems with economic growth and social stability appears to be unravelling. This volume speaks to public debates concerning the future of housing markets, policy and tenure, providing deep and provocative insights for academics, students and professionals alike.

Richard Ronald is Assistant Professor in Urban Studies at the University of Amsterdam and a Visiting Scholar in the Department of Housing and Interior Design at Kyung Hee University, Seoul. He is Review Editor of the *International Journal of Housing Policy* and Section Editor of the *International Encyclopedia of Housing and Home*. He has published widely on housing, urban and social change in Europe and Asia-Pacific, and in particular on international market and policy transformations concerning home ownership.

Marja Elsinga is Professor in the Faculty of Technology, Policy and Management at Delft University of Technology in the Netherlands. She is associate editor-in-chief of the *International Encyclopedia of Housing and Home* and editor-in-chief of the *Dutch Journal for Housing*. She has published widely on home ownership and risk, housing affordability, social housing and housing governance.

Housing and Society Series

Edited by Ray Forrest, School for Policy Studies, University of Bristol

This series aims to situate housing within its wider social, political and economic context at both national and international level. In doing so it will draw on the full range of social science disciplines and on mainstream debate on the nature of contemporary social change. The books are intended to appeal to an international academic audience as well as to practitioners and policymakers – to be theoretically informed and policy relevant.

Beyond Home Ownership
Edited by Richard Ronald and Marja Elsinga

Housing Disadvantaged People?
Jane Ball

Women and Housing
Edited by Patricia Kennett and Chan Kam Wah

Affluence, Mobility and Second Home Ownership
Chris Paris

Housing, Markets and Policy
Peter Malpass and Rob Rowlands

Housing and Health in Europe
Edited by David Ormandy

The Hidden Millions
Graham Tipple and Suzanne Speak

Housing, Care and Inheritance
Misa Izuhara

Housing and Social Transition in Japan
Edited by Yosuke Hirayama and Richard Ronald

Housing Transformations
Shaping the space of twenty-first century living
Bridget Franklin

Housing and Social Policy
Contemporary themes and critical perspectives
Edited by Peter Somerville with Nigel Sprigings

Housing and Social Change
East–West perspectives
Edited by Ray Forrest and James Lee

Urban Poverty, Housing and Social Change in China
Ya Ping Wang

Gentrification in a Global Context
Edited by Rowland Atkinson and Gary Bridge

BEYOND HOME OWNERSHIP

Housing, welfare and society

*Edited by Richard Ronald
and Marja Elsinga*

Routledge
Taylor & Francis Group

LONDON AND NEW YORK

First published 2012
by Routledge
2 Park Square, Milton Park, Abingdon, Oxon OX14 4RN

Simultaneously published in the USA and Canada
by Routledge
711 Third Avenue, New York, NY 10017

Routledge is an imprint of the Taylor & Francis Group, an informa business

British Library Cataloguing in Publication Data
A catalogue record for this book is available from the British Library

Library of Congress Cataloging in Publication Data
Beyond home ownership: housing, welfare and society/edited by Richard Ronald and Marja Elsinga.
p. cm.—(Housing and society series)
Includes bibliographical references and index.
1. Home ownership—Social aspects. 2. Housing—Social aspects. 3. Housing policy. I. Ronald, Richard. II. Elsinga, Marja.
HD7287.8.B49 2012
363.5—dc22
2011014982

ISBN: 978-0-415-58555-2 (hbk)
ISBN: 978-0-415-58556-9 (pbk)
ISBN: 978-0-203-18226-0 (ebk)

Typeset in Bembo
by Prepress Projects Ltd, Perth, UK

MIX
Paper from
responsible sources
FSC
www.fsc.org   FSC® C004839

Printed and bound in Great Britain by
TJ International Ltd, Padstow, Cornwall

CONTENTS

FIGURES

TABLES

CONTRIBUTORS

Rachel G. Bratt is Professor of Urban and Environmental Policy and Planning, Tufts University, where she has served as department chair for nearly ten years. Her research is focused primarily on housing problems facing low-income households and the role of non-profit organisations in supplying decent, affordable housing. She has written dozens of articles, and is the author or co-editor of three books: *Rebuilding a Low-Income Housing Policy* (Temple University Press, 1989), *Critical Perspectives on Housing* (Temple University Press, 1986) and *A Right to Housing: Foundation for a New Social Agenda* (Temple University Press, 2006). Rachel worked as a professional planner in the City of Worcester, Massachusetts and has served on a number of local, state and national boards and committees, including the Consumer Advisory Council of the Federal Reserve Bank. She received her PhD from MIT in Urban and Regional Studies.

John Doling is Professor of Housing Studies at the University of Birmingham. He has researched and published widely in a number of related fields, principally housing markets and housing policy, but also population change and welfare systems. The focus of attention has been on Britain and other advanced industrialised countries in Europe, North America and the Asia-Pacific region. He has undertaken research funded by a variety of organisations including the UK government, research councils and foundations. He has been coordinator of four projects under the EU's framework programmes, the most recent being DEMHOW (Demographic Change and Housing Wealth), which had 12 partners drawn from across the range of the member states. He is joint leader of the European Network for Housing Research working group on Home Ownership and Globalisation.

Marja Elsinga is Professor in Housing Institutions and Governance at the OTB Research Institute for the Built Environment at Delft University of Technology. She also teaches in the Faculty of Technology, Policy and Management. In addition she is the editor-in-chief of the Dutch housing policy periodical *Tijdschrift voor de Volkshuisvesting* and associate editor-in-chief of the *International Encyclopedia of Housing and Home*. Marja has published numerous journal articles on housing issues in Europe and has co-edited several books on owner-occupied housing. These include *Home Ownership: Getting In, Getting From, Getting Out* (IOS Press, Parts 1, 2 and 3; 2005, 2006, 2010 respectively) and, most recently, *Home Ownership: Beyond Asset and Security* (Delft University Press, 2007). She has also consulted on housing policy for the Dutch and Flemish governments as well as for the EU Commission.

Yosuke Hirayama is Professor of Housing and Urban Studies at the Graduate School of Human Development and Environment, Kobe University. He specialises in housing and urban change, home ownership and social inequalities, as well as comparative housing policy. His work has appeared in numerous Japanese and international academic journals and he is co-editor of *Housing and Social Transition in Japan* (with Richard Ronald, Routledge, 2007). He has received academic prizes from the City Planning Institute of Japan, the Architectural Institute of Japan and the Tokyo Institute of Municipal Research. He is also a founding member of the Asia-Pacific Network for Housing Research.

Srna Mandic is Associate Professor at the Faculty for Social Sciences at the University of Ljubljana in Slovenia, where she lectures on the sociology of social problems. She also heads the Centre for Welfare Studies. Her research interests include housing, quality of life and welfare provision and she is currently leading a project on quality of life and demographic change. She has participated in EU projects ENIQ and DEMHOW and was a principal researcher in a number of studies, including the 1996 Ljubljana Housing Survey and the Housing Survey 2005. She has served as a member of the Group of Experts on Access to Housing for the Council of Europe (1999–2001) and been a member of the Coordination Committee of the European Network for Housing Research.

Teresio Poggio is executive coordinator of the Research Laboratory of the Department of Sociology and Social Research at the University of Trento. He also carries out research on a freelance basis and in cooperation with other research organisations. His main research interests are housing and welfare systems and the role of wealth and its transmission in social stratification. He has written widely on the role of the intergenerational transmission of home ownership in the shaping of Mediterranean welfare systems and in the structuring of inequality.

Richard Ronald is Assistant Professor in Urban Studies at the University of Amsterdam in the Netherlands. He is the Review Editor of the *International Journal of Housing Policy* and Section Editor of the *International Encyclopedia of Housing and Home*. Richard has published extensively on housing and social change in Europe and Asia-Pacific. His recent books include a co-edited work on *Housing and Social Transition in Japan* (with Yosuke Hirayama, Routledge, 2007) and another on *Home and Family in Japan* (with Allison Alexy, Routledge, 2011). His monograph, *The Ideology of Home Ownership,* was published by Palgrave Macmillan in 2008. Richard has also been a recipient of the Japan Foundation Doctorial Fellowship and the Japan Society for the Promotion of Science Postdoctoral Fellowship.

Hannu Ruonavaara is Professor of Sociology at the Department of Social Research, University of Turku, Finland. His main interests in housing research are home ownership, comparative housing policy, historical sociology of housing, and qualitative methodology and theory in housing studies. He has published his work in English in numerous book chapters and international journals including the *European Journal of Housing Policy*, *Housing Studies, Housing, Theory and Society* and *Scandinavian Housing and Planning Research*. His recent and ongoing research projects deal with histories of Nordic housing policies, housing equity as a source of social welfare and neighbour relations and disputes in contemporary society.

David Thorns is Emeritus Professor of Sociology at the University of Canterbury, New Zealand, and Vice President of the International Social Science Council. His major research has been in the areas of housing, social policy, social inequality, comparative urban research, restructuring and change within advanced capitalist societies, urban sustainability, comparative welfare state policy analysis and globalisation and urban change. His work has been innovative and led to significant shifts in theoretical and research agendas. It also shows a consistent engagement with the implications of social science research for both public debate and disciplinary development.

Christine Whitehead is an internationally respected housing economist who has been working in the fields of housing economics, finance and policy for many years. Her current interests include international comparisons of home ownership finance, the impact of the financial crisis and the role of social housing, as well as a range of studies evaluating aspects of UK housing policies. She is currently Professor in Housing in the Department of Economics, London School of Economics. Until the end of 2010 she was also Director of the Cambridge Centre of Housing and Planning Research, which celebrated its twentieth anniversary in September that year. Her latest book, with Sarah Monk, is *Making Housing More Affordable*, published by Wiley Blackwell (2010).

PREFACE

Despite the political and cultural preoccupation with housing markets and house prices in recent years, studies of home ownership and housing systems have not been a central concern of the social sciences. The interconnections between the most recent housing bubble and global financial crisis have made it clear, nonetheless, that housing is intimately tied to social, economic and political affairs. There has consequently been a rush of publications since 2008 that have addressed housing (and networks of housing finance in particular) as a critical dimension of neo-liberalisation and globalisation and pointed to factors that, 'of course', should have been obvious before the crisis in mortgage lending and securitisation.

This book is not one of those publications. Indeed, it should be seen as a product of an existing research field that has been specifically concerned with housing systems and the social impact of home ownership for a number of decades already. The original idea for this text came from a meeting organised by the Home Ownership and Globalisation Working Group, which is part of the European Network of Housing Research. This group was inaugurated in the early 2000s and is currently coordinated by Marja Elsinga, John Doling and Richard Ronald, who have all contributed to this volume. The group is made up of housing specialists from diverse regions, mostly Europe, North America, Australasia and East Asia, who came together in November 2008 to discuss the latest developments in research. The meeting was nonetheless overshadowed by the crisis that was still unfolding following the collapse of Lehman Brothers two months earlier and subsequent to the failure of the US mortgage securitisation system.

The chapters in this edited book may be considered then as critical analyses of recent developments in national economies and housing policies and markets, by writers from related disciplines who have long been engaged in the study of housing systems. This is not, however, a book *about* the crisis. It deals with the recent boom and bust (or crunch) as simply the latest event in the ongoing transformation of housing systems. The main concern is how home ownership – particularly in the context of the intensified promotion of tenure in recent decades and its apparent centrality in neo-liberal transformations evident in various societies – contributes to social 'systems' and interacts with wider social, cultural, urban, political and economic processes.

Another feature of the book is its comparative inclusivity. This is not to say that it provides a comprehensive comparative overview, although the inter-national coverage of housing and home ownership is far broader than most publications in the field of housing studies. Countries and cases are largely considered in terms of their relevance to broader theories of housing systems and social change. While many of the usual suspects, such as the United States and England, are dealt with in detail, cases are also drawn from Mediterranean countries, post-socialist transition economies and Nordic societies of Europe, as well as Asia-Pacific nations, including Japan and New Zealand, where owner-occupied housing has long been privileged in policy and housing systems have played important parts in shaping social conditions. Although each chapter can be considered as an individual contribution, usually about a particular coun-try or region, there are clear links between them in the understanding of the role of home ownership in the shaping and reshaping of welfare regimes, the structuring and restructuring of socio-economic and political frameworks, and transformations in household and life-course patterns.

The title, *Beyond Home Ownership*, has multiple meanings as is explained in the introductory chapter. A particularly salient one is that there is far more to home ownership than simply a description of tenure. It is a way of organising dwelling and making a 'home', as well as a system that supports a particular pattern of housing production and consumption. The consequences can be both individually profound and, at an aggregate level, socially and economically radical.

A further implicit meaning is that, although this tenure has been normal-ised and recently embedded as the preferred form of housing in most societies, sometimes supplanting effective rental systems, its growth has been problematic. Inadequate regulation of circuits of housing finance along with the advance of housing markets have had detrimental effects, not only for economies, but also for households both inside and outside owner-occupied housing. Furthermore, the extension of home ownership to increasing swathes of low-income and eco-nomically vulnerable households has also proved questionable. The 'beyond' in this case represents a social and policy concern with what lies beyond existing approaches that have bluntly promoted home ownership as a panacea to prob-lems as diverse as economic inequality, social stability, declining pension funds and neighbourhood improvement, to name but a few. In the post-credit crunch milieu, governments have struggled to define new policy directions although the logic of neo-liberalism seems intact. Policy makers appear to remain 'stuck on' home ownership, even though the costs of subsidising this sector are becoming even heavier and the social divides it drives between different tenure and market sectors are challenging socio-economic stability.

This book does not provide any simple answers to these issues. It does, nonetheless, call for and speak to a debate on the position of home ownership in social and economic life. It elaborates theoretically and empirically on the diversity and outcomes of home ownership and mass owner-occupied housing sectors and by doing so contributes to understanding of contemporary social change. Specific attention is paid to the relationship between housing, welfare and society as we consider these elements to be deeply and intrinsically interrelated and fundamental to social scientific discussions of transformations underway in contemporary societies.

Of course, there are many people to thank for helping make this book possible, not least of whom are the members of the Home Ownership and Globalising Working-Group, both those who contributed directly and also those who provided challenging ideas in our meetings and discussions that helped to inspire this volume. We would also like to acknowledge our colleagues at the OTB Research Institute at Delft University of Technology and the Department of Geography, Planning and International Development Studies at the University of Amsterdam for sharing their knowledge and enthusiasm. Finally, we must thank Ray Forrest, editor of the Housing and Society series, and also Louise Fox from Routledge both for her work on this volume and for regularly chasing up the editors.

Richard Ronald and Marja Elsinga

1

BEYOND HOME OWNERSHIP

An overview

Richard Ronald and Marja Elsinga

Introduction

Even though it forms the financial, spatial and meaningful basis of household security for most families, it was not so long ago that owner-occupied housing was considered of relatively minor significance to social conditions and economic life. Post-war policy debates, especially in European contexts, largely understood housing issues in terms of shelter and focused on the welfare of working households. This stimulated a conceptual and material focus on subsidized rental housing provision, with home ownership considered preferable for those 'better off'. This model, however, has faded as housing, and home ownership in particular, has increasingly adopted a more central role in socioeconomic affairs and welfare issues.

First, in terms of housing welfare, governments have increasingly chosen to support home ownership and to reconsider the role of social rental sectors. This manifested in a drive to extend owner-occupied housing across the developed and developing world, largely by improving borrowing conditions, and consequently debt. Explicit state support of private home buying also intensified while funding for, and the role of, social rental housing has largely been residualized. Second, housing market booms, particularly the global boom that dominated the nascent years of this century, intensified the integration of housing markets with global economic and micro-household circuits of finance, reinforcing conceptions and uses of homes as market goods. To some extent the former and latter developments reinforced each other, with escalating state sponsorship of, growing demand for and intensified capital flows into owner-occupied housing. Crises in international housing markets in the late 2000s related to major failures in US subprime and mortgage securitization systems have, however, exposed the flaws in this model and been at the heart of the ongoing global economic crisis of the 2010s.

This book addresses inherent as well as emerging features of home owner-ship systems in order to look into and *beyond* the crumbling framework of the most recent housing epoch. Furthermore, it sets out to do so in international contexts both including and *beyond* the English-speaking homeowner societies that dominate debates on owner-occupied housing markets. Our concern is the broader impact of tenure systems and their ongoing influence on the structure and restructuring of society. While various social, economic and political issues are addressed, the changing relationships between home ownership and welfare relations as well as the reshaping of social inequalities are of particular con-cern. On the one hand, recognition of home ownership as a means to enhance household welfare capacity has advanced in recent years, but has manifested and impacted each society differently. On the other, the uneven growth of housing markets and housing prices, both spatially and temporally, has shaped particular distributions of wealth and debt between different tenures and dwellings, and across different generations of homebuyers and homeowners.

One of the main purposes of this volume is to elaborate on the significance of housing as a key dimension of social change and its centrality in socio-economic relations. In the emerging post-crisis context in which this book has been com-posed, it appears that, whereas it was once overlooked in socio-economic and academic analyses, housing, and home ownership in particular, has become central to the structure of international finance; the governance of national economies; the restructuring of welfare states; and the security, prosperity and well-being of individual households. This chapter sets the stage for what is to come in terms of the theoretical as well as empirical analyses, both national and international. It begins by assessing the growing influence of owner-occupied housing systems before going on to explore how and why this tenure has both expanded and become so influential in macro- and micro-socio-economic affairs. The reshaping of social inequalities as well as the neo-liberal restructur-ing of modes of welfare provision are further addressed. The last part considers emerging housing and welfare conditions and what lies ahead in the rest of this book.

The dominant tenure

The growth in owner-occupied housing sectors in recent decades has been quite remarkable. In Eastern European countries in particular, home ownership grew rapidly as a result of the post-communist transition in the early nineties, with housing privatization seen as a means to accelerate free market capitalism. Public housing was typically privatized, usually via sell-offs to sitting tenants at giveaway prices. Some of these countries now have home ownership rates of over 90 per cent. Compared with these societies, growth in home ownership in countries such as the United States and the United Kingdom has been modest but is still substantial. In 1970, home ownership accounted for just half of hous-ing in England and 63 per cent in the United States, but went on to reach around

70 per cent in both countries by 2005 (although it has subsequently begun to ebb). In Western Europe, too, although much later, many societies that developed large social rental housing sectors in the post-war decades went on to experience a rapid shift towards owner-occupation as well as substantial augmentations in aggregate mortgage debts. The Netherlands is particularly illustrative, with home ownership increasing from around 45 per cent of housing in 1990 to 56 per cent by 2006. With time, this market transformation became more intense, with the ratio of mortgage debt to gross domestic product advancing from 61 per cent to almost 100 per cent between 1998 and 2008. Across Europe, home purchase and borrowing for home purchase ballooned. By 2007, more than 60 per cent of households of the original 15 EU member states were homeowners and total mortgage debt had reached €13 trillion (Doling and Ford, 2007).

The proportionate rise in mortgage debt in European contexts is represented in Figure 1.1, while national differences in the size of owner-occupied housing sectors are outlined in Figure 1.2. The shift towards home ownership was not limited to Western societies and featured centrally in, among other places, the economic strategies of newly developed economies. In developed East Asia, growing owner-occupancy rates accompanied rapid industrialization and

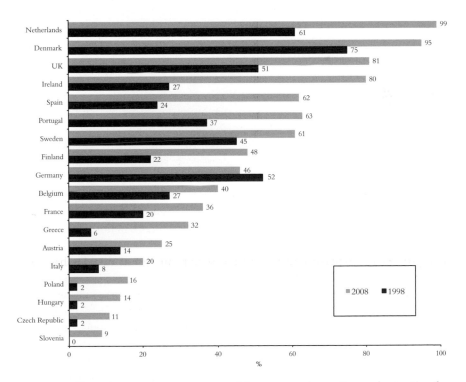

FIGURE 1.1 Changing aggregate mortgage debt to gross domestic product ratios for selected European countries.
Source: Adapted from EMF (2009).

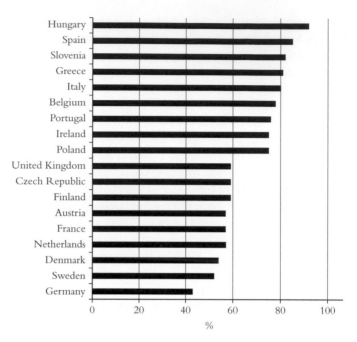

FIGURE 1.2 Share of home ownership, as percentage of housing stock, for selected European countries.
Source: Adapted from EMF (2009).

urbanization in the 1970s, 1980s and 1990s. Singapore is iconic in this regard (Chua, 2003), with the public home ownership programme, which houses over 80 per cent of all households, helping push the sector from 29 per cent to 92 per cent of all housing between 1970 and 2000. In China, where massive private housing construction and house price increases are still under way, the transformation has been seismic (see Wang and Murie, 1999; Ye *et al.*, 2010). While urban home ownership grew under market reform measures from 17 per cent to 45 per cent between 1985 and 1997, since 1998, after abolishing work-unit housing, owner-occupation has reached over 82 per cent among urban households.

A fundamental outcome of the super-rapid rise in housing commodification and, subsequently, market prices in these societies has been the emergence of massive affordability gaps, with intense price increases cutting younger households off from the housing market. Some East Asian societies, such as China, Hong Kong and South Korea, are now in the process of either developing or reinforcing existing social rental housing initiatives (Ronald and Chiu, 2010). Transition economies too are beginning to readjust housing policies in order to reduce macro-economic dependency on housing and construction sectors, and household vulnerability to market volatility. Yet even in the face of these experiences in the East, as well as market failures currently evident in most Western societies, the expansion of owner-occupied housing sectors as well as market deregulation continue to be a policy prescription – promulgated by agencies such as the World Bank and the Organisation for Economic Co-operation and Development (OECD) – for developing societies.

So what has been behind the spectacular and widespread orientation towards home purchase in recent decades? Economic approaches have traditionally emphasized global convergence, associating increases in home ownership with growing levels of national affluence (see Schmidt, 1989). However, the growth in home ownership has been far from even across affluent societies and in many, such as Sweden and the Netherlands, social rental housing continued to dominate policy until the 1990s. Furthermore, the correlation between national wealth and home ownership is far from linear, with, in Europe, for example, Germany[1] and Switzerland having the lowest rates – around 36–45 per cent – and Romania, Bulgaria and Albania the highest, with 90 per cent or more.

The expansion of owner-occupied sectors has been connected with the features of welfare regimes, although relationships are not always direct (Hoekstra, 2003; Kurz and Blossfeld, 2004; Norris and Domanski, 2009). Welfare regimes are understood to be the result of interclass alliances and power conflict resolutions in each society that lead to discernible relations between the state, economy and institutional structures (Esping-Andersen, 1990). In very simple terms, where labour is more influential, de-commodified forms of welfare provision – such as social housing – tend to be large, whereas where capital wins out, the welfare state is likely to be smaller and more commodified. Developed societies can be classified into three different types of welfare regime: *social democratic* societies with an emphasis on de-commodification; *liberal* ones emphasizing commodification; and *corporatist* countries where civil society plays a key role and where conflicts between left and right lead to contingent compromises in public provision. There are also countries where the state is considered less significant than the family in the provision of welfare (see Esping-Andersen, 1999).

In terms of housing systems, regime approaches would assume that liberal regimes, such as the United Kingdom and Ireland, and South European family-focused regimes, such as Italy and Greece, support large owner-occupied housing sectors, as is the case. However, in social democratic and corporatist regimes the relationship is far less obvious. For example, whereas both Belgium and Germany are considered corporatist conservative in terms of welfare regimes, Belgium is decidedly home ownership orientated (around 75 per cent of housing) compared with its neighbour. Norway is another good example and, although some indicators mark it as social democratic, around eight out of ten households are owner-occupiers, many of whom have been supported by tenure-biased policy measures.

Home ownership as a social project

Although variation in demand, supply and the availability of inputs such as land are usually emphasized (see Fisher and Jaffe, 2003), home ownership has grown most rapidly in each national context, albeit usually sustained by periods of economic growth, as a result of government support that has undermined the advantages of renting vis-à-vis buying, often through the subsidization of the market. In recent decades this has been evident in the European context as home ownership rates have advanced markedly in social democratic and corporatist societies that historically supported social rental housing but increasingly pursued privatization and deregulation policies. Atterhög's (2005) comparative analysis illustrates that the policy stimulation of home ownership has worked particularly well in non-Anglophone countries, whereas the limits of home ownership seem to have already been reached in the English-speaking societies. It is, however, not only policies favouring home ownership but, it seems, also those that change rental conditions that can really make a difference.

For example, rent and tax policies help facilitate private renting in countries such as Germany, Austria and Switzerland (see Lawson, 2010) where the rental sector continues to dominate urban housing markets. In the Netherlands and Sweden, on the other hand, governments have withdrawn support and funding for social rental housing and in some cases pressured housing associations to sell off their stock (Boelhouwer, 2002; Turner and Whitehead, 2002). There has been a marked shift in the role of social housing across European countries towards servicing the needs of the socially marginal rather than the needs of regular working households (Lévy-Vroelant, 2011). As the flow of public funds into social housing has receded, the overall pattern has been that subsidies for private housing[2] have expanded.

Providing opportunities for households to buy their own home has increasingly been embraced by policy makers who have pursued the proliferation of home owning, perceived as a means to spread wealth and financial responsibility throughout society. Increased home ownership has been seen as a means to improve neighbourhoods, the value of property and even the economic conditions of the poor (Retsinas and Belski, 2002).

Large-scale tenure transfers have become a common strategy among societies seeking to stimulate far-reaching socio-economic and political transformations. The 'right to buy' given to British social housing tenants under the Thatcher government – accounting for 1.8 million new homeowners between 1980 and 2000 – is emblematic in this regard (see Forrest and Murie, 1988). The massive transfers of East European housing stock from state to individual ownership during the post-communist transition of the 1990s also mediated a reorientation of households towards their homes in terms of asset accumulation and market relations (Clapham et al., 1996; Tsenkova, 2009). This was also a symbolic step for transition governments and marked the commodification of housing goods, the establishment of a housing market and the unburdening of the state of onerous responsibilities for housing maintenance and provision.

Extending access to home ownership has meant that increasing numbers of vulnerable or marginal households have been drawn into the tenure, helping push up prices and the cost of market entry. As rates of home ownership have expanded and values increased – making getting 'on the ladder' ostensibly more urgent – the more homebuyers have had to extend themselves. In the late 1990s and 2000s, with new flows of capital derived from non-traditional sources such as capital markets, banks became increasingly active – with encouragement from most governments – in lending to those who would have previously been excluded from owner-occupation. Such marginal homebuyers may well have felt that they benefited from steep price increases. However, during market downturn, which has typically accompanied trouble in the wider economy, they have been the most vulnerable to changes in lending conditions, unemployment and even family breakdown, leading to the loss of the home. Long-standing homeowners with substantial equity are often able to weather turbulent markets while those who buy at the peak of the housing price cycle with the highest loan-to-value ratios – typically younger, lower-income buyers – are usually the ones who pay the highest price (Bootle, 1996). In the United States, mass home foreclosures have characterized the most recent downturn[3] and have been particularly concentrated among the most marginal homebuyers, particularly among African American and Latino communities (see Bocian et al., 2010).

A feature of public discourses on home ownership has been an association between owner-occupied tenure status and improved citizenship. In this sense, too, increasing home ownership has represented a social project for governments and a means to re-moralize citizens as investors and property owners. International research, especially in the United States, has accentuated the positive outcomes of the transformation from renter to homeowner. These various effects run the gamut from improved psychological health and greater participation in voluntary associations and political affairs, to better school results and reduced delinquency among the children of owner-occupiers (see Rohe et al., 2002). Nonetheless, empirical findings often reflect the ideological context of research. With the escalation in subprime and other mortgage defaulters in the United States, research there has now begun to focus on the negative effects of home ownership, especially in poorer neighbourhoods (e.g. Immergluck, 2009).

The problem with researching the 'effects' of home ownership lies in the fact that tenure is difficult to isolate from the influences of, among other things, household and dwelling patterns and neighbourhoods effects. In the Netherlands, Kleinhans and Elsinga (2010), for example, illustrate how, among rental households offered the opportunity to purchase their rental home, those who became homeowners expressed a greater sense of empowerment than those who kept on renting. However, it was not necessarily the tenure change that empowered, but rather the tendency for more empowered households to buy. Moreover, becoming an owner-occupier can make households less mobile, embedding them more in the neighbourhood. It is therefore not necessarily the tenure that makes homeowners appear more satisfied or engaged with the community, although many studies have attributed positive individual transformations to tenure status.

Despite the loose connections between tenure and behavioural outcomes, political discourses on housing since the 1980s have gravitated towards a perception of homeowners as better citizens and superior kinds of consumers. This, it has been argued, has fit with emerging forms of neo-liberal governance (Flint, 2004; Langley, 2008; Ronald, 2008; Watson, 2009). The notion of the autonomous property owner invested in enhancing the value of their home has aligned with a particular type of governmentality that has sought not to intervene directly in social conduct but rather through the deployment of particular strategies and techniques to shape behaviour towards particular ends (see McIntyre and McKee, 2009). Expanding home ownership has represented an opportunity to transform individuals by stimulating their self-regulating capacities and aligning them to dominant norms of conduct. The market consumption of housing has thus been particularly significant in that its proliferation has contributed to the reordering of identities by constructing subjects as 'ethical citizens', as Rose (2000) puts it, responsible for their own well-being.

In the British political context the objective of linking housing tenure to neo-liberal forms of financial subjectivity and moral citizenship is quite transparent, and, although it was explicit under the Thatcher regime, it again came to the fore in post-2000 Labour government discourses:

> With home-ownership expanding into new areas and new groups, today I see Britain as one of the world's greatest wealth owning democracies where the widely held chance for not just some but all to own assets marks out a new dimension in citizenship and makes Britain a beacon for the world. Assets for all – enabling opportunity for all
>
> (Gordon Brown, ODPM, 2005)

Although, English-speaking societies are most associated with this perception of tenure, it has also become increasingly evident across Continental European societies, especially those that sought to marketize housing provision since the 1990s. In the following from a watershed Dutch housing policy memorandum, the link between housing privatization objectives and desirable social transformations is also clear:

> In general the control over and responsibility for the dwelling is largest in the case of home ownership. After all, homeowners do not only enjoy the utility of the home but also have possession. In this way home ownership can contribute to more housing satisfaction as well as the realization of socially desirable goals such as building up property and wealth.
>
> (Ministry of Housing, 2000, p. 88, author's translation)

With the reordering of socio-economic life around 'homeowner investor' subjects, more financialized or 'actuarialized' modes of being are argued to have been promulgated (Langley, 2008; Martin, 2002). For Watson (2009), the calculations of everyday life have come to mimic those of professional investors:

> how to treat life itself as a series of investment decisions; how to position the households assets on the right side of pricing trends; and how to plan for the long term by being able to continually trade up the value of assets.
>
> (p. 45)

The 'financialized self' has different expectations of governments and private corporations, and is more likely to support greater marketization of goods and services that enhance opportunities to invest and thus offset feelings of inse-curity. During market downturn, however, there are considerable chances of anomie and the subject is far more exposed, both ontologically and materially, to economic vicissitudes.

Just as the proliferation of homeowners has been associated with the reorien-tation of individual subjectivities, so too has the advance of home ownership been implicated in the socio-economic restructuring of capitalism in recent decades. For Peck and Tickell (2002), the post-Fordist reorientation of advanced capital-ist societies has featured, first, a rollback of welfare state provision, followed by a rolling out of new regulation that seeks to advance market-orientated practices and the commodification of social life more generally. To sum up, it has been a process of neo-liberalization that 'prioritizes market-based, market-orientated and market-disciplinary responses to regulatory problems; it strives to intensify commodification in all realms of social life; and it often mobilizes speculative financial instruments to open new arenas for capitalist profit making' (Brenner *et al.*, 2010, p. 328). Neo-liberalization has not diffused evenly, however, but instead has been mediated locally via regulatory experiments such as privati-zation and deregulation, trade liberalization, financialization, welfare reform and monetarist shock therapy. Housing policy reform, market deregulation and privatization from this perspective have played prominent parts in broader processes of transformation.

Home ownership has been at the forefront of neo-liberal experiments in regulatory restructuring. This is arguably because of the place of housing as the most market-orientated aspect of welfare state provision (Harloe, 1995). The promotion of home ownership in many contexts has not only represented neo-liberal ideology, but has also been effective in eroding public housing systems as a material and symbolic basis for the welfare state (Forrest and Murie, 1988). The focus on home ownership and concern with privatization in housing policy have played important roles in the commodification of the home and presenting housing as a consumer *choice*. Malpass (2006) argues that the state promotion of choice in housing has in reality been the 'choice' for social renters to become homeowners, and not the other way around. The increased commodification of housing has thus justified the withdrawal of collective forms of provision in favour of private ones. This has supported a reordering of relationships and obligations between citizens and the state. In the new model, autonomy and responsibility have been devolved from the state to active citizens, allowing for retrenchment in state-provided welfare.

The British example has often been considered typical and usually provides a point of reference in discussions of government retrenchment in the housing sector. However, patterns of change in welfare states are highly differentiated (Pierson, 2002). In Chapter 5 of this volume, for example, Ruonavaara illustrates the particular pathways for reforms in housing sectors of Nordic countries. All of the chapters in this book either directly or implicitly illustrate how the logic of neo-liberalism has permeated housing policy, as well as restructured relationships between governments, households and markets. This has, however, unfolded in each context in terms of indigenous features of housing systems and cultures. Each chapter in this way contributes to the broader understanding of housing and the diverse roles it is playing in the contemporary reshaping of capitalist economies.

Home ownership and welfare

The purpose of our analysis so far has been to consider the increasing prominence of home ownership not as a natural phenomenon or simple corollary of economic growth, but rather as an outcome of coordinated strategies that have restructured socio-economic relations that form the basis of contemporary governance, citizenship and economically centred subjectivities. To put it more simply, housing is not just housing! Home ownership has been a project that has social objectives and broad and complex socio-economic outcomes. As mentioned at the outset, the role of home ownership in the structure and restructuring of welfare relations is a particular concern of this book and is the focus of this section. The emerging consequences of housing system restructuring are explored further in the section that follows.

Many households across social classes have financially benefited from the massive house price increases of the early to mid-2000s, although those at the upper end of the property market enjoyed disproportionately larger rewards (see Dorling *et al.*, 2005). The inflation and bursting of the housing bubble of the 2000s nonetheless primed the spectacular financial crash in 2008. For some, the root of the housing market collapse lay in the imbalance between the structure of house prices and their fundamental value, whereas others point to mistakes made by overleveraged borrowers and irresponsible lenders (see Shiller, 2008; Wolf, 2009). Another suggestion has been that this housing bubble derived from, and drove forward, a particular restructuring in the logic and dynamics of the role of housing in the organization of welfare states (Ronald, 2008; Watson, 2009). The rise (and fall) of housing markets has thus been implicated as a consequence of recent welfare state restructuring under neo-liberal capitalism.

As we alluded to at the very beginning of this chapter, traditional understandings of housing welfare focus on public housing. As such, housing has been considered a feature within the welfare state. In the West European context most societies expanded subsidized rental sectors in the post-war period as a way of meeting housing shortages, but also as a reflection of citizenship rights and the desire to improve living conditions for working households.[4] Since the 1980s, however, support for and scales of social rental housing have experienced a marked decline. This shift has not simply represented a hollowing out of social provision, but has reflected broader transformations in governance and in particular a re-envisioning of the role of housing policy and the function of homes as welfare goods.

Whereas social rental housing has been the 'wobbly pillar' of the welfare state (Torgersen, 1987), private housing consumption in some contexts has come to be seen as a 'cornerstone' of household welfare conditions (see Groves *et al.*, 2007; Malpass, 2008). This involves thinking about the welfare outcomes of housing as a commodified rather than de-commodified good. The expansion of home ownership and property values has theoretically increased the overall economic capacity of households, which are, in principle, able to tap into this wealth to pay for welfare goods or retirement needs, potentially compensating for diminishing pensions and public services. Moreover, considering the growing pressures of ageing populations and expected public budgetary shortfalls, shifting the burden of welfare onto individual asset-building initiatives and market mechanisms has been particularly attractive to governments (Doling and Ronald, 2010). With the expansion of owner-occupation among lower- and middle-income classes in most developed societies since the 1970s, and following past observations of faster than inflation house price increases (in historic cycles at least), home ownership has come to represent, sometimes explicitly, a means for the state to offset onerous welfare demands on public coffers. This is achieved by supporting the ability of individual households to buy homes, trade up in the market and accumulate considerable equity of their own on the way.

The interchange between home ownership and welfare was initially considered by Jim Kemeny (1981, 1992) who observed in societies with high home ownership rates a particular distribution of housing costs over the life course for home-buying households. When the household is young, the costs of saving for a deposit and mortgage repayments are proportionately high relative to income, but, over time and with inflation, costs diminish and become minimal in retirement when the house is paid off. Homeowners essentially experience diminishing dependence on public welfare, offset by their growing private property asset wealth and because they no longer need to pay steep housing costs.[5] By contrast, in societies dominated by good quality, affordable rental housing where costs are relatively constant over the life course, support of public welfare provision and social housing services is likely to be higher and also more important to a larger proportion of the population in maintaining standards of living in old age. Castles (1998) extended this argument by focusing on how the income-in-kind enjoyed by un-mortgaged homeowners can substitute for a public pension income. Castles demonstrated statistical relationships between pension arrangements and home ownership rates, which often constitute what he refers to as the 'really big trade-off'.

What both Kemeny and Castles ultimately allude to is a particularly significant relationship between housing conditions and welfare relationships that has been notably absent in debates on welfare capitalism. Indeed, the role of the housing sectors in the constitution and development of welfare states has, historically, not been well integrated despite the obvious propensity for different types of housing tenure to commodify or de-commodify households. Broader empirical explorations have, however, stimulated greater concern over the role of housing in making households more or less dependent on the state for the satisfaction of non-shelter needs. In the developed countries of Southern Europe and East Asia especially, the welfare mix between state, family and market has proved to be strongly influenced by very high owner-occupancy rates.

In the Southern European regime the family plays a very important role in providing welfare of different kinds, and is integrated within broad kinship networks among extended family members (see Allen *et al.*, 2004; Elsinga and Mandic, 2010; Poggio, Chapter 3 this volume). In such a system the family home takes on a particular status as the locale of reciprocal exchanges of shelter and care, and plays a particular role in transfers and exchanges of wealth between generations, which is further emphasized by a context of relatively limited welfare provision outside the family. In East Asia, too, the ability of families to buy their own homes and build up property wealth through the housing market has been important in enhancing family asset capacity and welfare self-reliance, and also a notable feature of housing systems within indigenous welfare regime arrangements (Groves *et al.*, 2007; Ronald, 2007; Ronald and Doling, 2010). A central difference between Southern European and East Asian approaches has been the intervention of development-orientated states in Asian contexts, which have pursued elaborate public housing programmes centred on the extension of private housing development and ownership.

Offsetting underdeveloped public welfare by enhancing the uptake of owner-occupied housing and the advance of property markets, making households both more open to and capable of self-provision, is clearly a well-established practice in many developed societies. However, its explicit advance in liberal regimes has been more recent, and has been specifically associated with welfare rollback, legitimized through an 'asset-based welfare' agenda (Watson, 2009). This approach proposes that, rather than rely on state-managed transfers through taxation and welfare benefits, poorer households are best helped by getting them to accept greater responsibility for their own welfare needs by promoting saving and investment in financial products and property assets that augment in value over time. These can potentially be tapped later to supplement consumption and welfare needs when income is reduced (e.g. in retirement or in between employment) or used to acquire other forms of investment such as educational qualifications (Sherraden, 2003).

Asset-based welfare featured increasingly in policy initiatives in the 2000s, particularly in liberal regimes such as the United States and the United Kingdom. Although schemes included state-subsidised child trust funds and matched savings accounts (see McKay, 2001), individual owner-occupied housing property, as the largest asset a family normally owns and in recent years the most effective vehicle for net equity gains, has been a central target of policy reforms resembling asset-based welfare. Important to note is that, in order to achieve inclusivity for all households, the philosophy of asset-based welfare assumes that housing policy requires more than government emphasis on individual responsibilities. Rather, it calls for targeted policies for those excluded from housing asset strategies.

In countries associated with social democratic and corporatist welfare regimes, government discourses have erred towards improving opportunity and choice within the welfare state rather than welfare retrenchment. Nonetheless, many such countries have been particularly effective at deregulating and expanding housing markets. For Schwartz and Seabrooke (2008) this is significant as, although owner-occupancy may be comparatively lower, mortgage debt to gross domestic product ratios have increased rapidly (see Figure 1.1) and are often even higher than in traditional homeowner societies, illustrating a specific regime reorientation in some countries. Although social housing sectors may be large in these contexts, housing marketization marks a significant transformation and a growing awareness on all sides that homeowners can accumulate considerable wealth in homes, making housing a good investment against individual economic insecurity.

In this light, the 'really big trade-off' of Castles (1998) and Kemeny (1981, 2005) between state transfers and private housing wealth has taken on a new salience as neo-liberal policy agendas have progressed. The growing interest among governments in housing privatization essentially supported the advance of housing markets in the 1990s and 2000s, sustaining an unprecedented era of economic growth built upon the incorporation of the individual household wealth represented by owner-occupied property ownership into the macro economy. For Crouch (2009) this involved a restructuring of welfare relations in terms of a form of 'privatized Keynesianism', although 'house price Keynesianism' more specifically describes the role of owner-occupied housing consumption within emergent welfare relations. For Malpass (2008), developments in housing did not necessarily *cause* the adaptation of a particular form of welfare state but have allowed governments to pursue restructuring programmes that rely on the existence of 'substantial amounts of widely distributed housing wealth in order to secure political acceptance of changes in service provision' (p. 8).

The post-war Keynesian model of economic growth followed a demand management process supported by a welfare system facilitated by transfer payments. Social transfers protected households against economic upturns and downturns, making them more confident consumers and allowing firms to plan for the future, with the state playing a major role as insurer of last resort.

Crouch argues that in the 1990s, however, liberal governments, such as that of the United Kingdom, increasingly sought to shift responsibilities by writing down public debt and extending markets. The extension of credit provision played an important role in this regard and credit markets for low- and middle-income people were expanded dramatically. A complementary development in the financial sector was the acceleration in complexity and scale of high-tech derivatives among other speculative investment vehicles (Smith *et al.*, 2009). These innovations were thought to have reduced systemic risk, with the market price of risk assumed to be realistic, promoting more confident consumption and driving economic growth.

The housing market played a particular role as the new dynamic of growth specifically required loose lending for home purchase, pushing up demand and in turn property values. The potential assets represented by owner-occupied property market growth as well as expectations of continued house price inflation effectively became a basis for economic growth – with companies and banks expecting increasing house prices to erode household debt and support sustained demand – supporting rollback and state deregulation in terms of a smaller public welfare model. Rather than providing insurance through state-managed income transfers, governments supported home purchases and house price increases, which was achieved, in part, through the integration of commercial banking with investment banking. This was considered 'a way to reproduce stable conditions suited to the expansion of wealth held privately within the economy' (Watson, 2010, p. 414).

The house price bubble of the last decade, with an estimated increase in the total value of residential property in developed economies from $40 trillion to $70 trillion in the first five years of the century, has been hailed as the biggest bubble in history (*The Economist*, 2005). It has been proposed that, in the United States, the ability of the housing finance system to generate extra aggregate demand was central to above average rates of growth in the 1990s and 2000s (Schwartz, 2009). The success of housing finance in driving growth sustained a restructuring of capital flows and investment on a global scale. This was achieved by two key changes in housing finance. First, a revolution occurred, primarily through increased deregulation and securitization, in the interconnectedness of mortgage markets with other flows of capital and investment and other types of financial product, which became increasingly internationalized (Aalbers, 2008). Thus, although individual real estate transactions remained ostensibly parochial, they were increasingly mediated by a 'complex and diffuse institutional architecture' (Forrest, 2008, p. 40). Second, as Hannsgen (2007) argues, although lending for housing was once directed towards the social purpose of supporting home ownership and thus security and stability, it gave way – along with its increasing integration with global forms of capital circulation – to a profit-focused industry in which home ownership simply became a means of driving profit.

The assumption was that households would rationally manage their own housing equity and debt over the life cycle to offset individual disruptions in income and consumption. A whole new business innovating products that allowed households to release the equity held in their homes also advanced, making housing wealth more liquid and fungible. However, tapping into housing equity did not always serve the interests of household welfare management and has typically been transformed into enhanced lifestyle consumption or further speculative investment in housing. Moreover, research in the United Kingdom, where the industry proliferated significantly, shows that tapping into housing wealth does not enhance welfare as much as help households get by, with as many as one in three equity release customers, for example, using equity in their home in order to help service other debts (Overton, 2010).

In the late 2000s it became all too obvious that households mostly hadn't managed borrowing and asset building conservatively. Despite the explosion in house prices, people expected it, quite irrationally – as housing bubbles have proved before – to go on even further (Case and Schiller, 2003). At the same time, many large corporate investors had become particularly over-leveraged and over-extended in housing finance-related investment. The 2007–8 US credit crisis not only triggered the global recession that followed, but also began a process of realization of how far national governments, global financial networks and individual households had become exposed to and dependent upon housing markets.

The American subprime crisis and the financial meltdown in lending and securitization are dealt with in detail in this book by Bratt (Chapter 8). What this chapter, along with others in this volume, illustrate is that home ownership has become more broadly embedded in socio-economic systems and enmeshed with socio-political relations at a deeper level and across a far wider range of developed societies than previously imagined. Essentially, the imagining of home ownership as an asset base of individual welfare provision helped stimulate transformations in the structure of welfare systems and public finance. Housing markets are now integrated on quantitatively and qualitatively different levels with welfare conditions and the shaping of social inequalities and thus need to be addressed in academic research and public discussion with greater vigour than in the past. This book seeks to affirm these links and, moreover, begins to consider how the current reliance on housing markets and housing wealth – with no signs of reversal in commitments to home ownership policy and market practices – is continuing to shape new kinds of inequalities and trajectories in the evolution of welfare states.

Housing and emerging patterns of inequality

Arguably, although conditions are not stable, we are beginning to see the end of massive, crisis-related house price readjustments, revealing a new economic landscape reshaped by transformations in owner-occupied housing markets. Our concern in this book is not so much with the exact size and distribution of losses and gains (although Whitehead addresses differing outcomes of British house price booms in Chapter 6), but rather how the most recent boom accompanied a restructuring of the housing sector that is reshaping social relations and patterns of inequality. Many households across social classes ostensibly benefited from the massive house price increases of the 1990s and 2000s. Some estimates suggest that in the United States, for example, new homeowners buying between 1999 and 2005 saw an increase in median net wealth of $11,100–88,000 generated by changing housing market conditions. For incumbent homeowners, median net wealth nearly doubled from about $152,400 to $289,000 (Schwartz, 2009). As with previous fluctuations, however, the latest housing market boom concentrated risks and rewards (Hamnett, 2009). In particular, house price increases tended to reward those already better off, who were typically also more financially insulated when market trends reversed.

What has been unusual about the housing boom of the 2000s has been the extension of home ownership more broadly across social and income classes. Deregulation in finance stimulated many lenders to seek out those more marginal households in poor neighbourhoods that had previously been 'redlined' by mortgage companies as too risky to lend to (see Aalbers, 2011). Finding ways to lend money to low-income households was not simply a subprime issue; it also occupied regular lenders who became more involved in financing lending from capital markets rather than savings pools, as well as selling loans on through the securitization system (see Bratt, Chapter 8; Dymski, 2010; Martin, 2010). Governments also became explicitly concerned with getting low-income households into the owner-occupied housing system, although this took different forms in different contexts.

In the United States, the government put money into programmes such as the American Dream Down-payment Scheme, which aimed to support home purchase among non-white Americans. The HOPE VI programme also sought to extend home ownership in poor neighbourhoods by redeveloping public housing into mixed tenure communities. In England, too, many areas had demonstrated persistent low demand and appeared cut off from the mainstream housing market. Some rather extraordinary intervention measures were taken to reinvigorate these areas. More specifically, Housing Market Renewal initiatives set out to rebuild neighbourhoods with the objective of providing more attractive properties thereby stimulating real estate investment, although in doing so many low-income households were displaced (Allen, 2008). Another line of policy initiatives sought to help out individual households by offering to share ownership and thus reduce purchase costs.[6] The more house prices increased, however, the more the government had to become involved in helping those who could no longer afford to get into the market.

The irony is that, although housing market liberalization and the extension of home ownership was advanced as a means to make more households self-reliant and replace the state with the market in housing provision, the resulting imbalances and inequalities generated by the market called for even greater government action. First, greater economic imbalances between households caused by market distortions have typically required more spending on housing, but through user subsidies rather than supply.[7] Second, as markets took off, housing became less affordable, even for many middle-income households, meaning that governments have had to devise, and spend on, home purchase schemes, which help sustain unaffordable market levels. Third, during the credit crisis, saving the housing finance system (and the banking sector more broadly) required governments to pump massive sums into, or even take over, many lenders. Meanwhile, many post-crisis measures have involved the effective redirection of funds from welfare services to measures that target homeowners.[8]

The extension of home purchase to new classes of entrants was substantial, with, for example, around half of the lowest income decile in the UK now in home ownership. Nonetheless, the distribution of housing equity and exposure to market downturn remain highly uneven and it has been estimated that the wealthiest income decile of homeowners own, on average, five times the housing wealth of the lowest decile (Dorling *et al.*, 2005). This means not only that the impact of the housing market downturn now extends to a broader range of households than ever before, but also that those most adversely affected are normally made up of a larger proportion of poorer households. Those on lower incomes are more likely to have entered the market more recently (as lending became more accessible), were allowed to extended themselves the most financially (in individual rather than nominal terms) in order to buy – especially in the case of subprime lending – and have the least financial resources to draw upon should the worst happen (see Burrows and Wilcox, 2000; Schlay, 2006).

Furthermore, inflation and deflation in market values is not spatially unitary and prices move unevenly across countries and regions, and even across individual streets and neighbourhoods. More desirable areas and neighbourhoods attract better-off households, driving up prices more than in other areas in the boom (see Lees *et al.*, 2008), and sustaining greater resistance to decline during the bust. Booms thus tend to polarize losses spatially, with low-income buyers more likely to pay high prices in the peak for properties – usually in less desirable but more affordable neighbourhoods – that lose more proportional value with the bust. This polarization has been advanced in recent years by the growing transparency of neighbourhood quality determined by, in many societies, league tables and specialist web services (Butler and Robson, 2003). Although house prices have always reflected neighbourhood characteristics and promoted socio-spatial differentiation, the private housing market has increasingly become a core determinant of what type of neighbourhood people inhabit, intensifying the differentiation of areas and communities.

The patterns of home repossessions in the United States, which number in their millions since 2007, are a clear testament to the concentration of disadvantage among the poor, especially ethnic minorities (Bocian *et al.*, 2010; Immergluck, 2009). Similar patterns of concentrated proportional property value losses and, of course, mortgage arrears and repossessions among poorer homeowners are also evident across Europe and elsewhere. Although many low-income households have faced economic downturn and, possibly, unemployment before, never have so many been mortgaged homeowners. Although outright or high equity owners may be cushioned from further hardship by their properties, highly leveraged ones are rendered more vulnerable to losing their homes and mortgage deposits.

Family unity and generational divisions

Particularly evident in the most recent era of home ownership has been the marked impact of housing market shifts on relationships among family members. The clearest transformation has been the emerging divide between different generations in terms of housing and economic situations, with older generations on the whole having been disproportionately advantaged by historic policy and housing market developments, and younger ones likewise disadvantaged (Doling, Chapter 2). At the same time, this difference in conditions between young and old has helped re-enforce family relationships, with greater insecurity among one housing-poor generation enhancing dependency on the other housing-rich one. Transformations in home ownership and housing markets have thus important implications for understanding contemporary family relations.

In most developed societies, those born after World War II (usually referred to as baby boomers[9]) experienced a particularly favourable position with regard to the housing market. For this cohort, employment and economic conditions generally improved during their working lives. Meanwhile, welfare states were elaborated, improving both welfare conditions and, especially in parts of Western Europe, opportunities to enter subsidized rental housing. Many of this generation, and to a diminishing extent the one that followed, had good opportunities to get on the owner-occupied 'housing ladder', especially in contexts in which governments provided incentives to buy, or subsidies for tenants to become homeowners. These generations also benefited from exceptional periods of house price inflation that increasingly made entry to the market unaffordable to younger households.

Indeed, younger generations who formed independent households in recent years have found fixed employment conditions more elusive. Meanwhile, their chances of affording a home diminished as markets took off in the 2000s. Even among those who could buy their own homes, many had to extend themselves in terms of borrowing, paying out a larger proportion of their wages to service mortgage repayment demands, and have been more affected by changing equity conditions in the post-crisis context. In the English-speaking societies most transformed by neo-liberalization in the 2000s, changing home ownership conditions have led to decreases in aggregate home ownership levels, driven by falling home-purchase rates among younger people (Forrest and Hirayama, 2009). New Zealand is an illustrative context and is discussed in depth by

Thorns in Chapter 10. There, the rate of home ownership fell from 74 per cent in 1991 to 67 per cent in 2006, and is predicted to fall below 62 per cent by 2016. More significantly, owner-occupation among the 25- to 44-year-old group has declined by 44 per cent between 1991 and 2000. In Japan there is a similar story (Hirayama, Chapter 9), with the proportion of younger households entering the owner-occupied sector declining from as far back as the 1980s, but deteriorating further in the 1990s and 2000s.

An important outcome of changes in owner-occupied housing markets in many national contexts has been an increasing emphasis on family relationships. Concomitant with declining home ownership affordability has been the growing capacity of incumbent, asset-rich home-owning parents to draw upon their own housing wealth to assist their children in buying their own homes. In the UK context, Tatch (2006) estimates that 38 per cent of first-time homebuyers in England under 30 years old received financial assistance from their families in raising a deposit on an owner-occupied home in 2006, up from 10 per cent in 1995. In the post-financial crisis context it is likely that family help has become even more definitive to housing conditions as, following the credit crunch, lenders have demanded far more by way of security from new buyers, meaning significantly larger deposits.

Recent cross-European research has revealed that buying without help of the family is often almost impossible (Mandic and Elsinga, 2010). For those with parents unable or unwilling to assist them in buying a home, declining access to private housing has led to increasing numbers staying on longer in the natal home (Mandic, 2008). In Japan, the rise in such behaviour became conspicuous in the late 1990s, with such individuals labeled as 'parasite singles' (Yamada, 1999). More recently, however, singles staying on at home has come to be recognized as a reflection of the economic difficulties faced by young people.

Intergenerational dynamics may, however, be more complex, as in some cases the flow of assistance might be reversed, with housing-rich adult children helping out asset- and income-poor parents. In some countries, such as Hungary, the sharp shift towards the market may have shaped a pattern of high housing ownership and equity within one cohort, who through their housing status become important to other generations within the family in terms of providing shelter or assistance with purchase. In this sense, housing conditions may be driving the revival of multigenerational households as different generations pull together to share housing resources. Another factor reshaping the generational conditions has been the growing tendency for housing wealth to accumulate not only among certain generations but also along lines of inheritance. With fewer children to inherit (as fertility rates decrease meaning fewer children per couple) and greater focus on the family as a resource, the propensity is towards a growing divide between the children of homeowners, who are more likely to receive financial help in buying a home as well as inherit family property, and the children of non-owners.

In many developed countries the family has continued to be an important source of welfare. Privately owned family homes have been the spatial locale where welfare exchanges take place and shelter is shared, as well as an economic node through which family wealth is accrued, stored and passed on. In this volume, contributions by Poggio (Chapter 3) and Mandic (Chapter 4) elaborate on such arrangements in Italy and parts of South East Europe respectively. In these countries housing appears to be a key element in the family strategy. The recent transformation in home ownership and housing markets in liberal English-speaking countries arguably reflects a comparable reorientation towards family-based modes of welfare provision and exchange. Indeed, one suggestion has been that post-financial crisis economic stresses accompanied by the continued social and financial significance of home ownership are playing a part in the 're-familization' of society, with family assistance becoming more critical to accessing owner-occupied housing (Forrest and Yip, 2011). This is a remarkable observation considering that, although the last century featured a general decline in the family base of welfare in favour of collective provision, this trend now appears to be in reverse. It also challenges assumptions about individualization and the declining role of the family that feature in theories of late modernity (e.g. Beck, 1992).

Although re-familization has been emphasized, there has also been a decline in fertility associated with high home ownership societies. A number of studies have identified that, where home ownership is normalized, conjugal couples often see achieving buying a home as necessary to starting a family (Mandic, 2008; Mulder and Billari, 2010). In such contexts, rental sectors are more likely to be undeveloped, stigmatized, or at least not seen as suitable to forming a family household. Consequently, when home ownership becomes difficult to achieve, be it because of house price inflation or unstable borrowing or employment conditions, family formation, and thus the production of children, may be affected. Links between fertility and home ownership are particularly evident in Southern European countries where transitions to independent housing for new households have been slowed down by market conditions (Mulder and Billari, 2010). In East Asian societies, too, declining fertility rates have been associated with the growing inability of couples to marry and start families of their own resulting from tight housing market conditions (Forrest and Hirayama, 2009; Ronald and Hirayama, 2009). Similar patterns of (non)family formation may well become common to other European and North American home ownership-orientated societies as collective resources are eroded, lending and economic conditions become more austere and access to owner-occupied housing becomes more difficult to access.

The structure of the book

The rest of this book comprises individual chapters that address the changing role of home ownership, housing systems and policy frameworks in a number of exemplary societies. There is particular concern with housing market developments, shifting household and welfare relations, and social inequality, which we have attempted to connect in this chapter to broader, ongoing social transformations related to the growing embeddedness of housing, and especially home ownership, in social and economic life. Individual contributions are provided by leading academics recognized as experts on the specific national and international contexts they examine. Sociological, economic, demographic and geographic perspectives are also incorporated, reflecting the multidimensional nature of housing as well as the interdisciplinary nature of housing studies.

Although some chapters focus on individual countries, including England, the United States, Australia, New Zealand, Italy and Japan, others address specific groups of countries that have recently experienced similar housing sector transformations: the post-socialist countries of Central and Eastern Europe; and the Nordic countries.[10] These countries and regions demonstrate different alignments in the order of home ownership and different relationships between the state, households and housing systems. They also illustrate, notwithstanding the global development of housing markets and finance, the varied pathways that housing systems, policies and markets have followed in each country as home ownership has progressed, and how these historical contingencies and institutional legacies have shaped and continue to mould social transformations.

The first part of this book deals with demographic, family and welfare issues more explicitly. In Chapter 2, John Doling considers the dynamics of contemporary demographic changes in relation to the changing nature and distribution of home ownership and housing wealth. This chapter specifically addresses the significance of the increasing proportion of older people in European societies, how most of them are now homeowners and how this is reshaping relationships between housing wealth, pensions systems and policy frameworks. In particular, home ownership has become increasingly important to sustaining consumption in later life in the context of declining pension resources and state welfare capacity.

The next two chapters explore the relationship between home ownership, the family and welfare systems further. Teresio Poggio examines the role of home ownership sectors in Mediterranean Europe in Chapter 3, taking Italy as an empirical example. This region features a lack of secure and affordable rental housing alternatives and has had a focus on realizing home ownership via self-building or other non-market channels. Moreover, the family has performed a special role in both the production and funding of home ownership, which plays a particular part in family welfare overall. In Chapter 4, Srna Mandic extends the exploration of the family, home ownership and welfare in the context of post-socialist transition economies of Central and Eastern Europe. Although the macro-economic effects of housing privatization have concerned governments, Mandic illustrates the significance of family-owned housing, as in Mediterranean Europe, in constellations of welfare relations. She further establishes differences in how housing market restructuring shaped social transition as well as comparative differences in family support for home ownership across post-socialist Europe and the EU.

The second part of the book addresses relationships between the state, markets and home ownership more directly. In Chapter 5, Hannu Ruonavaara examines long-term trends in home ownership and housing policies in Nordic countries. Ruonavaara's analysis draws attention to the pathway dependence in the development of housing and policy frameworks. Housing tenures are seen as socially (politically and culturally) produced entities whose properties are quite dependent on the context in which they exist and develop. This has meant that policy retrenchment has been more or less successful in each Nordic country in relation to the local context and history of policy and politics, housing and home ownership.

In the next chapter, Christine Whitehead considers the dynamics of tenure in England and the viability of sustaining high levels of home ownership. She examines drivers of growth in owner-occupation in England over the last 30 years as well as the potential for future changes in this rate, given the current uncertain economic environment. The chapter specifically examines government interest in continuing to expand owner-occupation and the challenges that such a policy is likely to face.

In the next two chapters in this section Rachel Bratt addresses the situation in the United States. She does this first in reference to the historical position of home ownership in American public policy. Chapter 7 thus considers the diverse goals of home ownership-orientated policies that have sought, with varying emphasis over time, to give people a stake in society; enhance financial and personal well-being; promote confidence in the government; stimulate the economy; quell social unrest and racial tensions; rejuvenate neighbourhoods; and reduce economic inequality by promoting wealth accumulation. Chapter 8 focuses on more recent events including the antecedents of the most recent crisis in US housing finance and the lessons to be learned thereafter. Bratt underscores how the United States managed to create a mortgage finance system that shifted the risks away from the originator of loans to other investors, far removed from the lending decision. This resulted in a system that altered perceptions of how risks and responsibilities should be distributed between homeowners and lenders.

In the final part of the book, Asia-Pacific examples of mature homeowner societies are considered that illustrate emerging problems related to long-term bias in tenure policy and the interaction of housing systems and neo-liberalization. In Chapter 9, Yosuke Hirayama considers the housing careers being adopted by young Japanese households in light of declining opportunities to get into owner-occupied housing. In the Japanese context, prolonged economic downturn in combination with the legacies of a post-war home ownership-focused housing and welfare system have produced a significant divide between different generations in terms of housing status and conditions. As opportunities to get into the owner-occupied housing market have diminished, there has been a growing propensity for young people to rent cheap, compact, one-person apartments or stay on much longer in their parents' homes. In the final chapter, David Thorns turns to the development of home ownership in New Zealand and, to a lesser extent, Australia, as a means to asses how much owner-occupation continues to represent a political or personal 'dream'. Although there have been consistent government and individual preferences for owner-occupied housing provision, home ownership rates have been in decline for more than a decade. In New Zealand entry into home ownership has become particularly difficult for newly formed households. Chapter 10 thus explores whether this is a long-run structural and life-course change or a temporary adjustment brought on by current market conditions.

Conclusions

Inevitably, or even by definition, edited volumes are neither exhaustive nor definitive. This volume, nonetheless, attempts to contribute to important contemporary debates not only in housing, but also on government and governance, welfare and social policy, social change and neo-liberalization. Disentangling transformations in home ownership over recent decades from the latest financial crisis – especially in relation to diverse national configurations – constitutes something of a challenge. The danger is that, although the former is bound up with the latter, concern with the crisis has obscured perspectives on the wider roles that home ownership and housing systems play beyond circuits of credit and finance.

The emphasis in this volume is ultimately on the diverse nature of home ownership, which, as we have examined in this chapter, is far more than just a tenure or way of dwelling. Among other things it is a system that supports particular patterns of housing production and consumption which can have deep and far-reaching implications, both individually profound and socially and economically radical. The different chapters in this book illustrate various such outcomes in many different contexts, although all point to developments in housing and tenure as central components of contemporary urban and neo-liberal transformations.

The embeddedness of housing in socio-economic systems has become increasingly self-evident in recent decades and is likely to continue to shape future developments. Although global economic forces were relatively similar before and during the credit crisis, the arrangements of housing systems went along different pathways in each society and will of course continue to shape particular pathways through and beyond the economic crises of the 2010s. Of particular note is the mutual influence of home ownership, housing markets, welfare systems and family and household arrangements, which has for a long time been neglected, and is a critical concern that this book seeks to address.

References

Aalbers, M.B. (2008) The financialization of home and the mortgage market crisis, *Competition and Change*, 12(2), 148–166.

Aalbers, M.B. (2011) *Place, Exclusion, and Mortgage Markets*, Oxford: Wiley Blackwell.

Allen, C. (2008) *Housing Market Renewal and Social Class*, London: Routledge.

Allen, J., Barlow, J., Leal, J., Maloutas, T. and Padavani, L. (2004) *Housing and Welfare in Southern Europe*, Oxford: Blackwell.

Atterhög, M. (2005) The effect of government policies on home ownership rates, in J. Doling and M. Elsinga (eds) *Home Ownership: Getting In, Getting From, Getting Out*, Amsterdam: IOS Press.

Beck, U. (1992) *Risk Society*, London: Sage.

Bocian, D.G., Li, W. and Ernst, K.S. (2010) *Foreclosures of Race and Ethnicity: The Demographics of a Crisis*, CRL Research Paper, Washington, DC: Center for Responsible Lending.

Boelhouwer, P. (2002) Trends in Dutch housing policy and the shifting position of the social rented sector, *Urban Studies*, 39(2), 219–235.

Bootle, R. (1996) *The Death of Inflation: Surviving and Thriving in the Zero Era*, London: Nicholas Brealey.

Brenner, N., Peck, J. and Theodore, N. (2010) After neoliberalization, *Globalizations*, 7(3), 327–345.

Burrows, R. and Wilcox, S. (2000) *Half the Poor: Home Owners with Low Incomes*, London: Council of Mortgage Lenders.

Butler, T. and Robson, G. (2003) Plotting the middle classes: gentrification and circuits of education in London, *Housing Studies*, 18, 5–28.

Case, K.E. and Schiller, R.J. (2003) Is there a bubble in the housing market? *Brookings Papers on Economic Activity*, 2, 299–362.

Castles, F.J. (1998) The really big trade off: home ownership and the welfare state in the New world and the Old, *Acta Politica*, 33(1), 5–19.

Chua, B.H. (2003) Maintaining housing values under the condition of universal home-ownership, *Housing Studies*, 18(3), 765–780.

Clapham, D., Hegedus, J., Kintrea, K. and Tosics, I. (eds) (1996) *Housing Privatisation in Eastern Europe*, Westport, CT: Greenwood.

Crouch, C. (2009) Privatised Keynesianism: an unacknowledged policy regime, *British Journal of Politics and International Studies*, 11(3), 382–399.

Doling, J. and Ford, J. (2007) A union of home owners [Editorial], *European Journal of Housing and Planning*, 7(2), 113–127.

Doling, J. and Ronald, R. (2010) Property-based welfare and European home owners: how would housing perform as a pension? *Journal of Housing and the Built Environment*, 25(2), 227–241.

Dorling, D., Ford, J., Holmans, A., Sharp, C., Thomas, B. and Wilcox, S. (eds) (2005) *The Great Divide: An Analysis of Housing Inequality*, London: Shelter.

Dymski, G. (2010) Why the subprime crisis is different: a Minskyian approach, *Cambridge Journal of Economics*, 34, 239–255.

Elsinga, M. and Mandic, S. (2010) Housing as a piece in the old age puzzle, *Teorija in praksa: revija za druzbena vprasanja*, 47(5), 940–958.

EMF (European Mortgage Federation) (2009) *Hypostat 2008*, Brussels: EMF.

Esping-Andersen, G. (1990) *The Three Worlds of Welfare Capitalism*, Cambridge: Polity Press.

Esping-Andersen, G. (1999) *Social Foundations of Post Industrial Economies*, Oxford: Oxford University Press.

Fisher, L.M. and Jaffe, A.J. (2003) Determinants of international home ownership rates, *Housing Finance International*, September, 34–42.

Flint, J. (2004) Reconfiguring agency and responsibility in the governance of social housing in Scotland, *Urban Studies*, 41(1), 151–172.

Forrest, R. (2008) Globalization and the housing asset rich: geographies, demography's and policy convoys, *Global Social Policy*, 8(2), 167–187.

Forrest, R. and Murie, A. (1988) *Selling the Welfare State: The Privatisation of Public Housing*, London: Routledge.

Forrest, R. and Hirayama, Y. (2009) The uneven impact of neo-liberalism on housing opportunities, *International Journal of Urban and Regional Research*, 33(4), 998–1013.

Forrest, R. and Yip, N.M. (eds) (2011) *Housing Markets and the Global Financial Crisis: The Uneven Impact on Households*, Cheltenham: Edwin Elgar.

Groves, R., Murie, A. and Watson, C. (2007) *Housing and the New Welfare State: Perspectives from East Asia and Europe*, Aldershot: Ashgate.

Hamnett, C. (2009) Spatially displaced demand and the changing geography of house prices in London, 1995–2006, *Housing Studies*, 24(3), 301–320.

Hannsgen, G. (2007) A random walk down Maple Lane? A critique of neoclassical consumption theory with reference to housing wealth, *Review of Political Economy*, 19(1), 1–20.

Harloe, M. (1995) *The People's Home? Social Rented Housing in Europe and America*, Oxford: Blackwell.

Helbrecht, I. and Geilenkeuser, T. (2010) Homeownership in Germany: retirement strategies of households in a tenant society, *Toerija in Praksa*, 47(5), 975–993.

Hoekstra, J. (2003) Housing and the welfare state in the Netherlands: an application of Esping-Andersen's typology, *Housing, Theory and Society*, 20(20), 58–71.

Immergluck, D. (2009) *Foreclosed: High-Risk Lending, Deregulation, and the Undermining of America's Mortgage Market*, Ithaca, NY: Cornell University Press.

Kemeny, J. (1981) *The Myth of Home Ownership*, London: Routledge & Kegan Paul.

Kemeny, J. (1992) *Housing and Social Theory*, London: Routledge.

Kemeny, J. (2005) 'The really big trade-off' between home ownership and welfare: Castles' evaluation of the 1980 thesis, and reformulation 25 years on, *Housing, Theory and Society*, 22(2), 59–75.

Kleinhans, R.J. and Elsinga, M. (2010) 'Buy your home and feel in control': does home ownership achieve the empowerment of former tenants of social housing? *International Journal of Housing Policy*, 10(1), 41–61.

Kurz, K. and Blossfeld, H. (2004) *Home Ownership and Social Inequality in Comparative Perspective*, Stanford: Stanford University Press.

Langley, P. (2008) *The Everyday Life of Global Finance: Saving and Borrowing in Anglo-America*, Oxford: Oxford University Press.

Lawson, J. (2010) Path dependency and emergent relations: explaining the different role of limited profit housing in the dynamic urban regimes of Vienna and Zurich, *Housing Theory and Society*, 27(3), 204–220.

Lees, L., Slater, T. and Wyly, E. (2008) *Gentrification*, London: Routledge.

Levy-Vroelant, C. (2010) Housing vulnerable groups: the development of a new public action sector, *International Journal of Housing Policy*, 10(4), 443–456.

McIntyre, Z. and McKee, K. (2009) Creating sustainable communities through tenure-mix: the responsibilisation of marginal homeowners in Scotland, *GeoJournal*. Online. Available at http://www.springerlink.com/content/90xg83643pq14g79/fulltext.pdf.

McKay, S. (2001) The savings gateway: 'asset-based welfare' in practice, *Benefits*, 10(2), 141–145.

Malpass P. (2006) Housing in an 'opportunity society'. Home ownership and the amplification of inequality, in J. Doling and M. Elsinga (eds) *Home Ownership: Getting In, Getting From, Getting Out. Part II*, Amsterdam: IOS Press.

Malpass, P. (2008) Housing and the new welfare state: wobbly pillar or cornerstone? *Housing Studies*, 23(1), 1–19.

Mandic, S. (2008) Home-leaving and its structural determinants in Western and Eastern Europe: an exploratory study, *Housing Studies*, 23(4), 615–637.

Mandic, S. and Elsinga, M. (2010) Editorial, *Teorija in praksa: revija za druzbena vprasanja*, 47(5), 937–939.

Martin, R. (2002) *Financialization of Daily Life*, Philadelphia: Temple University Press.

Martin, R. (2010) The local geographies of the financial crisis: from the housing bubble to economic recession and beyond, *Journal of Economic Geography*, 11(4), 587–618.

Minstry of Housing (2000) *Nota, Mensen Wensen Wonen* [*White Paper on Housing: People, Wishes, Living*], The Hague: Ministry of Housing.

Mulder, C.H. and Billari, F.C. (2010) Home-ownership regimes and low fertility, *Housing Studies*, 25(4), 527–541.

Norris, M. and Domanski, H. (2009) Housing conditions, states, markets and households: a pan-European analysis, *Journal of Comparative Policy Analysis*, 11(3), 385–407.

ODPM (Office of the Deputy Prime Minister) (2005) *Homes for All*, London: ODPM.

Overton, L. (2010) *Housing and Finance in Later Life: A Study of UK Equity Release Customers*, London: Age UK.

Peck, J. and Tickell, A. (2002) Neoliberalising space, *Antipode,* 34(3), 380–404.

Pierson, P. (2002) Coping with permanent austerity: welfare state restructuring in affluent democracies, *Revue francaise de sociologie*, 43(2), 369–406.

Retsinas, N.P. and Belsky, E.S. (eds) (2002) *Low-Income Home Ownership: Examining the Unexamined Goal*, Cambridge, MA: Joint Center for Housing Studies and Brookings Institution Press.

Rohe, W.M., Van Zandt, S. and McCarthy, G. (2002) Home ownership and access to opportunity: a review of the research evidence, *Housing Studies,* 17, 51–61.

Ronald, R. (2007) Comparing homeowner societies: can we construct an East–West model? *Housing Studies*, 22(4), 473–493.

Ronald, R. (2008) *The Ideology of Home Ownership: Homeowner Societies and the Role of Housing*, Basingstoke: Palgrave Macmillan.

Ronald, R, and Chiu, R.H.L. (2010) Changing housing policy landscapes in Asia Pacific, *International Journal of Housing Policy*, 10(3), 223–231.

Ronald, R. and Doling, J. (2010) Shifting East Asian approaches to home ownership and the housing welfare pillar, *International Journal of Housing Policy*, 10(3), 233–254.

Ronald, R. and Hirayama, Y. (2009) Home alone: the individualization of young, urban Japanese singles, *Environment and Planning A*, 41, 2836–2854.

Rose, N. (2000) Community, citizenship and the third way, *American Behavioural Scientist*, 43(9), 1395–1411.

Schlay, A.B. (2006) Low income home ownership: American dream or delusion? *Urban Studies*, 43(3), 511–531.

Schmidt, S. (1989) Convergence theory, labour movements, and corporatism: the case of housing, *Scandinavian Housing and Planning Research*, 6(1), 83–101.

Schwartz, H. (2009) *Subprime Nation: American Power, Global Capital, and the Housing Bubble*, Ithaca, NY: Cornell University Press.

Schwartz, H. and Seabrooke, L. (2008) Varieties of residential capitalism in the international political economy: old welfare states and the new politics of housing, *Comparative European Politics*, 6, 237–261.

Sherraden, M. (2003) Individual accounts in social security: can they be progressive? *International Journal of Social Welfare*, 12(2), 97–107.

Shiller, R. (2008) *The Subprime Solution: How Today's Global Financial Crisis Happened and What To Do About It*, Princeton, NJ: Princeton University Press.

Smith, S.J., Searle, B.A. and Cook, N. (2009) Rethinking the risks of home ownership, *Journal of Social Policy*, 38, 83–102.

Tatch, J. (2006) *Will the Real First Time Buyers Please Stand Up*, CML *Housing Finance*, September, London: CML.

The Economist (2005) The global housing boom: in come the waves, 16 June.

Torgerson, U. (1987) Housing: the wobbly pillar under the welfare state, in B. Turner, J. Kemeny and L. Lundqvist (eds) *Between State and Market: Housing in the Post Industrial Era*, Stockholm: Almqvist and Wiksell.

Tsenkova, S. (2009) *Housing Policy Reforms in Post-Socialist Europe. Lost in Transition*, Heidelberg: Physica-Verlag HD.

Turner, B. and Whitehead, C.M.E. (2002) Reducing housing subsidy: Swedish housing policy in an international context, *Urban Studies*, 39(2), 201–217.

Wang Y.P. and Murie A. (1999) *Housing Policy and Practice in China*, London: Macmillan.

Washington Post (2009) Mortgage bailout to aid 1 in 9 U.S. homeowners. Online. Available at http://online.wsj.com/article/SB123617623602129441.html (accessed 1 April 2011).

Watson, M. (2009) Planning for the future of asset-based welfare? New Labour, financialized economic agency and the housing market, *Planning, Practice and Research*, 24(1), 41–56.

Watson, M. (2010) House price Keynesianism and the contradictions of the modern investor subject, *Housing Studies*, 25(3), 413–426.

Wolf, M. (2009) *Fixing Global Finance: How to Curb Financial Crises in the 21st Century*, New Haven, CT: Yale University Press.

Yamada, M. (1999) *Parasaito Shinguru no Jidai* [*The Age of the Parasite Singles*], Tokyo: Chikuma Shobou.

Ye, J.-P. Song, N.-J. and Tiang, C.-J. (2010) An analysis of housing policy during economic transition in China, *International Journal of Housing Policy*, 10(3), 273–300.

Part I

Demographic change, housing wealth and welfare

2

HOUSING AND DEMOGRAPHIC CHANGE

John Doling

Introduction

Following significant rates of growth in the Western member states over the entire post-war period, and in many of the Eastern member states over the period after the break-up of the Soviet Union, home ownership is now the predominant tenure in Europe; with some two-thirds of households now owning, Europe may be accurately described as a 'union of home owners' (Doling and Ford, 2007). Recent discussion about this growth and other developments in the housing systems of advanced economies have been markedly skewed towards the impact of globalisation and the associated rise of neo-liberalism (e.g. Doling and Ford, 2003; Malpass, 2006; Ronald, 2008; Stephens, 2003). One element of much of this discussion has been that these macro processes have underlain – in some interpretations, forced – the tendency for states to retreat from social forms of housing provision in favour of private forms, especially home ownership. Thus, Peter Malpass has argued that, although responding in different ways, each country is doing so in 'response to the pressures arising from globalisation . . . [resulting in] . . . a general tendency to cut back on universal services funded from taxation . . . Housing . . . has been at the leading edge of reform' (Malpass, 2006, p. 109).

Whatever the strength of such explanation, there is another macro process that has broadly progressed in parallel with the developments in home ownership: although following the baby boom in the decade or so immediately following the end of World War II fertility rates have had some cyclical variation, the general trend has been downwards, and this has been allied to a steady increase in life expectancy (European Commission, 2005). Fewer babies and longer lives have resulted in higher median ages in all member states, to the greying of Europe. This ageing of the populations of advanced economies has put their governments under pressure, as significant as globalisation, arguably, in its effect, to restructure their welfare systems. In reviewing the literature on population ageing and welfare provision, Castles (2004) indicates that 'the logic of [the] argument is transparent' (p. 4). On the one hand, pensions and cash benefits to older people combined with health and social care constitute the two largest programmes in most of the larger economies, amounting for about two-thirds of total social spending. On the other hand, the proportion of older people in those same economies is growing so there will be increasing upwards pressure on the costs of these elements of social spending. Moreover, because older people form a large potential voting block, it will be difficult for elected governments to resist their demands. In these circumstances, and given the twin pressures of globalisation and the fiscal implications that arise from a fall in dependency ratios, government spending on those welfare areas not directed at older people may be most vulnerable to cuts. In such a scenario, spending on social housing provision for young people and families might not be the highest priority and, whether through positive action to promote it or simply the withering away of other opportunities, home ownership may have come to occupy a larger share of national housing systems.

On this view, what can sometimes appear a rather mechanistic interpretation of globalisation as an independent variable that brings about an irresistible retrenchment of the social element in housing provision can be extended to an equally mechanistic interpretation that the same housing outcomes are the inevitable consequence of the ageing of populations.

The position taken in this chapter is that, although on the available evidence the ageing of populations in Europe appears to have had, and seems likely to continue to have, significant impacts on housing outcomes, the impacts are not necessarily, or only, in that direction or necessarily immutable. Indeed, the linkages between population and housing may actually be much more complex, including the possibility that the independent–dependent relationship is reversed.

It is elements of this complexity that the chapter explores. Following a presentation of the scale and extent of ageing populations, the chapter uses the life cycle model (LCM) as a vehicle for exploring the linkages between demographic structures and home ownership. Although the intention in this has been to focus on European experience, in practice the available evidential base is patchy and unsystematic so that studies from other advanced economies, especially the United States, are also drawn upon. From this, two types of linkage can be identified. The first is the possibility that home ownership has been a contributory cause of the ageing of populations as well as the challenges associated with ageing. This then sets home ownership as an independent variable that may influence demographic developments. The second linkage considers home ownership as a palliator, that is, the extent to which it may reduce the severity of some of the problems commonly deemed to result from an ageing Europe, specifically by meeting the income needs of the growing cohorts of older people. The argument is not that this characteristic of home ownership has somehow forced governments to promote home ownership, but rather that it has provided them with a reason to do so, and as such may have encouraged some actually to do so.

Although a central objective of this chapter is to promote the importance of demographic change in understanding housing system change, it is an objective based on recognition that the linkages are not always transparent, not necessarily uniform across countries and certainly not incontestable.

An ageing Europe

The ageing of the population of the European member states is part of a general, worldwide trend, taking place over the course of perhaps a century and through which there is a shift from high rates of fertility and mortality to low rates of fertility and mortality (Kinsella and Phillips, 2005). This demographic transition is bringing to an end an historically short period – much of the middle and latter part of the twentieth century – when European, and indeed other Western, economies, had, in economic development terms, an unusually favourable age structure. From the 1930s birth rates had been declining, thus moving away from the youth dependency of the past, while mortality rates had not yet reduced significantly, retired people were relatively few in number and age dependency was yet to emerge. In David Coleman's (2001) words, 'that benevolent phase of population structure, a transitional phase between the youth dependency of the past and the aged dependency of the future, is now going' (p. 2).

There are detailed differences in the extent of these trends between member states. The total fertility rate, the average number of expected births in a woman's lifetime, has dropped everywhere, but is particularly low in the southern and some eastern member states (Castles, 2004; European Commission, 2005). Yet overall the picture is uniform: everywhere the total fertility rate is below replacement levels and everywhere life expectancies have increased, with forecasts that they will continue to do so. In 1950, the countries that were to become the EU25 had, on average, only 9.1 per cent of their populations aged 65 and over, with 24.9 per cent under 15, whereas the forecast for a date a century later shows a reversal to 30.4 per cent and 13.13 per cent respectively (Table 2.1). Correspondingly, whereas for every one person of retirement age there were 5.52 younger adults aged 25–64 years in 1950, the expectation is that by 2050 there will be only 1.52.

The changes that have occurred already, no less the changes yet to come, are clearly dramatic and present significant challenges to member states, principally in terms of reducing economic growth potential below what it might otherwise be and of meeting the funding of health care and pension needs because of larger sections of the population requiring support and smaller sections creating the wealth and paying the taxes to fund them (European Communities, 2004; Malmberg, 2007). As the Kok report concludes:

TABLE 2.1 Distribution of the population (EU25) by age group (%)

Age (years)	1950	1975	2000	2025	2050
80+	1.2	2.0	3.4	6.5	11.9
65–79	7.9	10.7	12.3	16.2	18.5
50–64	15.2	15.4	17.2	21.3	18.5
25–49	35.0	32.7	36.9	31.1	28.2
15–24	15.8	15.5	13.0	10.5	9.7
0–14	24.9	23.7	17.1	14.4	13.3
Ratio of older (> 65 years) to younger (24–64 years) adults	1:5.52	1:3.79	1:2.85	1:2.31	1:1.52
Median age (years)	31	33	39	45	48

Source: European Commission (2005).

> these developments will have profound implications for the European economy and its capability to finance European welfare systems . . . the pure impact of ageing populations will be to reduce the potential growth rate . . . a GDP per head some 20% lower than could otherwise be expected . . . [and] an increase in pension and healthcare spending by 2050, varying between 4% and 8% of GDP.
>
> (European Commission, 2004, p. 13)

A life cycle approach

A model that facilitates the examination of linkages between these trends in demographic structures and the perceived threats they pose is one based on the human life cycle. Advanced economies have varying combinations of institutions, such as civil society organisations, that contribute to the well-being of people over the life course, from infancy and childhood when considerable help is needed with respect to basic biological needs as well as the acquisition of social and technical skills necessary for making a living later in the life course, through to old age when increasing frailty may limit the ability to independently sustain a livelihood. The modern welfare state can also be seen as in part fulfilling such functions. The pattern of taxation, particularly based on earned income, achieves a distribution horizontally over the life span that effectively pays for many of the consumption needs of those with little or no earned income: the young who particularly consume education and health care and the old who particularly consume pensions and health and social care. Notwithstanding elements of vertical distribution, in reality a large proportion of the welfare benefits received by individuals in many countries are self-financed, making each national welfare system a sort of 'savings bank' (Hills, 1993, p. 19). It is precisely because the savings bank is run on a social basis across generations that the shift in the numerical balance between the generations, requiring a shrinking working age population to support an expanding retired population, poses such large challenges.

In addition to, but not independent from, civil society and welfare state institutions, individuals and households appear to organise their financial affairs in a way that mirrors their life course. The life cycle model can be thought of as a strategy for the temporal redistribution of income, the basic premise being that, at any one time, individuals set their present level of consumption in relation to their present level of wealth and their expected future income (Deaton, 1992). In reality, because for most people the level of income over their life cycle approximates to an inverse U shape, the LCM can be characterised by a number of distinct stages. In the first of these, when individuals are young, their consumption (food, shelter, education and so on) generally exceeds their income so that, in effect, they borrow against future income. In the second stage, when they are in paid employment, their income exceeds their consumption, enabling them to save. In the final stage, that of retirement, consumption needs again generally exceed income so that to meet their consumption needs individuals draw from their savings.

Empirical studies involving many countries show that in practice the period of maximum saving tends to be in late middle age after the child-rearing years and before retirement, which points to a general relationship between saving and the age structure of national populations: the aggregate savings rate in a country tends to be 'lower when the population share of the elderly is high and when the population share of children is high' (Deaton, 2005, p. 13). From this, the impact of ageing populations is unclear: more older people would suggest a high level of dissaving – albeit with life expectancies increasing savings need to last longer so that dissaving may be at a slower rate – while fewer children would increase the saving capacity of adults in the child-rearing years.

Despite this uncertainty, it is clear that housing has the potential to play a particularly important role in the LCM, both in general and also in relation to the impact of different population age structures. In most countries housing costs, whether renting or purchasing, constitute a major, perhaps the largest, single item in household budgets. As such it determines the standard of living of the household both directly through the house itself and indirectly through its impact on the amount of the budget left over to consume non-housing goods. In turn, because housing is expensive relative to incomes it will also impact on the balance between consumption and saving. There is yet a further dimension in that housing is itself an item of both consumption and saving. Both renters and owners of dwellings (whether they are outright owners or repaying a housing loan) consume a flow of housing services; this equates to their housing standard of living. Owners additionally have an investment, which generally in advanced economies has experienced long-term growth and is tradable. People who buy their own homes are therefore both consuming its services over time and also, provided that house prices are rising in real terms, building up their wealth.

Empirical evidence of the role of housing wealth in household decisions about how much to consume can be found in statistically observable relationships between house price developments and consumer spending. Broadly, across the advanced economies, following periods of rapid house price inflation, levels of household consumption systematically increase (Catte *et al.*, 2004). This may be taken to indicate that households appear to treat home ownership as a form of saving, such that, as a result of an increase in house prices, if the level of their savings is boosted, they respond to the increased potential for consuming from savings later in the life cycle by increasing their consumption now.

Furthermore, from the evidence of this balancing it is possible to have some certainty about the consequences of ageing populations. What has been termed the wealth effect, or the impact of changes in the value of housing assets on the propensity to consume, has been found to be greater among older than younger homeowners, leading to the conclusion that 'as the population ages and becomes more concentrated in the old homeowners group, aggregate consumption may become more responsive to house prices' (Campbell and Cocco, 2004, p. 24). In short, with ageing populations, a given change in house prices is likely to have a more pronounced total effect on consumption.

Home ownership as a cause

Having established a demographic and life cycle context, we turn to the first of the two main arguments of this chapter: that population ageing, both as a trend and as a perceived problem for the fiscal foundations of welfare systems, may be a consequence, at least in part, of home ownership. This reverses the logic identified by Castles with housing systems shifting from being the dependent to becoming the independent variable and is explored in relation to fertility rates and early retirement.

Fertility rates

Much research, and indeed policy attention, has been directed at the question of why total fertility rates have dropped to their present levels. Some insights have been provided because not only have there been developments over time, but also there are differences between member states. Although all have low rates (below the replacement level of about 2.1), in some, for example the Southern European countries, rates have fallen to what has been termed 'lowest-low fertility' (below 1.3). Methodologically, this cross-sectional variation facilitates the search for national, institutional characteristics that underlie the decisions of those of child-rearing ages. Factors such as the nature of taxation systems and the degree to which they encourage women to be in paid employment, flexible working time arrangements that allow both men and women to combine working and caring roles, and the availability and costs of childcare facilities

– broadly what are termed 'family-friendly' policies – appear to play a significant part (Castles, 2004; Dingeldey, 2001; Sjoberg, 2004).

Combining both longitudinal and cross-sectional analysis, Castles (2004) has also argued the importance of shifts in values away from assumptions that women's primary role is motherhood and that work and child rearing are essentially incompatible, towards notions that men and women have equal rights and indeed an equal need to undertake paid employment. In his view, it is precisely because the southern countries have labour markets that are less conducive to female employment and cultural values that still consider combining work and motherhood as inappropriate that, in comparison with the greater gender equality of Scandinavian countries, there have been greater reductions in total fertility rates.

Underlying many of these explanations is the financial dimension of child rearing. The stark reality facing parents and would-be parents across Europe is that their children will impose a heavy financial burden that may not allow them easily to smooth consumption over the life cycle. Because children cannot support themselves their survival to adulthood is dependent on the ability and willingness of adults to provide them with financial and other resources (Malmberg, 2007). In some respects the burden has got larger. For earlier generations, for example, children were expected to contribute to the family income, but the raising of school leaving ages and the expectation of pursuing university-level education has now extended the number of years of their dependency (Malmberg, 2007).

Moreover, as Jim Kemeny (1981) pointed out some years ago, the financial burden of child rearing coincides temporally with the acquisition of home ownership, this arising because the housing stock in most countries is such that, in comparison with rental housing, the size, layout and location of owner-occupied housing offers greater benefits to young families than to singles and couples without children (Mulder and Billari, 2006). Consequently, European couples often move into home ownership in anticipation of or shortly after starting a family. But the financial costs of entry into home ownership are sometimes so great that they can actually lead to a decrease in the probability of having a child. Investigation by Mulder and Billari (2006) suggests that there may be significant cross-country differences in this effect, with those countries, such as Spain, Italy and Greece, in which finance markets are not very developed so that access to home ownership is financially difficult, whilst rental opportunities are relatively few, also having the lowest fertility rates.

These arguments are consistent with research which indicates that labour force participation rates for women in the childbearing years tend to be higher in countries where housing systems provide limited opportunities for acquiring good-quality rental housing at reasonable cost, pushing younger people towards home ownership (Doling et al., 2006). Once the decision has been made to opt for home ownership, however, it often locks both members of a couple 'into continuous employment in order to safeguard mortgage repayments' (Hakim, 2003, p. 258). These studies support the contention expressed by the European Commission that 'Europeans would like to have more children. But they are discouraged from doing so by all kinds of problems that limit their freedom of choice, including difficulties in finding housing' (European Commission, 2005, p. 2).

The developments in housing systems in Western countries, to the point that there are decreasing opportunities to enter rental housing along with house prices that, on the one hand, make entry into home ownership financially difficult and, on the other hand, make home ownership a good avenue for saving, appear to effectively force young households to consume less (other than housing) and save more than they would otherwise do. If this is the case, the assumption of the LCM that households set the level of present consumption with regard to their expectations about their future income and their current wealth is distorted because home ownership, which effectively has become a necessity for those wishing to rear children, is at the same time both consumption expenditure and saving: for many, its acquisition results in over-saving and crowds out non-housing consumption.

There is here, then, a contradiction. On the one hand, the home ownership stock in many countries seems, in comparison with rental housing, to provide a superior context in which to bring up children; from the point of view of a physical entity the promotion of home ownership could be reasonably described as a family-friendly policy. On the other hand, the front-loaded costs of entry into home ownership, which often necessitates the repayment of a loan that constitutes a high proportion of the combined sum of two incomes, mitigates against child rearing, so that from a financial perspective the promotion of home ownership can be considered a family-unfriendly policy.

Early retirement

A corollary of what we have identified as over-saving by younger adults as a consequence of home ownership is that, as they age to become older adults, home ownership provides opportunities that may exacerbate the impacts of ageing on the viability of welfare arrangements, specifically by facilitating the withdrawal from active participation in the labour market before the formal retirement age and thus effectively lowering the dependency ratio and reducing the tax base. Here, again, there are significant differences across Europe with member states such as France and Belgium, for example, having high early retirement rates.

The factors underlying individual decisions to stop working at a certain age are, like the factors determining fertility, complex. They include the state of health of the individual and the value they place on leisure time, the nature of pension and wider benefit systems and the incentives they give to carry on or stop work, and the nature of the labour market including the opportunities to work part time (Blondal and Scarpetta, 1997; Taylor, 2001). Here, also, home ownership appears to be a significant factor. The consumption aspect of home ownership means that the outright owner is able to continue to live in the home rent free so that they can, in comparison with renters, get by on a smaller pension (Castles, 1998). The investment, particularly if house prices have increased in real terms, also provides owners with at least the possibility of realising some or all of the equity to contribute to an income in old age. The result has been that, once other factors have been taken into account, in Western countries with high home ownership rates and high price increases, early retirement is more common (Doling and Horsewood, 2003). In LCM terms, therefore, over-saving at a young age, 'forced' by the nature of housing systems, may facilitate dissaving to take place earlier than might otherwise have been the case.

If the state promotion of home ownership is, with respect to young adults, a family-unfriendly policy, with respect to older adults it is a work-unfriendly policy. In the former case it may be seen as a factor contributing to the demographic trend of ageing by depressing fertility rates, and in the latter it may be seen as contributing to the fiscal consequences of falling dependency ratios by further reducing the proportion of the adult population in work.

Home ownership as a palliator

Insofar as home ownership may exacerbate the impact of ageing populations by facilitating lower participation rates for older workers, the same features of home ownership also provide a potential palliator. Because over the long run home ownership sectors have increased in size and house prices have increased in real terms, housing equity has come to constitute the single largest source of wealth held by the average European household. Although the precise amounts are unknown, rough estimates indicate that by about 2003 the net value of home-owned properties, that is, the gross value less outstanding loans, may have been around €15 trillion in the EU25 member states (Doling and Ford, 2007). More reliable estimates, but for a smaller group of states, show that in 2000 in France, Germany and Italy about half of total household wealth was housing wealth, with the proportion being about 65 per cent in Spain, just below 40 per cent in the Netherlands and the United Kingdom and just below 30 per cent in the United States (Boone and Girouard, 2002). In comparison, the value of the shares held amounted to a quarter or less of total household wealth. The wealth holdings of older Europeans, in their mid-fifties and over, are even more skewed towards housing assets (Lefebure *et al.*, 2006).

This is the second of the main arguments of this chapter: in principle, housing assets may be used to contribute to the income needs of older people; such dissaving could reduce the impact on individual households of the financial effects of withdrawing from paid employment, particularly where the level of formal pension systems has been reduced. Again, in principle, housing assets might attract the attention of national governments in seeking to deal with the fiscal consequences of ageing. In other words, some of the impacts of ageing populations could be relieved by the release of housing equity. This would be entirely consistent with the LCM: when working, households save so that, when retired, they can dissave and maintain consumption. Although the evidence is again patchy and incomplete as well as containing some contradictions, it does provide some support for concluding that the 'in principle' outcomes have sometimes, although certainly not always, become 'in practice' ones.

Dissaving housing assets: household behaviour

The first dimension of our examination concerns the extent to which European households see their homes in these terms: is home ownership universally seen as a financial asset? And, if so, how in practice do households use that asset?

The evidence here is particularly contradictory. On the one hand, recent research indicates that, over the last almost 30 years in each of ten Organisation for Economic Co-operation and Development (OECD) countries, whenever there has been a large annual increase in house prices, and therefore in the value of housing equity, this has had a downward effect on the amount of money that households saved in that year (Doling and Horsewood, 2008a). It might be concluded from this that households really do see housing as a form of saving and that they organise their affairs accordingly, reducing their additional savings in response to increases in the value of their housing equity. Moreover, the effect appears to operate across a range of European countries including southern countries. So, perhaps uniformly across Europe, households see home ownership as a form of saving.

On the other hand, the extent to which the use of housing assets varies with the age of the head of household has been examined in a number of econometric studies based on an LCM framework and suggests a reluctance to utilise that saving in old age. Many of these studies have used data for the United States or the United Kingdom for the 1980s and 1990s, with the results indicating that moving out of home ownership into rental housing, downsizing or otherwise drawing on equity in order to support consumption as households age was not widespread in those decades, an exception often occurring with the death of one partner or a move into a nursing home (Disney et al., 1998; Ermisch and Jenkins, 1999; Feinstein and McFadden, 1989; Rohe et al., 2002; Venti and Wise, 2001). More recent analysis with a European focus broadly confirmed these findings while also indicating important differences between countries. Most European households who are homeowners by their late fifties remain so throughout their remaining working and retirement years so that there is not evidence of large-scale dissaving or decumulation of housing assets. Nevertheless, there is evidence of some decumulation as people get older as well as significant regional differences. Particularly where housing costs are high and following the death of a spouse, the mobility rates of older Europeans increase, marking a general, but not large-scale, tendency to move into rental housing or to remain in home ownership but move to a smaller dwelling

(Tatsiramos, 2006). Older people in the southern member states (Italy, Greece, Portugal and Spain) are less likely than their counterparts in the other Western member states to move at all, or to move into a smaller dwelling or out of home ownership.

The general picture, then, is that older people have had limited propensity to use their homes as a source of wealth that might contribute to their income needs, leading to the intriguing question: if home ownership constitutes a form of saving, why don't people spend it in later life? There may be two sets of reasons for this reluctance to spend, one based in the nature of home ownership and of national housing systems, and one in the nature of different sources of wealth and household motives.

The nature of home ownership

The apparent reluctance of older owners to move out of their homes (to move downmarket or out of the market) may be a function of one or more housing and housing market attributes. The fact that home ownership is both a consumption and an investment good complicates the dissaving decision, because any form of dissaving that involves moving from the house necessarily changes the household's pattern of consumption. But it is a consumption that may have considerable psychic or emotional attachment. Established family and friendship networks and reliance on neighbourhood institutions along with a store of personal memories attached to the house itself can make changing one's home of a different dimension to changing the refrigerator or the car. In some countries the transaction costs involved in selling a house, and in purchasing another, including legal fees and taxation, are particularly high, making the realisation of this form of wealth more expensive than other forms. For example, transaction costs are relatively low in the United Kingdom and Scandinavia, and relatively high in Southern Europe (OECD, 2004). In some countries access to decent and reasonably priced rental accommodation may be restricted because of a shortage of supply or because of rules of access (Rouwendal and Thomese, 2010). Finally, and particularly in Southern European countries, housing is central to the larger, extended family project, not to be bought and sold but acquired on behalf of the whole family and passed through the generations. (Allen *et al.*, 2004; Earley, 2004).

The extent of such dampening effects on dissaving is significant because generally most equity withdrawal appears to occur when people move (Committee on the Global Financial System, 2006). This suggests that the full significance of housing as a palliator may rely on financial products, such as reverse mortgages, as they enable dissaving without moving. Whereas European financial institutions are expanding the number and range of financial products available to households (European Mortgage Federation, 2006), they are not uniformly available across Europe (ECB, 2003). At the present time, therefore, this is not an option for all Europeans and, even where it is, it is not widely pursued.

The nature of savings

The apparent reluctance to pursue strategies that release housing equity can also be attributed to the nature of different sources of savings or wealth. Wealth held by older people can usefully be divided into two categories. Annuity wealth provides an income stream, the level of which could be constant, in nominal or real terms, or subject to change imposed by an external agent, such as the government, and which would terminate on the death of the recipient. Generally, annuity wealth includes pensions and other social benefits. In contrast, bequeathable wealth, which includes housing assets, as well as other forms of savings such as cash, shares and durable goods, can be consumed at a rate determined by the individual and passed to an heir at death.

The bequest motive provides an addition to the LCM because it implies that individuals may not seek to reduce their wealth holding in old age but rather to hold on to their wealth or even to increase it. Somewhat confusingly, empirical examination of the rate of dissaving of older people – at least in the United States – indicates that, starting from the same level of resources, older people, whether single or couples, with children do not dissave more than their counterparts without children (Churi and Jappelli, 2006; Hurd, 1990).

In addition to the bequest motive, it is also possible that households pursue a precautionary savings motive, saving now against future financial shocks: housing as a sort of personal insurance or provident fund. This also provides an addition to the LCM:

> Uncertainty about the life-span, about health and health costs, and the extreme unpleasantness of poverty in old age, combine to make older people extremely cautious about running down their assets. Such behaviour also explains, at least partially, the important role of accidental bequests in the transmission of wealth.
>
> (Deaton, 1992, p. 192)

The bequest and precautionary motives, then, both offer a possible understanding of why older people may be reluctant to dissave in the way suggested by the LCM. But insofar as they are willing to dissave, might there be further reasons why they are more reluctant to use housing wealth than other wealth? One possibility lies in attitudes to risk. In comparison with younger people, older people tend to be less risk tolerant. In general, they are less willing to accept any risk with their investments, let alone higher than average risks, in return for the possibility of earning average, or higher, returns (Poterba, 1998). Given this, it can be anticipated that as people age they will tend to dispose of risky or volatile assets such as shares before less risky ones such as their homes, and both before the least volatile such as cash and government bonds.

For two further reasons it can be expected that couples will dissave less than people living on their own: first, because the living costs of two people sharing are less than twice the living costs of a single person, so that for a given standard of living there is less need to cash in savings; and, second, the probability that both members of a couple will die in the following year is less than the probability that a single person will die and so the expected time over which savings will need to be eked out is longer for the couple. Overall, the outcome could be 'a flat or slowly falling wealth path of the couple until one spouse dies. Then the survivor would switch to the more steeply falling path of a single' (Hurd, 1990, p. 613).

Changing attitudes

A common factor underlying the studies mapping the dissaving behaviour of older people is that they are based on historical data, much of it from the 1980s and 1990s. By definition, these data do not enable the identification of contemporary trends, one of which is the increasing tendency for households, at least in some countries, to view their home as a store of wealth that may be used to facilitate future consumption (Smith, 2005; Stone, 2003). Indeed, many of such claims are couched in terms of housing as a safety net, as a source of pension and as a vehicle for realising money when the owners want it. Moreover, there is evidence that, insofar as this is intended to fund future consumption, it is consumption for themselves rather than for future generations. In recent years the practice of SKIing (Spending the Kids' Inheritance) has gained some popular recognition, arguably reflecting a new reality in which the bequest motive has become less dominant. Moreover, it is possible that, as more people reach old age without having had children, questions of the home as a bequest and the significance of intergenerational transfers and solidarity take on a different hue: some might want to leave a bequest to do good things for their fellow man, or even the stray dogs of the neighbourhood, but evidence from the United Kingdom at least indicates that increasing numbers of people want to spend it on themselves (Rowlingson and McKay, 2007). In that way SKIing simply becomes Sing (Spending). Australian evidence on this is particularly interesting in that it indicates a clear distinction between the 50–65 and the 65+ cohorts, with the latter holding on to the notion of the house as a bequest for their children and the former very much more determined to ensure a continuation of the quality of life achieved during their working years, if necessary by using their housing equity (SEQUAL, 2008). It is possible, then, that future behaviour of European households with respect to their housing wealth may be very different.

Dissaving housing assets: government behaviour

The question of whether home ownership is viewed as a form of saving and how that saving is used can also be extended to governments. Although concern about the negative impact of ageing is clearly and frequently expressed by politicians and civil servants at the level of the European Union (e.g. European

Commission, 2005; European Communities, 2004), competence over the relevant policy fields is vested with the individual member states and, as usual in such circumstances, there is not an expression or a reality of a unified effort to use home ownership as a palliator. Perhaps the nearest to this was a communiqué issued at the end of a meeting in 1999 of the housing ministers of all of the then EU member states. Their position was that older homeowners should make use of their housing assets to pay for their old age:

> In most EU Member States, older people live in owner-occupied housing. This means that many older people possess capital in the ownership of their homes. The Ministers were aware of the need to explore new ways of helping older people to safely utilize their capital, for example, to obtain the housing and support services they need, to repair or adapt their existing homes or to release income to cover the costs of support services or to purchase new accommodation with support services available.
>
> (Finland, 1999, para 9)

Beyond this, statements have been *ad hoc* and country specific. Thus, the socialist party in Flanders has quite explicitly argued that further growth of home ownership should be encouraged because it provides the best way to live and to save for a pension (Sp.a, 2007). Some statements (ODPM, 2005) are consistent with a more general development of the systems of social protection in some member states through the promotion of asset-based welfare (Doling and Ronald, 2010). The point here is that home ownership can be seen as a means whereby individuals build up a sort of personal provident fund that can be called upon when needed. In that way, forced personal saving in the housing market may be viewed as substituting for tax and public spending.

Whatever the impact of explicit goals and *de jure* action to increase home ownership, it does appear that over the quarter of a century up to 2003 there has been a *de facto* substitution of housing assets for state expenditure on older people (Doling and Horsewood, 2008b). In the OECD countries, unusually large annual increases in house prices, and thus in housing assets, have been followed by reductions in state spending on pensions and other welfare benefits for older people. The corollary is that unusually small increases, or even decreases, in house prices are followed by increases in the generosity of state spending. In other words, housing appears to act as an independent variable causing, or leading to, a change in the level of state provision. Although it is not clear what processes lead to the trade-off, the size of the effect is greatest in those countries where, on the one hand, the government provides the most generous benefits and so there is numerically the greatest pressure on them to find ways of reducing the fiscal challenges of older people and, on the other hand, where pension and other benefit entitlements and housing wealth are distributed similarly. The reality, then, is that, even without being an overt policy, across the larger economies, both within and outside Europe, housing wealth appears to have relieved some of the fiscal pressures arising from population ageing.

Conclusions

This chapter has not argued that European governments have responded directly and overtly to the ageing of their populations by cutting social housing programmes and expanding home ownership. In that sense it does not support what Castles presented as the logic of the argument put forward by proponents of the view that ageing populations inevitably bring about welfare system development. Rather, the argument has been that the increases over recent decades in home ownership sectors across the EU are consistent with the attraction of home ownership as a palliator, in that it may be seen as having the potential to ameliorate some of the negative consequences of ageing populations.

The evidence presented in support of this argument is certainly not conclusive. This is partly because it is not drawn systematically from all European countries, let alone all West European countries; even so, there appear to be differences in their experiences. It is also partly a consequence of contradictions between different studies. Nevertheless, there appears to be some substance to the position that in some European countries increasing reliance is being put on the equity held in the form of home ownership, that this is in some ways substituting for pensions and other expenditures on older people and that, in at least some respects, this is being driven by demographic trends.

One pillar of the argument is that overall European households appear increasingly to be viewing home ownership as a source of wealth as well as a place to live. Moreover, as a source of wealth it is one that they may draw upon to support their consumption in old age. It is possible that the SKIing motive is eclipsing the bequest motive, perhaps not least because one of the features of demographic ageing is that fewer older Europeans will have children anyway. It is also possible that changing attitudes to the uses of housing are themselves driven in part by the concerns of households about the wisdom of relying on government support in a future of intense fiscal pressure.

The second pillar of the argument concerns governments. There is evidence relating to all those that were member states in 1999 of overt consensus around the use of home ownership to support older people's needs, as well as evidence of overt promotion of home ownership by some individual member states. Although this interest by European governments seems consistent with an equity-based welfare philosophy, it is not widespread. In addition to overt policy, there is evidence that increases in housing wealth over a number of decades have been followed by decreasing state expenditure on older people, and whatever the processes it points to a reality of home ownership substituting for pensions.

Such a conclusion points to the possibility that, in response to population ageing, European households and governments have been acting in a way that has promoted the expansion of home ownership. Insofar as that is the case then clearly explanations about the growth of home ownership and the decline of other sectors that have emphasised globalisation may need to be adapted to incorporate population ageing.

In addition to implications for theory, there are also implications for policy. The first concerns the consequences of substituting individual responsibility for pension provision through home ownership for state responsibility through pensions. In that this weakens the social insurance principles of pension systems the result may well be an increase in both inequality and the risk of poverty among older people. Such concern merits detailed and systematic examination of the distributional consequences of policy change.

A second implication is that throughout Europe the baby boomer generation, those born in the decade or so immediately following the end of World War II, have perhaps contributed greatly to the growth of asset prices, including house prices, from the mid-1990s onwards. Whether or not that has been the case, an issue of major significance concerns the possible consequence of the decumulation activities of the baby boomers as they move into the retirement ages. For the United States, Schieber and Shoven (1997) have developed the argument that, as pension systems move into a situation of being net sellers of assets, the result could be to depress asset prices, whether these be stocks, bonds, land or real estate. Insofar as life cycle savings constitute household pension systems, the same argument would apply to any mass selling of individually owned homes with a view either to moving to a cheaper house or to transfer into rental housing.

While stressing the role and consequences of viewing home ownership as a palliator, its significance as a cause of demographic change requires recognition. The impact that access to home ownership, with its financial implications, has on the ability of young people to get housing that is well suited to bringing up a family and meeting the other financial needs of child rearing is important. If in some respects the state promotion of home ownership can be viewed as a family-unfriendly policy, so its facilitating of early retirement might lead to the conclusion that it is a work-unfriendly policy also. Moreover, in a way these two are linked. Insofar as young people are forced to 'over-save', the pay-off is that they may be able to get by on lower incomes earlier than formal state retirement ages anticipate. It is here that home ownership as a cause and as a palliator are linked.

Finally, it should be noted that the arguments developed in this chapter are contingent not only on place (Western countries, particularly Europe) but also on time, with most of the empirical basis being related to the nineties and the noughties. But the last year or two have seen shifts in the macro-economic and political context that are so large in scale that they throw up questions about the continuation of existing trends and relationships. The credit crisis had its roots in the earlier expansion of home ownership sectors often fuelled by governments and the lending practices of the financial institutions. House prices commonly increased at rates far higher than underlying inflation, which made not only the sacrifice of entry that much stiffer but also the investment rewards so much greater. In these circumstances the relationships we have identified between demographic change and home ownership became prominent. The recent collapse of financial markets with reductions in the amount of money available to lend to house buyers – as well as to other economic activities – has also been common. In many Western countries this has been just part of the wider economic recession, public sector debt crises and re-evaluation of the neo-liberal model in which light regulation had been an ideal. Whereas it seems unlikely that these shifts in the economic and political tectonic plates will not have some impact on the behaviour of all of the main stakeholders in home ownership, the nature of the impact, both in the short and longer run, is uncertain. It is too early to say, for example, whether the belief, formerly widely held by European households, in the housing market as a safe and high return investment will return; or, equally, whether governments will continue to see home ownership as a palliator for the fiscal problems caused by ageing populations. What we can say is that demographic structures are extremely unlikely to remain constant and that they will continue to interact with housing markets.

Acknowledgements

This chapter is based, in part, on work carried out for the DEMHOW project, which is funded by the European Commission under its Framework 7 Programme (contract number SSH7-CT-2008–216865). I am grateful for the support of my research partners on the project, particularly my colleague Nick Horsewood.

References

Allen, J., Barlow, J., Leal, J., Maloutas, T. and Padovani L. (2004) *Housing and Welfare in Southern Europe*, Oxford: Blackwell.

Blondal, S. and Scarpetta, S. (1997) Early retirement in OECD countries: the role of social security systems, *OECD Economic Studies*, 29, 7–59.

Boone, L. and Girouard, N. (2002) The stock market, the housing market and consumer behaviour, *OECD Economic Studies*, 35(2), 175–200.

Campbell, J. and Cocco, J. (2004) *How Do House Prices Affect Consumption? Evidence from Micro Data*, Discussion Paper 2045, Cambridge, MA: Harvard Institute of Economic Research.

Castles, F.G. (1998) The really big trade-off: home ownership and the welfare state in the new world and the old, *Acta Politica*, 33(1), 5–19.

Castles, F. (2004) *The Future of the Welfare State*, Oxford: Oxford University Press.

Catte, P., Girouard, N., Price, R. and Andre, C. (2004) *Housing Markets, Wealth and the Business Cycle*, Economics Department Working Paper No. 194, Paris: OECD.

Churi, M. and Jappelli, T. (2006) *Do the Elderly Reduce Housing Equity? An International Comparison*, Working Paper No. 158, Fisciano, Italy: Centre for Studies in Economics and Finance, University of Salerno.

Coleman, D. (2001) Population ageing: an unavoidable future, *Social Biology and Human Affairs*, 66, 1–11.

Committee on the Global Financial System (2006) *Housing Finance in the Global Financial Market*, CGFS Papers No. 26, Basel: Bank of International Settlements.

Deaton, A. (1992) *Understanding consumption*, Oxford: Clarendon Press.

Deaton, A. (2005) *Franco Modigliani and the Life Cycle Theory of Consumption*, Research Program in Development Studies and Center for Health and Wellbeing, Princeton University, New Jersey. Online. Available at http://www.princeton.edu/-deaton/downloads/romelecture.pdf (accessed 19 July 2011).

Dingeldey, I. (2001) European tax systems and their impact on family employment patterns, *Journal of Social Policy*, 30(4), 653–672.

Disney, R., Johnson, P. and Stears, G. (1998) Asset wealth and asset decumulation among households in the retirement survey, *Fiscal Studies*, 19(2), 153–174.

Doling, J. and Ford, J. (2003) *Globalisation and Home Ownership: Experiences in Eight Member States of the European Union*, Delft: Delft University Press.

Doling, J. and Horsewood, N. (2003) Home ownership and early retirement: European experience in the 1990s, *Journal of Housing and the Built Environment*, 18, 289–308.

Doling, J. and Ford, J. (2007) A union of home owners [Editorial], *European Journal of Housing Policy*, 7(2), 113–117.

Doling, J. and Horsewood, N. (2008a) *Understanding Savings in EU Countries: The Role of Housing, Stock Markets and Demographics*, paper to the ENHR Working Group Conference, Istanbul.

Doling, J. and Horsewood, N. (2008b) *Home Ownership and Pensions: Testing the Trade Off*, DEMHOW Report to the European Commission. Birmingham: University of Birmingham.

Doling, J. and Ronald, R. (eds) (2010) Home ownership and asset-based welfare, *Journal of Housing and the Built Environment*, 25(2), 165–173.

Doling, J., Horsewood, N., Kassanis, A. and Vasilakos, N. (2006) Home ownership and labour force participation of younger people, in N. Horsewood and P. Neuteboom (ed.) *The Social Limits to Growth: Security and Insecurity Aspects of Home Ownership*, Amsterdam: IOS Press.

Earley, F. (2004) What explains the differences in home ownership rates in Europe? *Housing Finance International*, September, 25–30.

ECB (2003) *Structural Factors in the EU Housing Markets*, Frankfurt: European Central Bank.

Ermisch, J. and Jenkins, S. (1999) Retirement and housing adjustment in later life: evidence from the British Household Panel Survey, *Labour Economics*, 6, 311–333.

European Commission (2005) *Green Paper. Confronting Demographic Change: A New Solidarity between the Generations*, COM (2005) 94 final, Brussels: Commission of the European Communities.

European Communities (2004) *Facing the Challenge: The Lisbon Strategy for Growth and Employment*, Report of the High Level Group chaired by Wim Kok, Luxembourg: Office for Official Publications of the European Communities.

European Mortgage Federation (2006) *Hypostat 2005*, Brussels: European Mortgage Federation.

Feinstein, J. and McFadden, D. (1989) The dynamics of housing demand by the elderly: wealth, cash flow and demographic effects, in D.A. Wise (ed.) *Economics of Aging*, Chicago: University of Chicago Press.

Finland (1999) *11th Informal Meeting of EU Housing Ministers, Final Communique*, Kuopio, Finland, 27–28 September. Online. Available at http://presidency.finland.fi/netcomm/News/showarticle1127/.html (accessed 9 September 2008).

Hakim, C. (2003) *Models of the Family in Modern Societies: Ideals and Realities*, Aldershot: Ashgate.

Hills, J. (1993) *The Future of Welfare: A Guide to the Debate*, York: Joseph Rowntree Foundation.

Hurd, M. (1990) Research on the elderly: economic status, retirement, and consumption and saving, *Journal of Economic Literature*, 28, 565–637.

Kemeny, J. (1981) *The Myth of Home Ownership: Public versus Private Choices in Housing Tenure*, London: Routledge & Kegan Paul.

Kinsella, K. and Phillips, D. (2005) *Global Aging: The Challenge of Success, Population Bulletin*, 60(1), Washington, DC: Population Reference Bureau.

Lefebure, S., Mangeleer, J. and Van den Bosch, K. (2006) *Elderly Prosperity and Homeownership in the European Union: New Evidence from the SHARE Data*, paper to the 29th General Conference of the International Association for Research in Income and Wealth, Joensuu, Finland.

Malmberg, B. (2007) Demography and social welfare, *Journal of International Social Welfare*, 16, S21–S34.

Malpass, P. (2006) Housing policy in an opportunity society: home ownership and the amplification of inequality, in J. Doling and M. Elsinga (eds) *Home Ownership: Getting In, Getting From, Getting Out: Part II*, Amsterdam: IOS Press.

Mulder, C. and Billari, F. (2006) *Home-Ownership Regimes and Lowest-Low Fertility*, paper to the ENHR Working Group Conference, Delft.

ODPM (2005) Homes for all – expanding opportunities for home-ownership, press release 36/05, 1 April, Office of the Deputy Prime Minister.

OECD (2004) Housing markets, wealth and the life cycle, *OECD Economic Outlook*, June.

Poterba, J. (1998) *Population Age Structure and Asset Returns: An Empirical Investigation*, Working Paper 6774, Cambridge, MA: National Bureau of Economic Research.

Rohe, W.M., Von Shandt, S. and McCarthy, G. (2002) Home ownership and access to opportunity, *Housing Studies*, 17(1), 51–61.

Ronald, R. (2008) *The Ideology of Home Ownership: Homeowner Societies and the Role of Housing*, Basingstoke: Palgrave Macmillan.

Rouwendal, J. and Thomese, F. (2010) Home ownership, institutionalisation and mortality of elderly in the Netherlands, in J. Doling, M. Elsinga and R. Ronald (eds) *Home Ownership: Getting In, Getting From, Getting Out: Part III*, Amsterdam: ISI Press.

Rowlingson, K. and McKay, S. (2007) *Attitudes to Inheritance in Britain*, York: Rowntree Foundation.

Schieber, S. and Shoven, J. (1997) The consequences of population aging on private pension fund saving and asset markets, in S. Schieber and J. Shoven (eds) *Public Policy towards Pensions*, Cambridge, MA: MIT Press.

SEQUAL (2008) *'It's on the House'. A Consumer Study into the Attitude and Perceptions of Australians Aged over 60 Years*. Sydney: Senior Australian Equity Release Association of Lenders.

Sjoberg, O. (2004) The role of family policy institution in explaining gender-role attitudes: a comparative multilevel analysis of thirteen industrialized countries, *Journal of European Social Policy*, 14(2), 107–123.

Smith, S. (2005) *Banking on Housing? Speculating on the Role and Relevance of Housing Wealth in Britain,* paper prepared for the Joseph Rowntree Foundation Inquiry into Homeownership 2010 and Beyond.

Sp.a (2007) *Een kwestie van principe. Sp.a beginselverklaring 2007* [*A Matter of Principles. The Sp.a Principles Statement 2007*]. Online. Available at http://www.onzeperincipe.be (accessed 28 November 2007).

Stephens, M. (2003) Globalisation and housing finance systems in advanced and transitional economies, *Urban Studies*, 40(5–6), 1011–1026.

Stone, M. (2003) *Safe as Houses*, London: Prudential.

Tatsiramos, K. (2006) *Residential Mobility and Housing Adjustment of Older Households in Europe*, Discussion Paper No. 2435, Bonn: Forscchunginstitut zur Zukunft der Arbeit (IZA).

Taylor, P. (2001) Reversing the early retirement trend, *Labour Market Trends*, April, 217–220.

Venti, S.F. and Wise, D.A. (2001) *Aging and Housing Equity: Another Look*, NBER Working Paper No. 8608. Cambridge, MA: NBER.

3

THE HOUSING PILLAR OF THE MEDITERRANEAN WELFARE REGIME

Relations between home ownership and other dimensions of welfare in Italy

Teresio Poggio

Introduction

There are at least three important reasons for discussing the relations between home ownership and broader welfare systems with a focus on Mediterranean countries.[1] The first is that comparative welfare research has to a large extent ignored the housing domain, notwithstanding its importance both in classical thought on the welfare state and in real life, housing being a matter of great economic and social concern at both family and policy levels. Housing intersects in various ways with other dimensions of welfare and is particularly salient in conceptualizing the distinction between South European and Continental welfare regimes. In understanding welfare systems as a whole, home ownership and its place in the welfare mix marks an important boundary between Mediterranean and Continental European contexts. There are indeed significant differences between the two clusters of countries in home ownership rates, in the availability of affordable and secure alternatives in the rental sector and in the relative importance of the role played by the family in sustaining entry into owner-occupation. The implications of these differences are not restricted to the housing domain but are likely to inform the entire welfare system.

The second reason is that comparative housing studies have focused mostly on housing markets and policy – and hence on the English-speaking countries and on continental and Northern Europe – when analysing this form of tenure. Limited attention has been paid to the informal and family practices that support entry into home ownership, which are key factors in Southern Europe (Allen *et al.*, 2004). Here, housing support contributes to other forms of welfare, especially caring, often provided within family networks. It is then useful to investigate possible interactions between family support for home ownership and other forms of family help.

Finally, research on home ownership has recently acquired new impetus in relation to the retrenchment of the welfare state and the idea that welfare provision can also be granted by mobilizing individual assets, of which home ownership is a very popular one (see Doling and Ronald, 2010 for a recent discussion). In this perspective, the state is considered to actively support entry into home ownership not only as a form of housing provision but also as a way to sustain the accumulation of assets on which individuals can rely in order to purchase private welfare. Home ownership has historically played a wide social protection role in Southern Europe in the context of a rudimentary welfare state. Hence, discussing the relations between home ownership and the broad welfare system in this context can provide elements useful for the current debate focused on countries where this resource is expected to supplement the welfare state in the near future.

But what are the distinctive characteristics of home ownership in Southern Europe? The expansion of home ownership since World War II has been largely due to certain features specific to Mediterranean housing systems, besides generalized improvement in economic and living conditions. These features include a lack of secure and affordable alternatives in the rental sector; the opportunity to become a homeowner via self-building and other non-market channels; and an historical bias toward home ownership in housing policy. Last but not least, the family performs a key role in both the production of home ownership and its funding.

The expansion of this tenure has not happened in a vacuum. It also reflects peculiarities of national welfare systems, and it has interactions with them and consequences upon them. Asset building through home ownership has been a rational household strategy in a context of limited welfare provision – in which precautionary savings are necessary – and of limited alternatives for investment because of an underdeveloped financial market. Home ownership has performed a direct social security role for irregular workers who do not contribute to pension and insurance schemes. To a certain extent, social re-stratification has also taken place through home ownership in the past, because households with limited resources from the labour market have been able to convert their social and technical capital into housing wealth through self-building, which has often been illegal but tolerated (Bernardi and Poggio, 2004; Tosi, 1987).

Furthermore, there are relationships between the important role of family support for home ownership and the familialistic features of the Southern European care system. The intergenerational production and transmission of home ownership has been traditionally linked to the proximity between parents and their adult children (Poggio, 2008). This proximity enables the easier mobilization of in-kind resources that facilitate access to home ownership by the younger members of the family: a plot of land that can be built on; parents' and relatives' own labour for self-building; a family dwelling allocated for free. On the other hand, proximity is also a reliable foundation for further mutual support, and especially for care. Family support for home ownership is embedded in a family-based welfare system, and it also contributes to the reproduction of that model of welfare, especially when care is an issue (Poggio, 2008).

Co-residence between parents and adult children is certainly less common than in the past. Yet it is still a not infrequent way to share family resources – housing, income, and care – among family members. It also represents a typical route to home ownership, as younger members usually outlive their parents and inherit the house in which they have grown up and in which they form their own family. In general, intergenerational transfers supporting access to home ownership are a core component of the overall system of private transfers from ascendants to the new generation, and have redistributive effects.

If one 'zooms out' from the welfare state and considers the overall welfare system and the interplay among state, market and family in welfare provision, one finds that home ownership is a key element in this system and contributes largely to the shaping of the Mediterranean welfare regime.

This 'familialistic' home ownership model has intrinsic drawbacks. Given the lack of alternatives, households have to a certain degree been forced into owner-occupation, often irrespective of their economic resources. Low-income homeowners may experience poor housing conditions, suboptimal localization, and severe financial strain. Moreover, the family's role in sustaining access to home ownership acts as a not insignificant factor in the intergenerational transmission of social inequality.

Overall, families have represented an important informal agent in the housing system. In the Italian case, both the social production and the funding of home ownership have become progressively more market driven. Nevertheless, families are still major agents in the housing system as they are to a large extent responsible for funding home purchases within the market. Many are proving able to cope with changing contexts and with increased housing prices. There is some preliminary evidence, nonetheless, that the already-existing problems with the Mediterranean home ownership system are going to worsen, while new ones are emerging because of changes toward more market-driven forms of social production of home ownership. All these issues are discussed in the course of this chapter. The next section outlines the Mediterranean home ownership model and its implications for the broader welfare system. The following two sections discuss these issues in more detail with regard to the Italian case.

The 'familialistic' home ownership model and Mediterranean welfare systems

Mediterranean housing systems have several specific features in common when compared with the other West European countries. They have high home ownership rates (Table 3.1, column 1), and this form of tenure is widely distributed within all social strata. The distributive index in column 5 of Table 3.1 represents

TABLE 3.1 West European housing systems: selected countries and indicators

| | Occupied housing stock by tenure (%) | | | | (5) Home ownership distributive index[c] (2008) | (6) Real estate professionalization index[d] (2000) | (7) Per capita mortgage debt index (NL = 100)[e] (2008) | (8) Homeowners in 2004 (50 years and above) who acceded property by intergenerational transmission[f] (%) |
	(1) Owner-occupied	(2) Rented	(3) (Social rented)	(4) Other[b]				
Germany[a]	45	55	(n.a.)	0	0.50	3.7	39	21.8
Netherlands	55	45	(35)	0	0.55	4.3	100	3.3
Denmark	60	40	(20)	0	0.64	7.4	113	4.5
Sweden	61	39	(21)	0	0.58	8.4	60	6.4
Austria	58	39	(14)	3	0.69	3.4	24	27.8
France	56	38	(18)	0	0.61	5.3	31	13.9
UK	69	31	(21)	0	0.70	6.3	66	n.a.
Norway	77	24	(4)	0	0.56	5.1	101	n.a.
Italy	71	20	(4)	9	0.85	3.8	15	34.6
Portugal	75	21	(3)	4	0.92	2.7	28	n.a.
Greece	74	20	(0)	6	0.93	0.2	19	31.6
Spain	82	11	(1)	7	0.91	4.7	41	23.7

Sources: Own calculations on data from the National Board of Housing, Building and Planning (Sweden) and Ministry for Regional Development of the Czech Republic (2005), Statistics Norway, National Institute of Statistics (Italy) – estimates for the first few years after the year 2000 (1–4); EUROSTAT (5–6); European Mortgage Federation (2009) (7); Börsch-Supan et al. (2005) (8).

Notes:

a (1–4) excluding territories of the former GDR.

b Includes rent-free and usufruct dwellings.

c The distributive index presented is the ratio of the ownership rate for the low-income population (< 60% of median individualized income) to the rate for the remaining population (> 60% of median individualized income) based on EUROSTAT estimates from the Statistics on Income and Living Conditions (2008 survey).

d Number of employed persons in real estate per 1,000 inhabitants.

e Per capita mortgage debt data have been transformed into an index with the Netherlands as a baseline (NL = 100).

f Includes bequests, gifts and family help.

n.a., not available.

the odds ratio of being a homeowner between low-income individuals – the ones whose equivalized income is below 60 per cent of the median – and the remaining population with higher incomes. An index of 1 means that, on average, the two groups have the same probability of home ownership. If the index is lower than 1, low-income individuals are less likely to be homeowners than the better off.

In Italy, Portugal, Greece and Spain, low-income populations have, on average, chances of being homeowners that are close to those of the better off (index in the range 0.85–0.93). By contrast, in the Netherlands, Denmark and Sweden, being poor almost halves the probability of home ownership (index in the range 0.55–0.64) compared with the population with higher incomes. However, the 'democratization' of this tenure in Southern Europe is incomplete: social inequality still gives rise to variability within the home ownership sector with regard to, for example, the timing of home ownership, housing conditions and the implications for household budgets. Another shared feature is the limited incidence of the social housing sector, and of home ownership arrangements with social connotations (i.e. cooperatives in Norway, which account for 18 per cent of the home ownership segment). This is what distinguishes Southern Europe from the other countries considered that also have high home ownership rates such as the UK and Norway (Table 3.1, column 3).

A general lack of secure and affordable alternatives in the rental sector is due to both this underdevelopment of social housing and ineffective regulation – or non-regulation – of the private rental market (Allen *et al.*, 2004). Within this context, access to home ownership has been a rational strategy with which to satisfy housing needs and to invest savings in face of a relatively underdeveloped financial market. The availability of non-market channels to home ownership has enabled the expansion of this form of tenure also among low-income households. No strict land-use and building regulations and tolerance of illegal development have allowed self-building activities and direct commissioning (Tosi, 1987). This is particularly the case in rural areas, but in the past – at least in Italy – it was a not uncommon way to become a homeowner even in large cities and their outskirts (Alasia and Montaldi, 1960). In any case, until recently, housing-related markets were relatively unprofessionalized, creating space for the informal practices mentioned.

The number of employed persons in real estate per 1,000 inhabitants and the per capita residential mortgage debt (Table 3.1, columns 6 and 7 respectively) represent two rough indicators of the degree of professionalization of the housing market. Nevertheless, they can provide some preliminary evidence on cross-country differences. The distributional pattern of these two indicators is not perfectly linear, but it is apparent that Southern European countries rank at the lower levels of both of the distributions, a partial exception being Spain. Home ownership funding has traditionally had informal connotations as well. The mortgage market has performed a minor role in financing home ownership – as shown above – whilst personal savings and family wealth have been more important. Column 8 of Table 3.1 reports estimates from the *Survey of Health, Ageing and Retirement in Europe* (Börsch-Supan *et al*., 2005) on the importance of the intergenerational transmission – bequests, gifts and family help – for elderly homeowners. A high degree of variability exists in this respect, especially when the Mediterranean countries are compared with the Netherlands and Scandinavian countries. In general terms, the intergenerational transmission/ production of home ownership has historically been a key factor in the expansion of this form of tenure in Southern Europe.

The reproduction of social inequality is inherent to these intergenerational processes (Bernardi and Poggio, 2004; Poggio, 2008; Tosi, 1987). However, when the above-mentioned informal practices have been involved, a certain degree of re-stratification has taken place because working-class people have been able to convert their technical and social capital, and their time, into housing wealth (Bourdieu and de Saint Martin, 1990). The full implementation of land-use planning and building regulations, the increasing professionalization of housing-related markets and, in more recent years, the expansion of mortgage markets have given rise to a more market-driven system of production of home ownership. Little space is left for the informal production that in the past has allowed for some re-stratification. Home ownership on a market basis reflects the existing pattern of social inequality as it emerges from the labour market, whilst dedicated intergenerational transfers today tend to increase social inequality and give rise to a quasi-ascription of housing conditions (Bernardi and Poggio, 2004; Tosi, 1987).

But what about the relations between home ownership and the broader welfare system? Because of its peculiarity, housing has been regarded as a 'wobbly' pillar under the welfare state, considering the cases of those countries where both a comprehensive system of social citizenship and a large social housing sector – in the rental or in cooperative segments – have been developed (Torgesen, 1987). One relevant issue that has been raised is the contradictory distributive effect of housing policy vis-à-vis the general purposes of the welfare state.

Housing may be regarded as a 'wobbly' pillar under the welfare state also when considering Mediterranean countries, their general social protection framework and their housing policy. The last has historically been an underdeveloped sector of state intervention, to the point that non-policies have possibly contributed more to the shaping of housing systems than housing programmes. For these specific reasons, as well as for housing peculiarity, the distributive effects of housing policy are contradictory. However, if one considers the overall welfare system, and therefore also the roles performed by the market and the family, and the interplay among these three areas of resource allocation, housing is a key factor for the assurance of individual well-being, both because it satisfies specific needs and because it interacts with other dimensions of welfare. This seems to be especially the case in the Mediterranean countries, where the welfare state as a whole is relatively underdeveloped and where home ownership, as a major asset of households, is widespread.

As mentioned, home ownership is a way to satisfy housing needs in the face of a lack of secure and affordable alternatives in the rental sector. This kind of housing self-provision may well meet the need to accumulate precautionary savings, albeit in the form of bricks and mortar. If necessary, housing equity can be released in order to afford unanticipated expenditures and deal with social risks not covered by rudimentary welfare states. In a life cycle perspective, it is also a way to redistribute income to old age – when the imputed rent deriving from home ownership can supplement reduced earnings – so that home owner-ship is somehow functionally equivalent to a pension (Castles and Ferrera, 1996; Kemeny, 1981). This social security role is particularly important in countries where the informal economy – in terms of irregular workers and family-based small businesses, for instance – is an issue, and social security contributions are sometimes evaded. Self-employment (often in family-based small businesses) and unpaid family work are more common phenomena in Southern Europe than elsewhere (Table 3.2), as is irregular employment (OECD, 2004).

The expansion of home ownership has also brought a certain amount of re-stratification and asset building for households with limited incomes, at least when access to this tenure has been possible through non-market chan-nels. This explains the incidence of 'cash-poor, asset-rich' households in these countries. Moreover, the intergenerational transmission of home ownership from the elderly to the young members of the family redistributes resources between family generations, partially compensating for the bias against young

TABLE 3.2 West European labour markets: selected countries and indicators, 2006

	Labour force as % of population	Self-employment as % of total employment	Unpaid family workers as % of total employment
Germany	50.4	12.1	1.0
Netherlands	52.6	12.7	0.5
Denmark	53.4	8.8	0.6
Sweden	51.4	10.0	0.2
Austria	49.9	13.5	1.5
France	44.8	8.8	n.a.
UK	50.5	13.0	0.6
Norway	52.5	8.4	0.3
Italy	42.2	26.4	1.8
Portugal	52.8	23.9	1.2
Greece	43.8	36.3	6.5
Spain	49.0	17.8	1.3

Source: Own calculations on Organisation for Economic Co-operation and Development (OECD) data.

citizens that characterizes public transfers in Southern Europe (Attias-Donfut and Wolff, 2000; Castles and Ferrera, 1996).

Problematic interactions with other welfare areas also exist. In societies in which home ownership is widespread, and no affordable alternatives are available in the rental sector, this form of tenure tends to become the norm also for new entrants to the housing market. This increases the level of resources needed for the transition to adulthood[2] (Kemeny, 1981; Spilerman et al., 1993) and likely contributes to the postponement of family formation and to low fertility (Mulder and Billari, 2010). Limited alternatives in the rental sector also make mobility less likely, and hence the labour market more rigid (Cannari et al., 2000). New problems seem also to be emerging. These are linked to both structural changes within European societies and specific transformations of the Mediterranean home ownership model.

Home ownership and the welfare system in Italy

According to census data, the home ownership rate in Italy grew from 40 per cent in 1951 to 71 per cent in 2001. Moreover, about 9 per cent of the residential housing stock is currently allocated on a rent-free basis, mostly within family networks. This 'other tenure' is considered to represent an intermediate phase in the intergenerational transmission of home ownership. The expansion of the latter tenure has taken place within all regions of Italy and all strata of Italian society. However, significant differences still persist according to traditional distinction criteria in tenure distribution: small villages and towns have higher home ownership rates than big cities; low-income and young households are less likely – in relative terms – to be homeowners than affluent and elderly ones.

Cultural attitudes and a general improvement of economic conditions are among the factors most frequently cited in explaining the expansion of home ownership in Italy. However, a key role has also been played by the above-mentioned non-policies: on the one hand, because governments have been unable, or unwilling, to ensure secure and affordable housing within the rental sector, they have pushed households into the home ownership segment; on the other hand, households have been allowed to access home ownership via non-market, and more affordable, routes.

Since the early twentieth century, Italian housing policy has been biased towards home ownership and against social housing. On the ideological level, this policy has been largely inspired by the social doctrine of the Catholic Church, which considers the promotion of small property ownership and thrift to be the best solution for the 'social question'. As a result, assisted home ownership has always been part of social housing schemes, because new dwellings in this sector are allocated partly for renting and partly for home ownership through various kinds of leasing contract. The main beneficiaries of the allocation for home ownership have been civil servants and middle-class households (see Poggio, 2006 for a discussion). In the period 1951–70 about 800,000 public dwellings were constructed, and 850,000 were privatized during the same period (Padovani, 1996).

Rent regulation (1978–98) of the private rented market was unsuccessful in reconciling affordability and social protection for tenants with reasonable returns for landlords. Indeed, it possibly failed to achieve both these objectives (Poggio, 2005). The rental option has been socially constructed as an insecure tenure3 and still today, according to a recent survey, 'security and tranquillity of home ownership' is the modal (63 per cent) motivation reported by interviewed homeowners and/or tenants aspiring to this tenure, as a reason for their preference towards home ownership (Nomisma, 2007, p. 120). In this context, home ownership has prevailed over the rental option, even among middle- and low-income households, facilitated by the above-mentioned non-market channels (Tosi, 1987) and family support, especially in financial terms.

The data set out in Table 3.3 show the incidence of home ownership within Italian households by occupational class for various census years. The data refer only to households with a reference person active in the labour market. Differences in this distribution between classes are apparent, but so too is a converging trend towards home ownership. Table 3.3 also shows that housing tenure 'preferences' have changed, especially for the middle class. On decomposing the blue-collar class, it is possible to test for the importance of non-market channels. Because workers in the house-building sector are those who have – by definition – more technical and social capital available to enter home ownership via self-building or direct commissioning, they may be expected to exhibit a higher home ownership rate than manual workers in other industries and

TABLE 3.3 Home ownership rate (%) by occupational class and census year: Italian households with reference person in the labour market

	1951	1961	1971	1981	1991	2001
Bourgeoisie and service class	52.5	55.7	62.3	–	72.0	72.0
Middle class	21.7	35.4	41.7	–	70.5	70.8
Urban self-employed workers	40.4	48.5	53.2	–	69.3	69.6
Farmers	62.5	67.0	75.6	–	84.6	81.5
Blue-collar workers (all):	23.6	34.2	40.4	–	62.2	62.0
in industry	22.0	32.9	39.1	–	64.4	63.5
in house building	33.9	42.4	50.9	–	62.8	59.4
in services	18.1	27.5	33.7	–	60.7	61.4
Agricultural labourers	37.2	48.6	59.6	–	67.0	59.2
All	38.4	44.0	48.1	–	66.2	67.8

Source: Own calculations from Italian National Institute of Statistics, population and housing census, various years (1951–1971) and public use samples of the population and housing census (1991–2001). Data for 1981 are not available.

services. This expectation is borne out by the data in the table: until 1971, the home ownership rate for workers in the construction industry was at least 10 percentage points higher than that for blue-collar workers in other industries. This difference disappears from 1991 onwards, as a result of tightening up in this informal channel and partly because of compositional effects.[4]

Notwithstanding convergence towards home ownership, differences persist between occupational classes with regard to the timing of home ownership and modes of access to it (Bernardi and Poggio, 2004; Guiso and Jappelli, 1996; Poggio, 2008), the implicated housing conditions, the value of the property and the economic constraints on household budgets. As regards housing conditions, estimates based on the 'public use' sample of the 2001 census show that about 2 per cent of households owning their dwellings experience serious housing problems – living without drinkable water or without hot water or without a toilet in the dwelling – and that 5 per cent of them suffer from serious over-crowding. Some social groups are more at risk than others: the households of immigrant homeowners, for example, experience serious problems in 6 per cent of cases, and 16 per cent of them live in severely overcrowded dwellings.

Housing arrangements of couples at time of marriage and type of family support received have been investigated in a recent study using retrospective data (Poggio, 2008). Marriage still tends to coincide in Italy with leaving the parental home and with new family formation. It is therefore a crucial phase in housing careers. Survey estimates are presented in Table 3.4 by period of marriage. Because of the original research design, estimates refer only to couples with the following characteristics: husband aged 25–64 years; at least one parent of each partner alive at the time of the interview (2003); and both partners in their first marriage (97 per cent of couples in the selected sample).

A number of trends are evident when comparison is made of what happens in the three marriage periods. The incidence of both co-residences and rented dwellings has declined over time, while home ownership has increased. Purchasing a dwelling has become increasingly common among homeowners at marriage. All kinds of family support, except co-residence, have increased in importance. This is especially the case when financial assistance for purchase is considered. Within the more recent period of marriage, the overall housing support – co-residence, support for home ownership and allocation of a rent-free dwelling – provided by ascendants has involved 40 per cent of accommodations.

Housing assistance tends to be localized when support is provided in the form of in-kind resources. It is more likely that ascendants can help their adult children if the latter settle close to the former. The proximity required for family support to be given for home ownership is also a reliable foundation for further mutual support between generations, which is furnished in a kind of contract whereby care is exchanged for (anticipated) inheritance (Poggio, 2008).

Of particular note is that one kind of care-for-inheritance contract is institutionalized by inheritance and family law. Italian law establishes that descendants are the main inheritors, notwithstanding possible adverse wills, but also that

TABLE 3.4 Couples' accommodation at marriage and housing support received from their parents, by period of marriage (couples in their first or only marriage in 2003) (%)

	Period of marriage		
	Before 1983	1983–1992	1993–2003
Co-resident with parents	17.6	11.2	9.4
Independent accommodation: home ownership			
With parental support:			
home as a bequest	2.9	2.7	3.5
home received as a gift	3.1	4.8	4.2
financial help received for house building	1.1	1.7	2.2
financial help received for home purchase	3.5	7.5	9.5
Without parental support:			
built with their own means	4.2	3.7	2.8
purchased with their own means	5.8	9.5	12.9
inherited or received as a gift by others	0.1	0.3	0.6
already owned by one of the partners	5.5	8.3	10.0
Independent accommodation: rented for free			
by parents	8.6	11.9	11.6
by others	1.2	1.0	1.7
Independent accommodation: rented	46.3	37.3	31.6
All	100.0	100.0	100.0
Cases on which percentages are calculated	$n = 1,506$	$n = 1,789$	$n = 1,994$

Source: Own estimates from the ISTAT Famiglia e Soggetti Sociali (2003 survey). See rest of chapter for further information.

they should provide economic assistance to ascendants if needed. According to a 'subsidiarity' principle, the state provides assistance only in a second instance if no descendants are able to provide it. Adult children may pay for care services for their ascendants in order to preserve the housing that they will inherit, and which they will typically prefer not to see owned by strangers. Further, when local authorities provide care services and hospices for elderly homeowners, the latter can release their housing equity if there is nobody to cover the costs in other ways. In this case, the care-for-inheritance deal involves the state instead of descendants.

Recent trends and problematic outcomes

Recent trends in Italian home ownership and its relations with the welfare system can be distinguished analytically among socio-economic changes, structural changes in the housing system and endogenous developments within the national home ownership model. There are obvious interconnections among factors in these three groups, but this distinction serves to simplify the analysis.

First, among socio-economic changes, the ageing of the Italian population and immigration from other countries are important demographic factors to take into account. They are also directly connected with the distribution of housing wealth, in which the elderly are typically native outright owners whereas immigrants are new entrants to the housing market. Second, increased insecurity in the labour market, especially for young people, affects their capacity to have decent and stable incomes and to save, and borrow, money. Access to home ownership without support from the family seems to be more difficult than in the past, especially if house price dynamics are taken into consideration.

As regards housing-specific structural changes, land and urban planning, as well as building regulations, are now better implemented, and housing-related markets are becoming more professionalized than in the past. As already mentioned, this means that informal and low-cost routes to home ownership are disappearing, and that the re-stratification related to these informal processes no longer occurs.

The most dramatic change, however, has taken place in the mortgage market. Liberalization in the late 1990s led to a growth of mortgage provision and, in principle, to more favourable conditions for households looking to borrow. In the mid-1990s a typical mortgage had a 50 per cent loan-to-value threshold and a maturity of ten years. Furthermore, real interest rates were among the highest in Europe (Bernardi and Poggio, 2004). Since the late 1990s the credit market has offered mortgages with an 80 per cent loan-to-value threshold and maturities of 20–25 years and even longer. Interest rates – at least those components over which banks have some control – have been reduced by market competition. These changes in the conditions of mortgage provision have been made possible by a structural transformation in this service that increases the risks for borrowing households. Fund-raising has gradually shifted from a 'closed' system based on dedicated bonds to an 'open' system in which money comes from the international financial markets (Ball, 1990). This allows banks to lend more money, and for longer periods, to households, and it has also led to rapid growth of the mortgage market. Nevertheless, because banks now have less control over the cost of money, households are more vulnerable to volatility in international financial markets, especially when indexed interest rates are applied. Indexed interest rates enable some of the risks of operativeness to be transferred to households (Bonaccorsi di Patti and Felici, 2008). Further strategies in this regard include the securitization of loans on the secondary mortgage market. This is expected to lead to looser eligibility criteria for lending, and there is some preliminary evidence that this effect has come about.

Finally, the complete liberalization of the private rented sector anticipated this revolution in the mortgage market. These two factors[5] generated a dramatic increase in housing demand for purchase and boosted housing prices, as shown in Figure 3.1, substantially nullifying the effect of better mortgage conditions.

As an overall outcome of these changes in the mortgage market and of the rise in housing prices, the vulnerability of homeowners has arisen as a new problem in Italy. According to a recent study (Bonaccorsi di Patti and Felici, 2008), in 2007 3.5 per cent of mortgage loans taken out in the period 2004–7 resulted in repayment arrears; and a further 1.8 per cent resulted in severe arrears or mortgage defaults. Borrowers most at risk were young households (less than 30 years old) and immigrants. Arrears accounted for 10 per cent of the loans made to the latter. No systematic studies are available for subsequent years but newspaper reports and statistics on defaults provide some preliminary evidence for a worsening of the situation. It should be noted, however, that, notwithstanding structural changes in and expansion of mortgage markets, Italian households still largely rely on their own savings and family wealth to fund home purchase and renovation; at least, compared with European standards.

Two different influential surveys estimate that only 12–13 per cent of all Italian households were repaying a mortgage in 2008 (Banca d'Italia, 2010a;

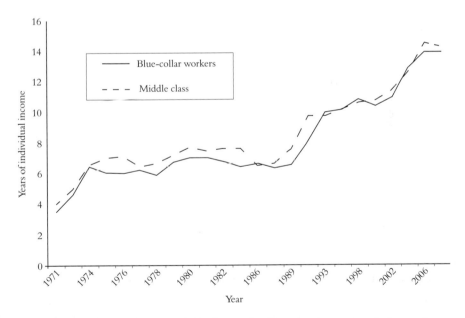

FIGURE 3.1 Years of income needed to buy a dwelling, by occupational class and year (1971–2008).
    Notes: ratio between aggregate mean values (self-assessed) of dwellings occupied by blue-collar and clerical workers and aggregate average individual earnings for these occupational categories.
    Source: own calculations from Bank of Italy, *Supplementi al Bollettino Statistico*, various years; based on estimates from the Surveys on Household Income and Wealth.

ISTAT, 2010). This contrasts with corresponding figures for other European countries – 26 per cent in Germany, 29 per cent in France and 38 per cent in the Netherlands, for instance (European Central Bank, 2009) – and is even more divergent when different national home ownership rates are taken into account (see Table 3.1). Further, not all households take out a mortgage even when they purchase a home on the market. Since 2009, the Bank of Italy has been monitoring the housing market with a quarterly survey on real estate agents. These surveys continue to estimate that about 30 per cent of housing purchases in the real estate market are not funded by a mortgage (Banca d'Italia, 2010b).

Although the current economic context is negatively affecting the Italian economy as a whole, and subsequently household economic capacity, the credit crunch seems to have had fewer dramatic consequences in comparison with other European countries. The main reason is probably the limited importance, in relative terms, of the mortgage market. The tightening of credit standards for loan approvals has been reported by the Bank Lending Survey for Italy.[6] Current mortgage conditions, nonetheless, remain far better at present than before 1998. The demand for loans to households has decreased but it is progressively recovering. The apparent growing vulnerability of homeowners on the Italian scene is nevertheless a clear matter of concern, not only in the current economic crisis but also in the long run, as it marks a structural transformation.

To conclude, some of the changes that have taken place, or are taking place, are also somehow endogenous to the Mediterranean home ownership model and may represent a 'natural' development that could somehow have been foreseen. In societies with high home ownership rates – and few or no affordable alternatives in the rented market – the distribution of housing wealth has a major impact on living conditions. More specifically, the value of the property of those who are already homeowners sets the threshold of what is needed by new entrants to the housing market (Facchini and Villa, 2005; Kemeny, 1981; Spilerman et al., 1993). Wealth distribution becomes a factor that directly affects the capacity to satisfy certain needs. This is considered a major external constraint on the transition to adulthood and for family formation and fertility. The boom in house prices that began in around 2000 has exacerbated this distributional problem. It is also likely to widen existing cleavages in Italian society and to create new ones.

Conclusions

This chapter has addressed various relations between home ownership and welfare systems in Southern Europe. The Italian case has been assumed as exemplary and has been subjected to more detailed scrutiny. Three significant points have been developed: the centrality of home ownership in the Mediterranean welfare regime; the importance of informal and family practices in comparative housing research, at least when considering Southern Europe; and the potential role of home ownership in an asset-based welfare system. Some provisional conclusions are now drawn according to these different perspectives.

It has been argued that home ownership is an important and multifaceted resource, and contributes in multiple ways – not just housing – to individual well-being and social protection, and to the shaping of the entire welfare system. Family practices and intergenerational transfers supporting entry into home ownership perform a key role in Italy. Macro evidence from comparative welfare and housing research suggests that there are similarities in this respect with other Southern European countries. However, more systematic comparative research based on micro data is needed before the discussion conducted here can be generalized to the entire cluster of countries corresponding to the Mediterranean, or familialistic, welfare regime. What does already seem clear – at least when considering Southern Europe – is that there is no justification for comparative welfare research that ignores housing, nor for comparative housing research that ignores the role of the family and informal practices in the housing systems.

The foregoing discussion has outlined some problematic features of the role performed by home ownership. To some extent they are linked to recent changes in housing-related and credit markets. The increased vulnerability of households repaying loans is one of them, and has been recognized in public debates. The distributional outcomes of housing wealth, its transmission and possible cumulability with other forms of capital – and the importance of home ownership as a relatively independent factor in the structuring of inequality – is a less widely addressed but nevertheless very important issue.

When considering home ownership in an asset-based welfare perspective, the Italian experience can provide some significant insights that inform the current debate. The 'popularization' of home ownership in Italy, the expansion of this housing tenure within all social strata, has not represented a form of 'democratization'. Differences still exist in the likelihood of accessing this form of tenure, and in the timing and manner of access. Distinct living conditions, housing values, localization and commuting constraints derive from these differences. Other economic implications for household budgets and their role in the structuring of social inequality are also significant. Well-off households are more likely to receive family support and transfers, whereas low-income ones committed to home ownership are more likely to experience a financial strain that may undermine their capability to satisfy other important needs. Overall, there is considerable evidence to suggest that home ownership is a factor in augmenting social and economic inequality.

Some of the connections between home ownership and other welfare domains have also been discussed, highlighting that this resource represents one pillar of private, often family-based, welfare provision in the context of an underdeveloped welfare state. Home ownership is evidently a crucial resource for families that are required to guarantee social protection for their members. On the other hand, relying on home ownership as a pillar in a mixed system of welfare provision seems largely incompatible with social citizenship in the Marshallian sense (Marshall, 1949 [1964]). Even if some compensatory effects may derive from dedicated policies or informal practices supporting access to home ownership by low-income households – as has happened in the Italian case – it is unlikely that any policy targeted towards low-income households will be able to compensate satisfactorily for inequality arising from the labour market or from the additional cumulative inequality inherent in the distribution of home ownership and in the processes of its intergenerational transmission.

References

Alasia, F. and Montaldi, D. (1960) *Milano, Corea: inchiesta sugli immigrati*, Milano: Feltrinelli.

Allen, J., Barlow, J., Leal, J., Thomas, M. and Padovani, L. (2004) *Housing and Welfare in Southern Europe*, Oxford: Blackwell.

Attias-Donfut, C. and Wolff, F.C. (2000) The redistributive effects of generational transfers, in S. Arber and C. Attias-Donfut (eds) *The Myth of Generational Conflict*, London: Routledge.

Ball, M. (1990) *Under One Roof. Retail Banking and the International Mortgage Finance Revolution*, New York: Harvester-Wheatsheaf.

Banca d'Italia (2010a) I bilanci delle famiglie italiane nell'anno 2008, *Supplementi al Bollettino statistico. Indagini campionarie* (new series), 8.

Banca d'Italia (2010b) Sondaggio congiunturale sul mercato delle abitazioni in Italia. Gennaio 2010, *Supplementi al Bollettino statistico. Indagini campionarie* (new series), 12.

Bernardi, F. and Poggio, T. (2004) Home ownership and social inequality in Italy, in K. Kurz and H.P. Blossfeld (eds) *Home Ownership and Social Inequality in Comparative Perspective*, Stanford: Stanford University Press.

Bonaccorsi di Patti, E. and Felici, R. (2008) *Il rischio dei mutui alle famiglie in Italia: evidenza da un milione di contratti, Questioni di Economia e Finanza*, Occasional Paper No. 32. Rome: Banca d'Italia.

Börsch-Supan, A., Brugiavini, A., Jürges, H., Mackenbach, J., Siegrist, J. and Weber, G. (eds) (2005) *Health, Ageing and Retirement in Europe. First Results from the Survey of Health, Ageing and Retirement in Europe*, Mannheim: Mannheim Research Institute for the Economics of Aging, Strauss GmbH.

Bourdieu, P. and de Saint Martin, M. (1990) Le sens de la propriété. La genèse sociale des systèmes de préférences, *Actes de la recherche en sciences sociales*, 81/82, 52–64.

Cannari, L., Nucci, F. and Sestito, P. (2000) Geographic labour mobility and the cost of housing: evidence from Italy, *Applied Economics*, 32, 1899–1906.

Castles, F.G. and Ferrera, M. (1996) Home ownership and the welfare state: is Southern Europe different? *South European Society and Politics*, 2, 163–184.

Doling, J. and Ronald, R. (2010) Home ownership and asset-based welfare, *Journal of Housing and the Built Environment*, 2, 165–173.

European Central Bank (2009) *Housing Finance in the Euro Area*, Occasional Paper Series, 101. Frankfurt: European Central Bank.

European Mortgage Federation (2009) *Hypostat 2008*, Bruxelles: EMF.

Facchini, C. and Villa, P. (2005) La lenta transizione alla vita adulta in Italia, in C. Facchini (ed.) *Diventare adulti. Vincoli economici e strategie familiari*, Milano: Guerini.

Guiso, L. and Jappelli, T. (1996) Intergenerational transfers, borrowing constraints and the timing of home ownership, *Temi di Discussione (Banca d'Italia)*, 275. Rome: Banca d'Italia.

ISTAT (2010) *L'abitazione delle famiglie residenti in Italia – anno 2008, Statistiche in breve – Famiglia e Società*, Rome: ISTAT.

Kemeny, J. (1981) *The Myth of Home Ownership: Private Versus Public Choice in Housing Tenure*, London: Routledge and Kegan Paul.

Marshall, T.H. (1949) *Citizenship and Social Class*, Marshall lecture, Cambridge, reprinted in *Class, Citizenship and Social Development* (1964), Garden City, NY: Doubleday.

Mulder, C.H. and Billari, F. (2010) Home ownership regimes and low fertility, *Housing Studies*, 4, 527–541.

National Board of Housing, Building and Planning (Sweden) and Ministry for Regional Development of the Czech Republic (2005) *Housing Statistics in the European Union 2004*, Karlskrona, Sweden: Boverket, National Board of Housing, Building and Planning.

Nomisma (2007) *La condizione abitativa in Italia: Fattori di disagio e strategie d'intervento*, Rome: Nomisma.

OECD (Organisation for Economic Co-ordination and Development) (2004) *Informal Employment and Promoting the Transition to a Salaried Economy*, OECD Employment Outlook, Paris: OECD.

Padovani, L. (1996) Italy, in P. Balchin (ed.) *Housing Policy in Europe*, London: Routledge.

Poggio, T. (2005) La casa come area di welfare, *Polis*, 2, 279–235.

Poggio, T. (2006) Proprietà della casa, disuguaglianze sociali e vincoli del sistema abitativo, *Rivista delle politiche sociali*, 3, 27–40.

Poggio, T. (2008) The intergenerational transmission of home ownership and the reproduction of the familialistic welfare regime, in C. Saraceno (ed.) *Families, Ageing and Social Policy. Generational Solidarity in European Welfare States,* Cheltenham: Edward Elgar.

Spilerman, S., Lewin-Epstein, N. and Semyonov, M. (1993) Wealth, intergenerational transfers, and life chances, in A.B. Sørensen and S. Spilerman (eds) *Social Theory and Social Policy. Essays in Honor of James S. Coleman*, Westport, CT: Praeger.

Torgesen, U. (1987) Housing: the wobbly pillar under the welfare state, in B. Turner *et al.* (eds) *Between State and Market: Housing in the Post-War Industrial Era*, Stockholm: Almqvist and Wiksell.

Tosi, A. (1987) La produzione della casa in proprietà: pratiche familiari, informale, politiche, *Sociologia e ricerca sociale*, 22, 7–24.

4

HOME OWNERSHIP IN POST-SOCIALIST COUNTRIES

Between macro economy and micro structures of welfare provision

Srna Mandic

Introduction

In those countries generally referred to as 'post socialist', home ownership entered policy agendas in the early 1990s, with housing reforms embodying a departure from socialism and the advancement of markets. The promotion of, and proliferation in, rates of home ownership were central to reform efforts and often also served at that time as a measure of transitional success. Meanwhile, in the last three decades in Western developed countries, home ownership has evolved into a frequently discussed phenomenon and is considered in terms of a more diverse array of issues. Debates on home ownership have reflected broader developments in social sciences, with a particular concern being integrative concepts, most notably 'welfare regimes' that link housing and families in terms of welfare capacities and conditions (Esping-Andersen 1990, 1999; Matznetter, 2002; Vogel, 2002; Allen *et al.*, 2004; Berthoud and Iacovou, 2004; Ronald, 2007). This concept is significant because of its ability to combine housing and housing tenure with different issues, providing a basis for cross-national comparisons. These debates went along with the recent increase in the output of survey data, providing more cross-nationally comparative empirical information both on macro as well as micro levels.

In this chapter we focus on home ownership in post-socialist countries and in particular its specificity in comparison with developed Western countries. We first examine how discussions of home ownership in post-socialist countries are situated within the broader framework of theoretical debates and their shifting foci. An overview of these debates is thus presented and the argument put forward, in the context of post-socialist countries, that home ownership has received uneven analytical treatment: namely, home ownership remains primarily discussed in terms of macro-economic issues while its relation to the micro level of household and family welfare continues to be largely unrecognized. The second half of the chapter concerns itself with the empirical exploration and analysis of the role of the family in sustaining home ownership in post-socialist countries. A further objective is to compare variances in and the significance of patterns of owner-occupied family housing across countries in the EU. To establish the features and strength of family support for home ownership comparatively, reference to other groups of countries, based on the data of the European Quality of Life Survey (2003), will be made.

In post-socialist countries important features in home ownership systems have been recently highlighted, such as very high owner-occupancy rates (Stephens, 2003; Lowe and Tsenkova, 2003; Hegedus and Teller, 2006; Domanski *et al.*, 2006) and a high incidence of unfit housing and material deprivation in Eastern Europe (Norris and Shiels, 2007; Mandic, 2010a), yet discussion of home ownership in these countries still faces a number of challenges. Post-socialist countries have not been evenly included in welfare regime typologies or related debates, and until recently were not included in cross-national comparative survey data. There has been a significant shortage of data and, most importantly, micro-level data on welfare provision and the transfer of resources within family frameworks. Thus, there seems to be a substantial gap in knowledge that has impeded comparisons with Northern as well as Southern Europe with regard to welfare contexts. Particularly interesting in this regard is comparisons with Southern European countries as many more similarities may be expected with these countries than with others because of the incidence of retrenched welfare states and weak markets. Nonetheless, comparisons appearing in the literature are relatively few.

Conceptual background

In the discussion of home ownership, different approaches can be identified, each bringing to the forefront of analytical attention some features of the phenomenon while neglecting others. How an object of observation is defined and framed is however a significant issue for both policy and the development of social science (Parsons, 1995). In this section, three perspectives on, or approaches to, home ownership are outlined, pointing to dissimilarities between the post-socialist and the West European countries in the treatment and understanding of home ownership. A major difference is that in post-socialist countries home ownership has been primarily perceived as an issue of macro-economic efficiency. In contrast, in Western developed countries, home ownership has typically been seen, and in various ways discussed, as an issue of welfare, whereas such a perspective has been almost absent for post-socialist countries. However, in recent debates there have been notable attempts towards further integration of approaches.

Home ownership as an issue of economic efficiency

Attention to home ownership in post-socialist societies grew in the early 1990s when the phenomenon of 'housing reforms' and 'housing privatization' in countries in transition in Eastern and Central Eastern Europe entered the European housing research agenda. In these countries the rate of home ownership was frequently a core issue among transitional policies and served as a tangible measure of their progress. In a number of cases this led to a drastic rise in home ownership rates, far exceeding those of the countries previously considered exemplars of home-owning societies. Indeed, this rise in rate of home ownership among the post-socialist countries has been frequently documented and discussed as an outcome of privatization policies, mostly consisting of the sale of public rented housing to sitting tenants, on the one hand, and of restitution of rental property to the original pre-war private owner or their inheritors, on the other (Turner *et al.*, 1992; Hegedus *et al.*, 1996; Clapham *et al.*, 1996; Struyk, 1996).

Other issues frequently discussed in relation to the increased rate of home ownership in most post-socialist countries were the causes of and explanations for these changes. The logic of this transformation, with the rising home ownership at the core, was most impressively articulated in terms of the East European housing model (EEHM) and its dissolution (Hegedus *et al.*, 1996; Hegedus and Tosics, 1996). According to this, privatization was seen as a necessary response to the problems inherent in the EEHM: production, consumption and allocation of housing dominated by the state; restrictions on the market and private property; unsustainably high state subsidies for housing; poor upkeep and maintenance of existing stock; bad quality newly built stock; and lack of individual choice. Privatization of rented housing was seen as a means to boost private property and the housing market, bringing more efficiency to the entire housing system. In other words, privatization was seen as an element of an overall shift from the command to the market-based economy, transforming the entire housing system being a starting point and a shift to home ownership a precondition. However, very few authors were critical about the wider outcomes of housing privatization in countries in transition.

To sum up, it was the macro-economic perspective that dominated discussions of housing with regard to transitional reforms. This perspective was clearly articulated in the thesis that housing served as a 'shock absorber' for the whole economy during transition (Struyk, 1996). Later discussion of home ownership in the region was still influenced by such macro-economic perspectives that served to frame the debate around the issue of efficiency in the housing system. Only recently, with a widening spectrum of themes and authors discussing home ownership in this region (see, for instance, Lowe and Tsenkova, 2003; Norris and Shiels, 2007; Doling and Horsewood, 2005; Pichler Milanovic, 2001; Cirman, 2006; Hegedus and Teller, 2006; Elsinga *et al.*, 2007), have discussions gradually departed from this macro-economic perspective.

Home ownership as a privatized structure of welfare provision

In early 1980s Kemeny (1981) brought home ownership into the analytical and social scientific limelight in Western developed countries. He focused on the very nature of home ownership tenure and highlighted both its inherent and its context-dependent characteristics by contrasting arrangements in Anglo-Saxon societies with those in Sweden. To some extent, and more extensively elaborated later (Kemeny, 1992, 1995), Kemeny established in this work the relation between housing tenure and wider social structures, as well as between housing and welfare. Distinguishing between collectivist and privatized forms of social structures, he maintained that the rate of home ownership, being a privatized form of housing provision, is strongly related not only to the nature of the national housing system and to urban structures, but also to the entire welfare system, particularly to health and pension insurance systems. More specifically, high home ownership rates impact on society, creating 'a life style based on detached housing, privatized urban transport . . . and strong resistance to public expenditure . . . to fund quality universal welfare provision' (Kemeny, 2005, p. 60).

This influential early work on housing opened, at the time, a new and profound avenue for reflection on home ownership in modern societies. However, although recognizing the link between home ownership and public welfare provision, even highlighting the possible role of home ownership as a substitute for old-age pensions, and warning that 'housing is strikingly absent from comparative welfare research' (Kemeny, 1992, p. 80), Kemeny seems to have inspired housing debates of the time around another focus. It was the capacity of home ownership to characterize entire national housing systems, leading to a very influential distinction between 'home-owning societies', in which 'home ownership became normal tenure for all but the poorest households' (Kemeny, 2005, p. 60), and 'cost-renting societies', in which renting was made attractive also for significant numbers of middle- and higher-income households. This distinction, together with the subsequent concept of rental markets as 'integrated' versus 'dualist', framed most subsequent cross-national comparative analyses of home ownership among developed Western societies.

Home ownership as a family welfare issue

The third distinctive approach to home ownership is related to wider debates surrounding welfare regimes and can be attributed to recognition of Southern European specificities. This is best articulated in the concept of the South European housing model (Allen *et al.*, 2004). This concept was developed in response to the mainstream welfare regimes debate, which did not sufficiently cover either South European countries or the role of housing in welfare. Castles and Ferrera (1996) made the case that in Southern Europe the extended family played a significant role in the delivery of welfare to households with regard to old-age pensions, health care and housing. Allen and colleagues (2004) went further, maintaining that 'understanding family strategies is as important as understanding formal housing policies in grasping the nature of the housing system' (p. 99). By thoroughly analysing common housing strategies they confirmed the strong role of the (extended) family and of kinship networks in providing resources in the form of financial aid, self-construction and building sites, all of which were determined by home ownership status and conditions. They argued that in South Europe, in the provision of welfare, the family is 'an important organizing principle' and 'housing is one of the domains where its role is more developed' (Allen *et al.*, 2004, p. 126). Essentially, the South European home is not only a dwelling, but also 'a safety net for the family's welfare' (Allen *et al.*, 2004, p. 161).

To sum up, the specific contribution of this line of reasoning was a clear emphasis on provision of welfare as a broader framework, necessary to fully comprehend the role of housing and of home ownership in South European societies. Moreover, within this welfare framework, family and micro-level strategies were recognized as equally important as the welfare state. This perspective, emphasizing the micro level, increasingly appeared in analyses in which housing, demography and certain aspects of welfare meet to produce very specific outcomes in South Europe, such as the pattern of family forma-tion and living arrangements (Iacovou, 2004), late leaving of parental home by young adults (Berthoud and Icacovou, 2004; Vogel, 2002), three-generational households (Saraceno and Olagnero, 2004) and a specific intergenerational flow of resources (Albertini *et al.*, 2007). Also noteworthy is the comprehensive over-view of ways that home ownership is subject to intergenerational transmission and how housing is related to other forms of support within broader families (see Poggio, 2008).

Combining perspectives

These three approaches broadly differ in period of time, in geographic cover-age and in the characteristic perspective that framed mainstream discussions of home ownership. In the most general sense these different waves reflect the focus of cross-national comparisons during given periods. The first wave focused on Western developed countries and articulated the divergence in home ownership between them. The second wave introduced the transitional Eastern European countries, while expressing a specific concern with home ownership as the new basis of the housing system and its efficacy. In other words, West–East diver-gence was perceived as a macro-economic issue. The third wave introduced South European societies and the role of home ownership articulated within the framework of welfare provision. However, it was the micro level where family and kinship welfare practices were specifically emphasized and recognized, distinguishing a North–South European divide. In other words, the North–South European divide in the role of home ownership was articulated in terms of the micro-level strategies within the framework of welfare provision.

Some of the explanation for the existence of such diverse and separate perspectives can be found already in Kemeny's observation from almost two decades ago concerning the neglect of housing by comparative welfare researchers. He argued that 'housing is so deeply embedded in social structure and so difficult to disentangle from other forms of welfare' (Kemeny, 1992, p. 80) that it causes problems of analysis, and 'therefore housing tends to be either omitted entirely or included as one item among welfare areas' (Kemeny, 1992, p. 80). He also emphasized that 'a more theoretically grounded housing studies must take welfare issues and problems centrally into account' (Kemeny, 1992, p. 81).

Recently, however, there has been a strong and increasing tendency in the social sciences to combine housing and welfare into a more integrated picture and to observe home ownership within it. There has been a series of discussion about different trade-offs between home ownership and welfare in Western developed countries (Kemeny, 2005; Doling and Horsewood, 2005; Castles, 2005). Also important is a line of analysis linking home ownership to broader structures of global capital and risk and observing possible convergence across a broader range of societies around home ownership and asset-based welfare (Doling and Ford, 2003; Ronald, 2008; Doling and Elsinga, 2006; Elsinga *et al.*, 2007; Doling and Ronald, 2010). However, the most general and most integrative framework is the one relating housing to welfare regimes, inspiring a number of recent works (for overview see Ronald, 2007) and proving very relevant also for comparisons of West and East Asian home ownership models.

However, for the post-socialist countries such integrative developments are still only emerging. It should be pointed out that, for some post-socialist countries, the role of family support in housing provision has been acknowledged (see Cirman, 2008; Hegedus and Teller, 2007). Most recently, the significance of family housing equity in provision of old-age security for its members has been highlighted for Hungary (Hegedus and Szemzo, 2010) and Slovenia (Mandic, 2010b), and comparisons made to some West European countries (Elsinga and Mandic, 2010). Yet the topic has yet to be systematically and comprehensively examined, particularly regarding similarities and differences across post-socialist countries and their possible subgroups. Two shortcomings have specifically contributed to this situation. First, these countries have been virtually absent from debates on welfare regime typologies. So for these countries the role of the family as a complementary force to the market and the welfare state has not been elaborated nearly as much as for South European countries. Second, these countries face a great shortage of empirical micro-level data on welfare provision and on the transfer of resources within the family framework. Thus, there seems to be a substantial gap, still not allowing comparisons with Northern as well as Southern Europe with regard to the welfare context.

Linking home ownership and family welfare: post-socialist countries in a comparative perspective

It has already been recognized that in post-socialist countries rates of home ownership are generally very high, denoting 'super home ownership' housing systems (Stephens, 2003; Hegedus and Teller, 2006). Although the importance of the macro level – most notably privatization policies launched by the state – in supporting high levels of home ownership has already been thoroughly discussed and acknowledged, at the micro level, the family and the support it provides for and through home ownership has remained largely neglected. In this section we empirically explore how significant the family is in sustaining home ownership in post-socialist countries and estimate, as far as the data allow, how strong it is in comparison to other countries and groups of countries in the EU.

We can essentially hypothesize that, in post-socialist countries, the significance of family in sustaining home ownership is more similar to that in South European countries than it is to that in other European countries. Because the significance of the family in housing in South European countries has already been recognized and reported, this group of countries can be used as a yardstick against which to measure the strength of the phenomenon elsewhere.

Because of the widely recognized lack of comparable data for new member states, it is possible to carry out only a simple analysis. In our examination of the family as a micro foundation of home ownership we are very limited by the available data and only rather indirect indicators can be used. Because of that, and because of the scarce pre-existing research findings, this examination is of an exploratory nature; it can provide only rudimentary estimates that, nonetheless, provide some substantial new insights.

Data, methods and indicators

Our analysis employs data from the European Quality of Life Survey (2003).[1] This is presently one among very few available data sets covering all 27 European member states. It provides basic information about households and their quality of life in various domains including housing and family. In this survey 'home ownership' stands for the self-reported housing tenure of the household, so home ownership indicators refer to population (i.e. households) and not to housing units. As a consequence, these data cannot be directly compared with other data sources in which home ownership and its rate typically refer to housing stock.

As our aim is to estimate the strength of family support for home ownership in post-socialist countries in a comparative way, that is, by reference to other groups of countries in Europe, our method is a simple comparative analysis. This basically means that groups of countries are examined for possible internal similarities and differences in particular chosen characteristics. Afterwards, groups are compared, for which simple arithmetic unweighted group averages are used. However, where relevant, attention is called to cases in which a group member is very different to others ('outliers'). Although insightful, the group average should be used with caution.

European 27 countries were grouped in the following way (Figure 4.1):

- South European countries: Cyprus, Greece, Italy, Malta, Portugal and Spain. Although there is often much dispute over how to classify the South European group according to welfare regime typology, categorization in this case was not problematic; however, we added two new member states to the usual members of the group.
- Subcategories of West European countries were taken as counterparts to the South European group. They were classified into three subgroups that are, in addition to the South European group, broadly in line with welfare

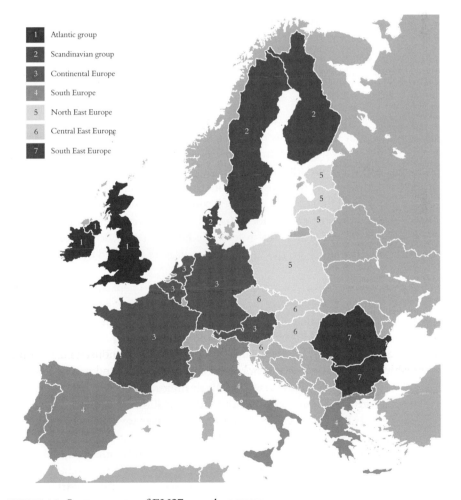

1   Atlantic group

2   Scandinavian group

3   Continental Europe

4   South Europe

5   North East Europe

6   Central East Europe

7   South East Europe

FIGURE 4.1 Seven groups of EU27 member states.
   Source: Adapted from European Quality of Life Survey (2003).

regime typologies (Esping-Andersen, 1990; Allen *et al.*, 2004; Berthoud and Iacovou, 2004). These groups are: Atlantic (or liberal) with the United Kingdom and Ireland; Scandinavian (or social-democratic) with Denmark, Finland and Sweden; continental (or corporatist) with Austria, Belgium, France, Germany, Luxembourg and the Netherlands.

- Last is the group of post-socialist countries, comprising ten new member states. Because of its size (number of member states) and because not much is known about their diversity, this group was divided into three subgroups: North East European (NEE) with Estonia, Latvia, Lithuania and Poland; Central East European (CEE) with the Czech Republic, Hungary, Slovakia and Slovenia; and South East European (SEE) with Bulgaria and Romania. This subdivision follows geographical lines, but has also proved useful in monitoring housing developments in this region (see Hegedus *et al.*, 1996). It should be noted, though, that in the case of Poland our classification diverges from many others. We did not classify Poland as CEE, but rather as NEE, which is geographically still adequate, but is also justified because of similarities found with regard to systems of welfare provision (Mandic, 2008).

To examine the extent to which home ownership is underpinned by family and kinship, four indicators were selected. They each provide specific insights into how the ways and mechanisms of achieving home ownership status are backed up by family and kinship and how owned homes are part of the welfare economy. Although the first observed indicator is a rather direct one, the other three are more indirect. What these circumstantial indicators denote is not direct evidence of what family does; instead, they convey the circumstances in which the presence and an active role of the family are very common, as both the state and the market are lacking. These indicators included the following:

- *Use of owner-occupied housing by extended family.* There are two forms of such use detectable in the database. The first is the incidence of three-generational households in owner-occupied housing. This signifies that an adult person with children shares accommodation with parents. The second is the incidence of accommodation provided rent free. This implies that a household is neither owner nor renter, but uses a unit owned by another private person, normally a relative. Both indicators explicitly denote sharing of housing resources within the framework of the broader family and particularly among diverse generations. This gives way also to sharing and exchange of other services and goods in the context of family economy and welfare. It has been pointed out already that in South Europe the role of the (extended) family is very significant and that this is manifested in the highest incidence of co-residence of parents and adult children and of three-generational households (Allen *et al.*, 2004; Saraceno and Olagnero, 2004; Iacovou, 2002; Poggio, 2008).

- *Coverage of home ownership by mortgages.* In terms of access to home own-ership, and frequently also in the maintenance of homes, the mortgage represents a key prerequisite for entry into home ownership via the market. There are, by contrast, two other means of entry into home ownership – inheritance/gifts and self-provision construction – both of which entail the family. Thus, a low percentage of mortgages among homeowners indicates the presence of other sources, coming from family and kinship – in mon-etary form or in kind, such as labour, material, and so on.
- *The rate of home ownership in rural versus urban areas.* This figure gives an indi-cation of the extent to which home ownership, in contrast to renting, is predominantly a rural phenomenon. Conversely, it can also be equally an urban phenomenon. As a predominantly rural phenomenon, home owner-ship may be driven by different mechanisms related to pre-industrial forms of family structure and economic production.

The use of owner-occupied housing by extended family

How a member of an extended family can make use of housing owned by other members could be observed in two ways in the available data, shown in Figure 4.2 (individual countries) and Figure 4.3 (the group averages).

The first indicator of the use of owned housing by extended family is the percentage of three-generational households in owner-occupied housing found for each country. The figures show that in South European countries this ranges from 2 to 5 per cent, somewhat exceeding the rate in other West European countries (which most frequently report 1 percent). However, the most marked West European exception is Ireland, with a high presence of three-generational households, but this country has been already recognized as quite 'South European' regarding its family formation patterns (see Iacovou, 2004). Somewhat similar, yet less marked, is the exception of Luxembourg. However, the post-socialist countries exhibit even higher percentages of three-generational households, reaching as high as 15 per cent in Poland and 14 per cent in Bulgaria. To sum up, the figures indicate that the three-generational household is a phenomenon that is almost non-existent in Northern Europe (exceptions being Ireland, Austria and Luxembourg), but somewhat more sig-nificant in Southern Europe and even more significant among post-socialist countries. These differences can be relatively well summarized by group aver-ages (Figure 4.3), varying from zero in the Scandinavian group to 10 per cent in the South East European group.

The second indicator – percentage of households in accommodation pro-vided rent free – follows quite a similar pattern to the first indicator. The phenomenon is very scarce in the Atlantic and Scandinavian groups and most of the continental group, a marked exception in the last being Austria. In Southern Europe the phenomenon is slightly more pronounced, with it being even more manifest among post-socialist countries. The extremes are Hungary, with a rate

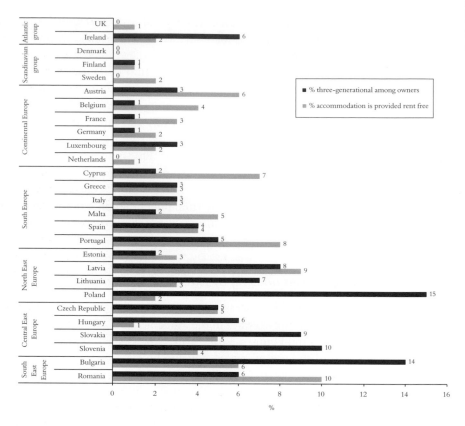

FIGURE 4.2 Three-generational households and households in rent-free accommodation: individual countries.
Source: Adapted from European Quality of Life Survey (2003).

as low as 1 per cent, and Romania, with a rate as high as 10 per cent. In terms of group averages, the percentage of households in rent-free accommodation stretches from 1 per cent in the Atlantic and Scandinavian groups to 8 per cent in South East Europe. So for both indicators, post-socialist countries as a group are found to be much closer to the South European groups of countries than to other West European groups.

Coverage of home ownership by mortgages

In this section we distinguish between those homeowners who have a mortgage and those who do not. The relative size of these two categories, expressed as a percentage of the total population, is compared across countries. Figure 4.4 shows individual country rates, and Figure 4.5 presents group averages.

Figures show that countries differ very much within each category. When the two categories are expressed as a simple ratio, extremely large differences

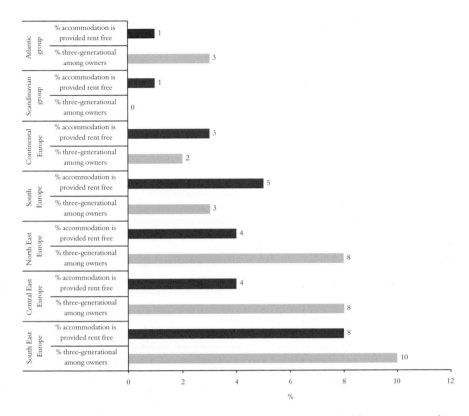

FIGURE 4.3 Three-generational households and households in rent-free accommodation: group averages.
Source: Adapted from European Quality of Life Survey (2003).

appear. These differences can be illustrated by the two most extreme cases: in the Netherlands the ratio is 4:46, whereas in Bulgaria it is 89:0. In the first case, homeowners without a mortgage represent a marginal share of 4 per cent of the total population, whereas those with mortgages comprise almost half of the total population. In contrast, in Bulgaria homeowners without mortgages represent the vast majority of the population, almost 90 per cent, whereas those with a mortgage are few and were not even detected in the survey sample.

Among all 27 member states, the share of homeowners with a mortgage exceeds the share of those without a mortgage in only four countries: the United Kingdom, Denmark, Sweden and the Netherlands. In all other countries the opposite is the case, and the balance between these two categories varies strongly. However, it is possible to distinguish between three types of situation:

• High coverage of mortgages can be defined by a situation in which the majority (or close to the majority) of homeowners have mortgages, or this category represents at least 33 per cent of the total population. This indicates

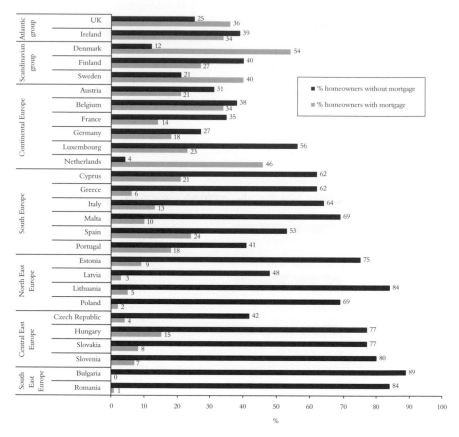

FIGURE 4.4 Homeowners with and without mortgages as a percentage of the total population: individual countries.
Source: Adapted from European Quality of Life Survey (2003).

that a significant proportion of the total population belongs to this category. This is the situation in six countries: in all of the Atlantic countries, in most of the Scandinavian ones and in two of the continental ones.

• Medium coverage can be defined as the situation in which mortgages are well developed, but not prevalent among homeowners: mortgaged home-owners represent between 10 and 25 per cent of the total population. This situation can be found in ten countries – the majority of the continental and South European countries, with only one post-socialist country (Hungary) belonging to this group.

• Low coverage of mortgages implies that only a minority of homeowners, representing up to 10 per cent of the total population, have an outstanding loan. There are 11 countries in this situation, nine of them being post-socialist and two of them South European. Among post-socialist countries, it is only Hungary that does not have such a situation.

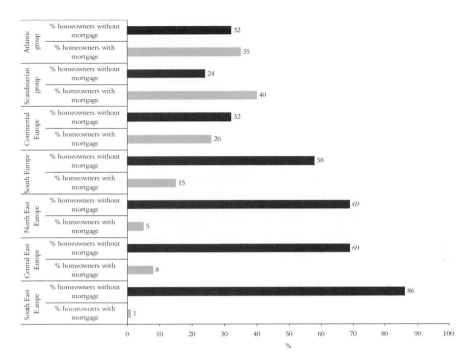

FIGURE 4.5 Homeowners with and without mortgages: group averages.
Source: Adapted from European Quality of Life Survey (2003).

Groups of countries appear relatively homogeneous and, notwithstanding a few 'outliers', group averages are a reasonable measure of how similar and diverse they are. Thus, post-socialist countries are quite homogeneous (Hungary being an exception) and have a low proportion of homeowners with mortgages. These countries are clearly on the lower end of the scale and lie in the vicinity of the South European group, whereas the Atlantic, Scandinavian and continental groups sit at the upper end. Again, the South European group has an intermediary position. Such ranking of groups of countries also implies an inverse ranking in terms of other non-monetary sources of housing assistance coming from the family.

Rural versus urban home ownership rates

Home ownership rates in rural and urban areas for each country are presented in Figure 4.6. As a general rule, home ownership rates are higher in rural than urban areas where rental alternatives are mostly located. However, when figures are compared for a single country, three distinctive situations can be found.

In the first situation urban and rural areas strongly diverge. This is most marked in six countries – Austria, France, Germany, Netherlands, Portugal and the Czech Republic, where home ownership is the major tenure (exceeding 50

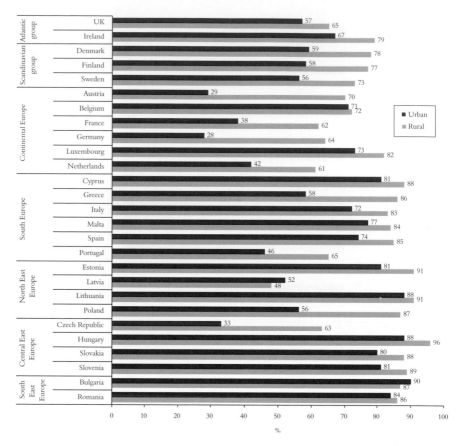

FIGURE 4.6 Percentage of homeowners in urban and rural areas: individual countries. *Source:* Adapted from European Quality of Life Survey (2003).

per cent) in rural areas, but is only minor (below 50 per cent, and often much lower) in urban areas. This situation is therefore found in most of the continental group (Austria, France, Germany, Netherlands), as demonstrated by its group average (Figure 4.7). In these countries urban areas have not been invaded by home ownership and some of them embody Kemeny's concept of 'cost-renting societies'. The two other countries with this situation are Portugal from the South European group and the Czech Republic from the Central East European group. Both countries represent remarkable exceptions in their groups.

The second situation is the opposite, meaning that between urban and rural areas home ownership rates differ very little or not at all. If the margin is set to up to 10 percentage points difference, this situation can be found in 14 countries: nine of them are post-socialist, the other five come from the Atlantic (United Kingdom), continental (Luxembourg and Belgium) and South European (Cyprus and Malta) groups.

The third situation is the intermediary situation. This is found in the

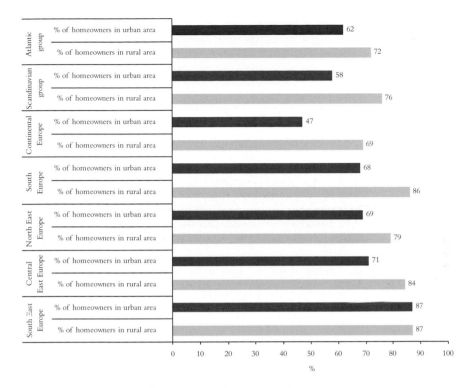

FIGURE 4.7 Percentage of homeowners in urban and rural areas: group averages.
Source: Adapted from European Quality of Life Survey (2003).

remaining seven countries, of which three are in the South European group, three in the Scandinavian group and one in the Atlantic group.

With regard to urban and rural differences, the comparison of groups is not simple and no straightforward conclusions can be made. Groups of countries are found to be markedly less homogeneous than when considering other conditions. In contrast to the relatively homogeneous Atlantic, Scandinavian and South East European groups, the other groups are heterogeneous and there is a notable presence of outliers. However, two conclusions can be drawn for post-socialist countries. First, given the difficulties in comparing groups, post-socialist countries are not found to be closer to South European groups than to other groups. However, although this holds for the urban/rural comparison of home ownership, in the overall level of home ownership they are much closer. Second, in the majority of post-socialist countries, home ownership is an urban as much as a rural phenomenon.

Discussion and conclusions

In the first part of the chapter various perspectives in home ownership have been summarized, demonstrating how different the standpoints that characterize discussions of home ownership in post-socialist countries have been. Specifically, the major focus has been on the macro level and on the role that home ownership has had in improving the economic efficiency of the entire housing system, while its relation to the micro level and family welfare was not really recognized.

In our empirical consideration we have turned to the micro level and, using available data from the European Quality of Life Survey, have explored how significant the family is in sustaining home ownership in post-socialist countries. Thus, we observed some indicators of how owned homes are integrated into the economy and into the welfare strategies of extended families. These microeconomic foundations of home ownership have received very little attention in research, while the part that macro processes play in producing high levels of home ownership – particularly housing privatization policies undertaken by transitional governments – has been generally well recognized.

The significance of the family as a micro base of home ownership was estimated for post-socialist countries in a comparative way – with reference to the South European countries where it has already been recognized as very important (Iacovou, 2004; Vogel, 2002; Saraceno and Olagnero, 2004; Allen *et al.*, 2004). We hypothesized that post-socialist countries are more similar to the South European countries than to the West European countries in this respect.

The data observed indicate – directly and indirectly – that extended family is a significant micro foundation of home ownership in post-socialist countries. Among these countries the role of the family in sustaining home ownership was found to be even more pronounced than in South European countries, well known for the prominent role of the family in provision of housing and welfare for their members.

The use of owned homes by extended family – manifested as three-generational households and rent-free accommodation – was found to be specifically high among post-socialist countries. Although, not surprisingly, it exceeds rates among the Atlantic and Scandinavian groups, where the phenomenon is hardly even detected, it also far exceeds rates in the South European group. Among the three post-socialist groups the incidence of these two forms together reaches an average of 12–18 per cent. Although these figures might not seem very high per se, they prove significant compared with the size of the social rented sector, which in most post-socialist countries does not reach even as high as 10 per cent of households.

Also, the coverage of home ownership by mortgages was found to be specifically low in post-socialist countries, where homeowners without a mortgage represent a huge majority of the total population and those with a mortgage only a tiny proportion. This is quite the reverse in the Atlantic and most Scandinavian countries where mortgages are very frequent among homeowners. The fact that the coverage of home ownership by mortgages is specifically low in post-socialist countries points to two further issues. The first is exposure to the recent and ongoing global financial crisis. With fewer current loans, homeowners in post-socialist countries seem to have been less vulnerable to the financial aspects of the credit crunch. The second is the significant role of other monetary and non-monetary mechanisms that support entry to – and the sustaining of – owner-occupied housing, particularly self-help practices and strategies of sharing diverse housing and non-housing resources within family networks. Again, post-socialist countries were found to be more similar to South European than to West European groups of countries.

Lastly, the issue was raised about the rural versus urban base of home ownership in post-socialist countries. It was found that in most post-socialist countries home ownership has invaded urban areas to practically the same extent as traditional rural areas. Home ownership proves to be an urban as much as a rural phenomenon. This indicates a need to further explore the specific urban drivers of home ownership, that is, other than those related to traditional production and family structures, and highlighting new forms of kinship solidarity in sharing resources and risks in time.

To summarize, in post-socialist countries there are many indications that owned homes frequently serve as a housing resource shared by members of the extended family. The owned home – both as accommodation and as financial equity – is one of the various welfare resources that are shared and exchanged within the family network and particularly between generations. To recognize how home ownership is backed up on the micro level in post-socialist countries, its micro foundations must be sought within the broader framework of welfare provision within family networks. As already highlighted for South Europe and as is becoming increasingly recognized for East Asia, housing and particularly home ownership has a specific and significant role in this framework, that is, in the ways that the family 'procure, use and share other welfare goods' (Ronald, 2007, p. 477). However, given the major shortage of empirical data, this insight into these issues in post-socialist countries is very limited, calling for further examination that would allow for cross-national comparisons and generalizations.

Acknowledgements

The author is grateful to the UK Data Archive for permission to use data from the European Quality of Life Survey 2003 and acknowledges that the original data creators, depositors and copyright holders, the founders of the data collections and the UK Data Archive bear no responsibility for their further analysis or interpretation. This chapter is based on research conducted in the EU 7th Framework Program DEMHOW and supported by the Agency for Research and Development of the Republic of Slovenia PS P5–0200.

References

Albertini, M., Kohli, M. and Vogel, C. (2007) Intergenerational transfers of time and money in European families: common patterns – different regimes? *Journal of European Social Policy*, 17(4), 319–334.

Allen, J., Barlow, J., Leal, J., Maloutas, T. and Padovani, L. (2004) *Housing and Welfare in Southern Europe*, Oxford: Blackwell.

Berthoud, R. and Iacovou, M. (2004) *Social Europe*, Cheltenham: Edward Elgar.

Castles, F. (2005) The Kemeny thesis revisited, *Housing, Theory and Society*, 22(2), 84–86.

Castles, F. and Ferrera, M. (1996) Home ownership and the welfare state: is southern Europe different? *South European Society and Politics*, 1(2), 163–185.

Cirman, A. (2006) Housing tenure preferences in the postprivatization period: the case of Slovenia, *Housing Studies*, 21(1), 113–134.

Cirman, A. (2008) Intergenerational transfers as a response to changes in the housing market in Slovenia, *European Journal of Housing Policy*, 8(3), 303–315.

Clapham, D., Hegedus, J., Kintrea, K. and Tosics, I. (eds) (1996) *Housing Privatization in Eastern Europe*, Westport, CT: Greenwood.

Doling, J. and Ford, J. (2003) *Globalisation and Home Ownership: Experiences in Eight Member States of the European Union*. Delft: Delft University Press.

Doling, J. and Horsewood, N. (2005) Housing opportunities and welfare provision: testing causality, *Housing, Theory and Society*, 22(2), 80–83.

Doling, J. and Elsinga, M. (eds.) (2006) *Home Ownership: Getting In, Getting From, Getting Out*, Amsterdam: IOS Press.

Doling, J. and Ronald, R. (2010) Property-based welfare and European homeowners: how would housing perform as a pension? *Journal of Housing and the Built Environment*, 25(2), 227–241.

Domanski, H., Ostrowska, A., Przybysz, D., Romaniuk, A. and Krieger, H. (2006) *First European Quality of Life Survey: Social Dimensions of Housing*, Dublin: European Foundation for the Improvement of Living and Working Conditions.

Elsinga, M. and Mandic, S. (2010) Housing as a piece in the old age puzzle, *Teorija in praksa*, 47(5), 940–958.

Elsinga, M., De Decker, P., Teller, N. and Toussaint, J. (eds) (2007) *Home Ownership beyond Asset and Security*, Amsterdam: IOS Press.

Esping-Andersen, G. (1990) *The Three Worlds of Welfare Capitalism*, Cambridge: Polity Press.

Esping-Andersen, G. (1999) *Social Foundations of Postindustrial Economies*, Oxford: Oxford University Press.

European Quality of Life Survey (2003) Principal Investigators: European Foundation for the Improvement of Living and Working Conditions and Wissenschatszntrum Berlin Fur Sozialforschung; Data Collector: Intomart GFK (Hilversum, Netherlands); Sponsor: European Foundation for the Improvement of Living and Working Conditions; Distributed by UK Data Archive, University of Essex, Colchester; February 2006. SN: 5260.

Hegedus, J. and Tosics, I. (1996) The disintegration of the East European housing model, in D. Clapham, J. Hegedüs, K. Kintrea and I. Tosics, with H. Kay (eds) *Housing Privatization in Eastern Europe*, Westport, CT: Greenwood.

Hegedus, J. and Teller, N. (2006) Managing risks in the new housing regimes of the transition countries – the case of Hungary, in J. Doling and M. Elsinga (eds) *Home Ownership: Getting In, Getting From, Getting Out*, Amsterdam: IOS Press.

Hegedus, J. and Teller, N. (2007) Hungary: escape into home ownership, in M. Elsinga, P. De Decker, N. Teller and J. Toussaint (eds) *Home ownership beyond Asset and Security*, Amsterdam: IOS Press.

Hegedus, J. and Szemzo, H. (2010) Households' strategy in old-age: financing retirement and care in Hungary, *Teorija in praksa*, 47(5), 1062–1077.

Hegedus, J., Mayo, S. and Tosics, I. (1996) *Transition of the Housing Sector in the East-Central European Countries*, Budapest: USAID, Metropolitan Research Institute.

Iacovou, M. (2002) Regional differences in the transition to adulthood, *Annals of the American Academy*, 580(1), 40–69.

Iacovou, M. (2004) Patterns of family living, in R. Berthoud and M. Iacovou (eds) *Social Europe*, Cheltenham: Edward Elgar.

Kemeny, J. (1981) *The Myth of Home Ownership: Public Versus Private Choice in Housing Tenure*, London: Routledge.

Kemeny, J. (1992) *Housing and Social Theory*, London: Routledge.

Kemeny, J. (1995) *From Public Housing to the Social Market: Rental Policy Strategy in Comparative Perspective*, London: Routledge.

Kemeny, J. (2005) 'The really big trade-off' between home ownership and welfare: Castles' evaluation of the 1980 thesis, and a reformulation 25 years on, *Housing, Theory and Society*, 22(2), 59–75.

Lowe, S. and Tsenkova, S. (eds) (2003) *Housing Change in East and Central Europe*, Aldershot: Ashgate.

Mandic, S. (2008) Home-leaving and its structural determinants in Western and Eastern Europe: an exploratory study, *Housing Studies*, 23(4), 615–637.

Mandic, S. (2010a) The changing role of housing assets in post-socialist countries, *Journal of Housing and the Built Environment*, 25(2), 213–226.

Mandic, S. (2010b) Household's views on security in old age and the role of housing in Slovenia, *Teorija in praksa*, 47(5), 1011–1027.

Matznetter, W. (2002) Social housing policy in a conservative welfare state: Austria as an example, *Urban Studies*, 39(2), 265–282.

Norris, M. and Shiels, P. (2007) Housing inequalities in an enlarged European Union: patterns, drivers, implications, *Journal of European Social Policy*, 17(1), 65–76.

Parsons, W. (1995) *Public Policy*, Cheltenham: Edward Elgar.

Pichler Milanovic, N. (2001) Urban housing markets in Central and Eastern Europe: convergence, divergence or policy 'collapse', *European Journal of Housing Policy*, 1(2), 145–187.

Poggio, T. (2008) The intergenerational transmission of home ownership and the production of the familialistic welfare regime, in C. Saraceno (ed.) *Families, Ageing and Social Policy. Generational Solidarity in European Welfare States*, Cheltenham: Edward Elgar.

Ronald, R. (2007) Comparing homeowner societies: can we construct an East–West model? *Housing Studies*, 22(4), 473–493.

Ronald, R. (2008) *The Ideology of Home Ownership: The Role of Housing in Homeowner Societies*, Basingstoke: Palgrave Macmillan.

Saraceno, C. and Olagnero, M. (2004) *Quality of Life in Europe – First Results of a New Pan-European Survey*, Dublin: European Foundation for the Improvement of Living and Working Conditions.

Stephens, M. (2003) Globalisation and housing finance systems in advanced and transition economies, *Urban Studies*, 40(5–6), 1011–1026.

Struyk, R. (1996) *Economic Restructuring of the Former Soviet Bloc: The Case of Housing,* Aldershot: Avebury.

Turner, B., Hegedus, J. and Tosics, I. (eds) (1992) *The Reform of Housing in Eastern Europe and the Soviet Union,* London: Routledge.

Vogel, J. (2002) European welfare regimes and the transition to adulthood, *Social Indicators Research,* 59(3), 275–299.

Part II

Government, markets and policies

5

HOME OWNERSHIP AND NORDIC HOUSING POLICIES IN 'RETRENCHMENT'

Hannu Ruonavaara

Introduction

At the time of writing all of the Nordic countries are struggling with the consequences of the US banking crisis. The crisis, created partly by the housing finance boom in the United States, has upset the whole of the global financial order. This has repercussions that concern very crucially the housing sector and especially home ownership in Nordic countries (Denmark, Finland, Iceland, Norway and Sweden). The most extreme example of this is to be found in the smallest of these countries, Iceland. In recent decades Iceland enjoyed a rather spectacular economic success that was brought to an end with the crisis in the private banking sector. When the economic boom came to an abrupt end this meant severe problems not only for Icelandic businesses but also for those indebted homeowners whose loans were in foreign currency. With the loss of value in Icelandic currency the cost of mortgage debt went up suddenly, thus increasing almost overnight the debt load of indebted households. In none of the other Nordic countries have the repercussions of the financial crisis been so dramatic as in Iceland. However, severe economic volatility has also been experienced in the other Nordic countries. Redundancies, temporary dismissals, closing down industrial plants and problems in the construction sector, as well as temporary house price decreases, have also happened in these countries. An increase in homeowners' debt and repayment arrears is also a possibility, through either rising unemployment or rising mortgage interest and declining equity values. However, on the whole the scale and nature of influence of the global financial turmoil on home ownership and housing in the Nordic countries cannot be readily observed, and is as yet not well researched.

The focus of this chapter is, however, not on the recent crisis but rather on the longer-term trends in owner-occupied housing sectors and housing policies in Nordic countries, especially the role that home ownership plays in these policies. Unless otherwise indicated, the empirical detail and most interpretations in this chapter derive from a comparative historical study of Nordic housing policies carried out by a team of researchers coming from each of the five countries: Denmark, Finland, Iceland, Norway and Sweden.[1] I utilise the findings from the country studies (Annaniassen, 2006; Bengtsson, 2006a; Jensen, 2006a; Ruonavaara, 2006; Sveinsson, 2006), as well as those from comparative analyses made in the project (Bengtsson, 2006b; Jensen 2006b).

The approach adopted in these studies was influenced by what has recently been called *comparative historical analysis* (see Mahoney and Rueschemeyer, 2003), a label adopted by some institutionalist political scientists and historical sociologists. As an approach, it places special emphasis on institutions and their *path-dependent* development. The central housing institution we are concerned with is *housing tenure*, understood as the sets of practices and rules that provide residents in a society legitimate access to housing. Therefore, of special interest are policy events and processes that somehow change the content of housing tenures or their respective relations. Housing tenures are seen as socially (politically and culturally) produced entities whose properties are highly – although not entirely – dependent on the context they exist in (see Ruonavaara, 1993).

Is there a Nordic housing regime?

As is well known, Sweden, as well as its Scandinavian neighbours, Denmark and Norway, form part of a specific welfare state model, identified as a social-democratic (Esping-Andersen, 1990) or Scandinavian model. As two neighbouring countries that are historically closely connected to these three Scandinavian countries, and tied to them by a number of political and cultural links, but which do not geographically belong entirely (Finland) or at all (Iceland) to Scandinavia, politicians, media and researchers, as well as the general public in these countries, often speak of a *Nordic*, rather than a Scandinavian, model of welfare. The central features of the Nordic model of welfare are benefits provided for all people irrespective of wealth and income (universalism), high levels of compensation, wide coverage of services, redistribution of income, and so on. As Jon Kvist has pointed out, the Nordic model is best seen as an ideal type that summarises the central principles of Nordic thinking concerning the welfare state. The reality of various Nordic welfare policies is, however, more complex and variable than the idea of the Nordic model would suggest. Kvist has shown how different Nordic societies at different times and in different policy areas move closer to or further from the ideal typical Nordic model (see Kvist, 1999). In spite of this there is a core of the Nordic model that helps us to understand the nature of welfare arrangements in the Nordic countries.

If the Nordic welfare model is an ideal type that only vaguely accounts for the characteristics of real welfare states, how do we go about understanding the Nordic *housing regime*? Is there such a thing? In a recent comparison of the Nordic housing systems, *Housing and Housing Policy in the Nordic Countries*, Martti Lujanen (2004)[2] asserts that, in spite of apparent differences, there is nevertheless a common foundation to Nordic housing policies. He describes the unifying features as follows:

> All the Nordic countries seek to provide housing of a decent standard for the whole of their population. The division of responsibilities between different housing market actors is similar. National government – the state – and local government – the municipalities – have a fundamental responsibility for the development of housing provision, while the private sector is responsible for areas where this sector functions effectively.
>
> (Lujanen, 2004, p. 15)

Apart from these features Lujanen mentions the role of municipalities in planning and infrastructure provision and the state's role as financers of housing production and renovation. Although there might be some special characteristics of Nordic countries concerning these features of the housing system, it is doubtful whether they actually single out Nordic housing arrangements as a housing regime distinct from what other European societies have. Moreover, although Lujanen's introduction needs only one page to summarise the common foundation, it takes five pages to summarise the differences between the Nordic countries.

As a matter of fact, Nordic housing researchers have tended to regard Nordic housing policies as rather different from each other. For example, when the most prominent representative of the housing provision approach (see Ball and Harloe, 1992) in the Nordic countries, Matti Niva, compared Swedish and Finnish housing policies, he tended to view the two housing regimes as largely opposed to each other. In this comparison, Sweden represented a de-commodified housing policy in which speculation at the point of production was eliminated, whereas Finland represented a kind of market-driven policy that had open doors to speculative housing production (see Niva, 1986). Although the contrast between Finland and Sweden in housing policy has usually been regarded as a rather clear one, the other Nordic countries have not been seen as completely similar either.

That there are considerable differences between Nordic housing regimes is actually rather puzzling – assuming that there is indeed something that can be called the Nordic model of welfare or welfare regime. Our research indicates that these differences are embedded in the histories of the different Nordic housing policies but also that on a general level there are some features that all of the Nordic housing policies share. One of them is a certain policy bias against private renting: in all of the Nordic countries the housing policy regime that developed after World War II tended to treat private renting as speculative activity that needed to be controlled and regulated for the protection of residents. This, like other features of the post-war policy regime, has been changing. For example, in Finland, private rental housing was in a way rehabilitated in the mid-1990s with the removal of the remains of state regulation of that sector. A telling sign of this changing attitude was a recent advertisement on the front page of a major Finnish newspaper urging citizens to invest their savings in rental housing enterprise. The advertisement was signed by both the Finnish real estate owners' and the Finnish tenants' interest organisations. A business profiting on people's need for housing that, until relatively recently, was thought to require control and regulation exceeding that exercised in other markets seems now to be regarded as action in the public interest. This reflects the challenge that all of the Nordic housing policies have faced in recent decades: the pressure towards a more market-oriented housing regime.

Home ownership in the Nordic countries

The Swedish housing model is internationally much better known than those of the other Nordic countries, not least through Jim Kemeny's comparative studies in which Sweden was (favourably) compared with other countries, with institutional arrangements and housing policies favouring home ownership (see, for example, Kemeny, 1981). It is usual to point out that home ownership is much less dominant in Sweden than in many other countries, most significantly the large English-speaking countries: the United Kingdom, the United States and Australia. In Sweden there is a large sector of municipal non-profit rental housing and, apart from the main tenures of renting and owner-occupation, there is an intermediate form of tenure, sometimes translated simply as cooperative housing (sometimes termed *tenant-ownership*). However, the Swedish system of housing tenure, which many know of, is not the *Scandinavian* (or Nordic) system of tenure. As a matter of fact, there are marked differences between the Nordic countries in the role that owner-occupation plays in housing provision.

Table 5.1 shows the tenure structures of the Nordic countries around the year 2000 (Karlberg and Victorin, 2004).[3] In the table the various national forms of housing tenure have been classified into a typology of four kinds of

TABLE 5.1 Distribution of housing stock by category of owner in 2000 (%)

	Direct ownership	Indirect ownership	Public and social rented	Private for-profit rented	Other	Total
Denmark	51	6	20	19	5	100
Finland	64	–	17	15	4	100
Iceland*	81	5	4	10	–	100
Norway	63	14	5	18	–	100
Sweden*	38	16	23	17	6	100

Source: Karlberg and Victorin (2004, p. 58).
* Estimated figures.

relations of possession of housing: direct ownership, indirect ownership, public and social rented sector and private for-profit rented sector. Fitting the forms of tenure found in the Nordic countries into this typology requires *translations* that in some cases are open to discussion (see Ruonavaara, 2005). Although open to some problematic interpretation, the table gives a good approximation of what we are interested in here: the extent of owner-occupation in the Nordic countries. What needs to be explained is the distinction between direct and indirect ownership. An example of direct ownership is the usual type of owner-occupation of detached housing found in all countries: the adult members of the household living in the house are its legal owners. By indirect ownership Karlberg and Victorin mean ownership of housing in which 'the building or property is owned by a legal entity of which the residents are members or joint owners' and 'shareholding in the legal entity is linked to the right to the dwelling' (Karlberg and Victorin, 2004, p. 62). The Swedish tenant-ownership, as well as Norwegian, Danish and Icelandic forms of cooperative housing, are classified into this category (but not Finnish tenant-ownership, about 1 per cent of the housing stock!). What is important here is that where cooperative forms of tenure are particularly important (i.e. in Sweden and Norway) the forms of indirect ownership have gradually developed from regulated housing sectors into more market-driven ones, *thus making them more and more similar to direct ownership.* So when looking at the significance of owner-occupation as a general type of tenure, one should not focus only on direct ownership.

Looking at the table, it indeed seems to be the case that Sweden has a rather low rate of home ownership, if that is understood simply as direct ownership. Moreover, Sweden seems to be alone on this level of direct ownership: the other Nordic countries have a rate of direct ownership ranging from 51 per cent in Denmark to 81 per cent in Iceland. Thus, in a European comparison, an exceptionally low rate of *direct* home ownership is not at all characteristic of the Nordic housing regime, but only of Sweden. Iceland is the home ownership society *par excellence* among the Nordic as well as European countries, but rates of direct home ownership also approach two-thirds in Finland and Norway. But are the differences as big as they seem?

To assess the importance of ownership as an institution of access to housing we should take into account also indirect owner-occupation. What is actually a distinctive feature of Sweden, but also of Norway, is the internationally high percentage of indirect home ownership, that is, tenant-ownership and cooperative tenure. However, in both countries these forms of tenure have gradually evolved from being housing sectors partly de-commodified by regulation of prices and transactions into ones that resemble, more and more, direct ownership. For example, it can reasonably be argued that the Finnish *limited housing company*, which is a form of tenure for owner-occupation of flats in multi-family housing in Finland, is rather close to the present form of Swedish *tenant-ownership*, usually understood as cooperative housing (see Ruonavaara, 2005). Looking at owner-occupation more broadly, as a type of tenure based on the institution of ownership, it seems to be dominant in all of the Nordic countries, including Sweden. The highest proportions of rented housing, found in Denmark and Sweden, are not more than 40 per cent of all housing.

To sum up, there are large differences between Nordic countries in the importance of home ownership in the housing system, but how large these are depends on what forms of tenure are actually counted as home ownership proper. When 'cooperative' forms of ownership are counted as owner-occupation, then the differences are smaller. However, the fact that people live in different kinds of owner-occupied housing does not exclusively determine the social and economic nature of their housing arrangements. For example, owner-occupation cannot be equated with speculative housing markets. For example, in both Iceland and Finland there have been government-supported 'social' forms of owner-occupation in which access is needs tested and price levels and resales regulated.[4] To investigate the social and economic nature of owner-occupation one should look at the social and institutional arrangements around different tenures. Here we will focus on how they, and especially owner-occupation, figure in the housing policy of a country.

Housing policies and tenures

One of the defining characteristics of the Nordic model (ideal) has been the focus on general or universal provision of benefits and services in contrast to serving only the needs of those that need them the most. The latter kinds of selective policies use means and needs testing in the allocation of benefits and services so that those who can provide for themselves are not entitled to them. The distinction between universal and selective policies can, of course, be applied also to housing policies. For example, non-profit rental housing where residents are chosen selectively on the basis of housing need and income level, and not simply on a 'first come first served' basis, while public housing loan subsidies are provided for special categories of residents or builders. The core idea of selective policies is that they are targeted to the least well off. Their justification is simple: it is fair to use the scarce resources on those who are disadvantaged and not use them for those who can afford to provide the good or service for themselves. The justification of universal policies is based on another norm of fairness stressing equal rights and obligations: everyone should be entitled to the same benefits and services irrespective of her or his social position. When this is the case, enjoying the publicly provided benefit or service should not, in principle, be stigmatising in any sense – which can be, and often is, a problem with selectively allocated benefits and services. To put the difference of policy orientation in a nutshell: universal policies are targeted to all households, selective policies to the needy households.

Sweden has been well known for its reluctance to apply selective housing policy instruments. For example, the relatively large municipal rental housing sector in Sweden is not strictly speaking social housing as it has not been allocated, in principle, according to needs and means testing – although in practice it has increasingly been responsible for housing less well-off households. Also, Swedish policy has had an ambition to make direct and indirect public subsidies for housing as tenure neutral as possible. Apart from Sweden, Denmark also has a predominantly universal housing policy approach. This, however, does not mean that all of the housing policy instruments in these countries are universal. Both countries also use selective housing policy measures. For example, in Denmark and Sweden, as in other countries, housing allowances are not allocated to all households but only to those that are entitled to them. To say that a country has a universal housing regime means that its housing policy has a mixture of universal and selective policy instruments where universal ones are predominant – similarly, selective housing policy regimes may also use universal benefits (Bengtsson, 2006b, pp. 328–329).

Of the five Nordic countries, Finland and Iceland represent most clearly the selective model. In Finland housing policy has mostly been understood as social policy aiming primarily to provide decent housing for those who cannot acquire it in the market and to even out differences in housing standards among affluent and disadvantaged households. In the Finnish housing policy discourse, 'socially responsible' has usually meant 'selective', and concern about the stigmatising effects of selective policies have not at all been as distinctive or as central as in Swedish policy discourse. Both Finland and Iceland have *dualist* housing regimes in a broader meaning than Kemeny gives the term. Instead of there being only a dualist system of *rental* housing, in which one part of rental housing is private and profit driven and another part is public and non-profit driven (Kemeny, 2006, p. 2), in Finland and Iceland this has concerned all housing. In both countries there has been a subsidised sector of 'social' owner-occupation in which access has been means tested, prices have been administratively determined and transactions controlled. In Finland, production of state-financed owner-occupied housing, where such regulations were applied, was replaced by a less regulative system of interest subsidy loans in 1996, and in Iceland, transactions of workers' dwellings were deregulated in 2002. These changes, nonetheless, do not alter the basic point: selective policies are historically not restricted only to public rental housing. Therefore, housing tenure orientation and policy orientation are distinct aspects of the housing regime.

There is also the case of Norway and how it fits into the general/selective typology. The housing regime that evolved in Norway during the three decades after 1945 developed towards the Swedish model, which Norwegian policy makers were directly influenced by – but, as will be seen later, this has subsequently changed.

Nordic housing regimes are at present in a state of change. A new regime is emerging but in most countries it has not yet fully formed. Table 5.2 cross-tabulates each Nordic housing regime with regard to institutional basis (in terms of housing tenure) and policy orientation: universal or selective. The institutional basis refers to the housing tenures that housing policy mainly

TABLE 5.2 The policy orientation and institutional basis of Nordic housing regimes

		Institutional basis		
		Ownership	Ownership/renting	Renting
Policy orientation	Universal	Norway	Sweden	Denmark
	Selective	Iceland	Finland	

Source: Bengtsson (2006c, p. 328).

works through, and tenures in this ideal–typical scheme are reduced to only two: ownership and renting. The ownership category thus includes the 'intermediate', more or less cooperative, forms of tenure. Housing regimes are not stable and unchanging entities, and the table here attempts to portray the housing regime that evolved in the late twentieth century *at its high point*, that is, at the point before the recent pressures towards retrenchment of housing policies started to affect the Nordic systems. The high point was reached at slightly different times in different societies, but, broadly speaking, the high point was reached in the 1970s and 1980s.

All combinations seem to exist except a case of selective policy focus with a basis in renting. However, in recent times Finland has been moving in this direction as state involvement in housing has to a large extent shifted towards the more focused support of social renting. This is well in line with the selective orientation of Finnish policy. Rental housing is an option for less well-off households, and targeting resources to rental housing thus represents the focusing of welfare on the most in need. Nevertheless, until the 1990s, state financing of owner-occupied housing was as important a tool for Finnish housing policy as state financing of rental housing. Actually the divide between state-financed and 'freely financed' housing has been more important in the Finnish housing policy than the tenure divide. State housing finance has in the past included regulations that have created both state-financed owner-occupied and rental housing sectors that do not operate entirely on market principles.

Apart from Finland, Sweden is also a country where housing policy has operated through both renting and ownership. The municipal rental housing sector, which covers about one-fifth of the housing stock in Sweden, has been the central policy instrument in Swedish housing policy. Such housing also exists in selective housing regimes but there it has the character of social housing serving the needs of the most vulnerable groups. In Sweden municipal rental housing is open for everyone. In fact, the difference between the municipal and commercial rental housing is not as important as elsewhere as both are a part of an integrated rental market with an internationally unique system of rent negotiations between the organised parties of the rental housing market. Rent setting is based, on the one hand, on the historic costs of housing and, on the other, on assessment of the 'use value' of housing. There are two reasons, however, why the Swedish policy is not based entirely on renting. As pointed out above, the marked policy objective of the Swedish housing policy has been tenure neutrality in the distribution of state subsidies to housing. Moreover, the Swedish form of cooperative housing – tenant-ownership – has here been classified into ownership (see Bengtsson, 2006a, pp. 101–153.)

In the two other Scandinavian countries with universal housing policies, the institutional basis of policy is grounded in just one tenure. For Danish housing policy the basis is in non-profit rental housing, which in this case accounts for about one-fifth of dwellings. The distinctive feature of the Danish system is that it is not municipalities or national non-profit developers that are the owners of rental housing but publicly subsidised and regulated voluntary associations. Associations operate independently of, but in close contact with, municipalities, and are the instrument through which the municipality works to fulfil its duty to house all citizens in its area. Local associations are also nationally organised and act as an important interest group in national housing policy (see Jensen, 2006a, pp. 45–96.)

In Norway, unlike its Scandinavian neighbours, housing policy has been institutionally based on ownership. In Norway the structure of tenures is dominated by ownership to a larger extent than in neighbouring Scandinavian countries – or even Finland. As the social rental housing sector is rather small, 5 per cent of the housing stock, its importance as a policy instrument can be limited. Central to the late-twentieth-century Norwegian housing regime was the housing policy's bias against private renting: profiting on 'other people's homes' has not been considered appropriate. If renting has not been a central policy instrument, cooperative tenure has, especially in urban municipalities. The cooperative sector constituted for most of the post-World War II period a de-commodified housing sector with low entry costs and regulation of prices. The Norwegian bias against renting has nurtured a favourable attitude towards owner-occupation in general, not only cooperative tenure. The universal ambitions of the Norwegian housing policy were realised through a public housing finance system that provided subsidised housing finance mainly for owner-occupied housing (see Annaniassen, 2006, pp. 159–211).

Iceland resembles Finland in its selective policy orientation but there the institutional basis of policy is towards ownership, as in Norway. The majority of dwellings have been owner-occupied since at least 1940, and the major alternative that existed, private renting, has diminished to one-tenth of all dwellings. A tradition of self-building is characteristic of the Icelandic housing regime, and the position of home ownership as the natural solution for satisfying housing needs is taken even more for granted than in the other Nordic homeowner societies. Accordingly state and municipal housing policies were never oriented towards creating a Scandinavian-type non-profit rental housing sector, but rather on supporting citizens' wishes to become homeowners. Consequently, only about 5 per cent of dwellings are social rental housing. The marginal role of rental housing in Icelandic policy is visible in the fact that Iceland got its first permanent legislation concerning all rights and duties in rental housing as late as 1979 (see Sveinsson, 2006, pp. 279–320).

There is one final point to be said about universal and selective housing policies. In all of the countries with universal housing policies there have been strong organisations that have functioned as a driving force in national housing policy: tenant organisations, social housing organisations and cooperative organisations. Sweden, with its corporatist rent negotiation system as well as the exceptionally high degree of organisation in the tenant movement, is a unique case in this sense, as Bo Bengtsson has identified (see Bengtsson, 1995). In Sweden, housing is embedded in civil society in a way that is exceptional internationally. To a lesser extent the two other Scandinavian countries share similar features. Very little of this exists in the Nordic countries with selective regimes, Finland and Iceland. Certainly, some *non-housing* organisations, especially labour unions, have played an important part in housing policy, often for employment rather than housing policy reasons, but the importance of organisations that directly connect with housing, such as tenant movements or homeowners' associations, has been rather limited.

Policy retrenchment and home ownership

The development of housing policies can be analysed in terms of an ideal type that distinguishes four phases: (1) the introduction or establishment phase; (2) the construction phase; (3) the administration phase; and (4) the privatisation or retrenchment phase (Bengtsson, 2006c, pp. 21–22; Jensen, 1995, pp. 229–230). In the first phase political interventions in the housing market are introduced. In the second phase the primary concern is to eliminate housing shortage by producing as much housing as possible. In the third phase attention shifts to the management and maintenance of the housing created, and in the last phase the responsibility for housing the population is gradually shifted from public powers back to the market. This model seems, to a certain extent, to apply to all of the Nordic countries. The timing of phases is different in different countries and sometimes the boundaries between phases are hard to distinguish, but the ideal type nevertheless provides a fruitful framework for analysing the development of housing policies.

Retrenchment started in different times and progressed in various forms in each Nordic country. It can reasonably be argued that its impacts have been less dramatic on housing regimes with selective housing policies. After all, retrenchment means diminishing public involvement in the housing market and targeting what is left of it at those considered to need it the most. In the case of already selectively oriented policies this means a diminishing scale and deepening selectivity, but no fundamental alteration of policy principles. For example, in the case of Finland, four developments could be seen as policy retrenchment: public financing of housing was scaled down; direct public financing was targeted to social rental housing; support for owner-occupation was transformed from direct financing to interest subsidies; and the private rental market was deregulated (see Ruonavaara, 2006). The last of these can be considered a significant change of past principles. In the mid-1990s, when liberalisation of the private rental market was completed, it affected some 15 per cent of households. Although there was political controversy about the reform, it was not enduring.

In the post-World War II period in Norway, the state housing bank, Husbank, was a major player in the housing regime. Between 1945 and the end of the millennium about half of Norway's 2 million dwellings had been built with low-interest Husbank loans granted to cooperatives and individuals alike (Gulbrandsen, 2004, pp. 166–167). Husbank financing was accompanied by regulations concerning costs, standard and size of dwellings. Any applicant making an application conforming to Husbank criteria was eligible for a subsidised housing loan. This meant that no means testing was applied to individual applicants. A significant element of deregulation was the removal of the general interest subsidy in Husbank loans in 1995. The abolishment of the general subsidy from Husbank housing finance was accompanied by an emphasis on the *effectivity* of housing policy measures: the resources used to subsidising housing should be effective in levelling housing inequality and therefore selective direct subsidies were preferred. This argument had been presented already in the 1980s in Norway, at the time when another retrenchment reform was introduced. Up to 1982, the reselling prices in the market for cooperative flats were regulated whereas those of owner-occupied flats were unregulated. This caused problems – especially the operation of under-the-counter payments and dissatisfaction among cooperative owners who felt themselves unjustly treated – that were solved by deregulating the second-hand cooperative market. This was partly a justification for the later deregulation: with subsidised loans the state was *de facto* supporting household equity building. With these changes in policy, Norway moved *significantly towards a selective housing policy* (see Annaniassen, 2006).

In Denmark, retrenchment manifested itself in attempts to privatise social rental housing. Creating possibilities for tenants in social rental dwellings to buy their homes was one of the central goals of housing policy of the new non-socialist government in 2001. The government's plan aroused stern opposition on the part of the rental housing associations' interest organisation, as well as the municipalities' central organisation and opposition parties. The social political consequences of the reform were scrutinised but there were also difficult legal obstacles to a reform that in a sense meant expropriating an independent association's property and making it a private one. The law was passed in 2004 but in a much watered-down form. A proposal offering the possibility for a tenant who so wished to purchase his/her dwelling from the association was transformed into law that gave the right to buy to tenants only if the local housing association and the municipality agreed. The veto right of associations and municipalities made the proposal for a general law a voluntary experiment for those organisations and municipalities that happened to support the government line. This meant that very few dwellings were actually privatised (see Jensen, 2006a). Thus, in Denmark, entrenchment policies had a very difficult start. The government has not, however, given up in its determination to undermine the social rental sector's position (Gomez Nielsen, 2010).

It is of special interest to investigate how the trend towards housing policy retrenchment observable across Europe has affected Sweden, the country that, more than any other, embodies the Scandinavian model. The Swedish housing regime has been under pressure for a 'system change' (as they call it in Sweden) since the early 1990s. The non-socialist government that came to power in 1991 started a project making Swedish housing provision more market driven: for example, parts of the previously very generous (and costly) subventions to the housing sector were abolished, state housing loans were replaced by state loan guarantees and the special position of municipal rental housing companies was removed in legislation. Groups within government also had plans to demol-ish the corporatist rent negotiation system and introduce market rents in rental housing. Reforms in that direction met with stern opposition from the tenants' movement and had little support from the public. What became passed in law represented only a small change in the rent negotiation system without chang-ing its central principles, such as the leading role of the municipal rental housing companies in the determination of rent levels. Since the social democrats' come-back to power in 1994 none of the changes made by the previous government has been cancelled. However, heated political debate concerning the corporatist rental housing system and the position of the non-profit rental housing sector has continued (see Bengtsson, 2006a, pp. 145–153).

With the possible exception of Denmark, in all of the Nordic countries retrenchment has progressed and housing policies have moved towards selective measures instead of universal ones. One part of this change is the abandon-ment of the past focus on production. Not only in Sweden, but also elsewhere, housing policy has become more a policy of residence, that is, a policy that is concerned less with producing as many dwellings as possible and more with maintenance and renovation of existing housing, housing management and the social composition of residential neighbourhoods, and so on. This develop-ment is understandable in light of the 'life cycle' of housing policy that was outlined above. However, another part of the change is an ideological one: in all Nordic countries, traditional social democratic policies are being challenged by neo-liberalist, new public management. Not only the successful bourgeois parties but also social democrats themselves have come to emphasise the market instead of state provision.

How has retrenchment affected the position of owner-occupation in the Nordic countries? In Denmark the most important sign of policy retrench-ment concerns social rental housing. It was to be privatised and turned into owner-occupied housing – which, of course, would have made Denmark more of a homeowner society. However, the attempted privatisation has so far been a failure and thus it has not had much impact on the tenure system. There have been some changes in the subsidy system that are not strictly a part of housing policy but which have an important housing policy element: from the late 1990s onward, Denmark has reduced the right to deduct housing loan interest in taxation, thus limiting the previously substantial tax subsidy to owner-occupation. In Sweden the retrenchment policies have largely been concerned with the corporatist rental market system and the position of municipal rental housing companies. Although substantial changes to the Swedish system have occurred, the basic principles of the Swedish housing regime have been maintained. The non-profit sector has remained significant even though tenure conversions into cooperative housing and sometimes private rental housing have become more common, especially in the largest urban municipalities. There is also a recurring discussion about whether direct ownership of flats in multi-family housing should be allowed. According to Swedish law such ownership is not possible. Tenant-ownership has largely come to serve in the place of ownership-based tenure in such housing. Retrenchment reforms have thus attempted to strengthen not only the position of the market but also of owner-occupation in the Swedish housing regime.

In Norway retrenchment has meant a change from wide state involvement in the provision of housing to all people through the state housing bank, to a regime in which the main role of the state is to help special groups to gain access to the housing market. The scale of state financing of new-build production has decreased from 75 per cent to 25 per cent of new housing (Annaniassen, 2006, p. 214). Home ownership in various forms has been dominant in Norway for some time, and the state still provides loans for self-builders but now without any special subsidy. The level of housing in Norway is now higher than ever, and the present policy considers the market-led homeowner society to be able to provide housing successfully to most households in the country. The state now seeks to distinguish special groups that are unable to enjoy the benefits of growing housing welfare and to target them with special policies. This runs the risk of polarisation among households with segregation between relatively well-off owner-occupiers and social tenants dependent on public support. Moreover, the safety net that homeowners can rely on has worn quite thin – but that is the case in the other Nordic homeowner societies as well.

In the Finnish case the trend towards retrenchment has in a way crystallised the principles of the Finnish housing regime: that most people provide housing for themselves through the private housing market or self-building, and the role of the state is to help those that cannot help themselves. In the Finnish case this change happened in the context of *declining* rates of owner-occupation. This rather unique development was caused by the economic depression and the accompanying housing and property market crisis that Finland experienced at the end of the 1980s and early 1990s. Since the mid-1990s until the new recession the Finnish economy has fared very well, and people's confidence in home ownership as a solution to their housing needs seems not to have been eroded.

Conclusions

It seems questionable whether there is one Nordic housing regime, and just as questionable is whether there is one Nordic pattern of housing tenure. In terms of owner-occupation the Nordic countries have a fairly large number of different forms of tenure that can be classified as such. However, distributions of types of tenures are not very informative about what a country's system of housing is like. The content of tenures is largely shaped by the social arrangements that are connected with them. In this chapter this was illuminated from a rather narrow perspective: what is the role of tenures, and especially home ownership, in a country's housing policy. In more or less all of the Nordic countries housing policies have faced pressures towards retrenchment.

One core idea of the research project that this chapter has been based on was that of housing policies' *path-dependent* nature. To put it very simply, path dependence means that the nature of an institution, policy or whatever social process the concept is applied to is to a great extent determined by its history. Development processes are such that when one path is taken it becomes increasingly difficult to choose another in the junctures that eventually open to the actors involved. There are special reasons why housing policies can be considered particularly path dependent: housing is long-lasting, slow and expensive to produce; its locational and physical structure as well as features of ownership cannot be changed overnight; houses are not only consumption goods to be used but also something that people get attached to; and so on. (see Bengtsson and Ruonavaara, 2010). Both the material and special social characteristics of housing as a good to be used in satisfying basic needs create a lot of *inertia* that housing policies have to deal with.

The failure of retrenchment policies in some Nordic countries is due directly to the path dependence of housing policies and institutions. This is seen most clearly in the case of Denmark where an ambitious plan to privatise rental housing was watered down into a compromise with little effect on the provision of rental housing in the country. The stern opposition by various organisations and political parties and the practices institutionalised in law as well as popular resistance made it so difficult to pursue reform that the government had to establish a rather poor compromise (and to seek indirect ways to pursue its policy). Much the same can be said about Sweden, where retrenchment policy has been more successful. However, there too, the basic pillars of the housing system have been left intact. In the Nordic home ownership societies with selective policies the retrenchment pressures have not been as great as in Denmark and Sweden as the principles of the housing regime are not in stark contradiction to retrenchment. Nevertheless, it has also been difficult in these countries to abolish institutions. For example, in the case of the Finnish state housing finance, retrenchment first took the road of conversion rather than that of abolishing (about conversion, see Thelen, 2003, pp. 225–230). The old housing system of direct state housing finance for new production of all kinds of housing was first scaled down to a system of producing social rental housing and was then, after about ten years, completely abolished.

Where retrenchment policies have been successful, home ownership has emerged more than before as a housing tenure liberated from state regulation – or, alternatively, a tenure left to the mercy of market forces. Whether this proves to be to the detriment of the millions of homeowners in Nordic countries remains to be seen. Most Nordic countries experienced an economic and banking crisis, growing unemployment and household credit problems about ten years ago, in the early 1990s. If indeed there is another, similarly deep crisis approaching, these countries should be prepared. There is little that housing policies can do to prevent the crisis, but there is considerable potential to relieve the housing-related consequences of such a crisis.

Acknowledgements

I thank my Nordic colleagues Bo Bengtsson, Erling Annaniassen, Lotte Jensen and Jón Rúnar Sveinsson for useful comments and encouragement.

References

Annaniassen, E. (2006) Norge – det socialdemokratiska ägarlandet [Norway – the social democratic homeowner society], in B. Bengtsson (ed.), E. Annaniassen, L. Jensen, H. Ruonavaara and J.R. Sveinsson, *Varför så olika? Nordisk bostadspolitik i jämförande historiskt ljus* [*Why so Different? Nordic Housing Policies in Comparative Historical Light*], Malmö: Égalite.

Ball, M. and Harloe, M. (1992) Rhetorical barriers to understanding housing provision. What the 'provision thesis' is and is not, *Housing Studies*, 7, 147–165.

Bengtsson, B, (1995) *Organisationerna och bostadspolitiken i Sverige – ett avvikande fall?* [*Organizations and Housing Politics in Sweden – A Deviant Case?*], Research Report 1, Upsala: Institutet för bostadsforskning, Uppsala universitet [English summary].

Bengtsson, B. (2006a) Sverige – kommunal allmännytta och korporativa särintressen [Sweden – municipal non-profit housing and corporative interests], in B. Bengtsson (ed.), E. Annaniassen, L. Jensen, H. Ruonavaara and J.R. Sveinsson, *Varför så olika? Nordisk bostadspolitik i jämförande historiskt ljus* [*Why so Different? Nordic Housing Policies in Comparative Historical Light*], Malmö: Égalite.

Bengtsson, B. (2006b) Fem länder, fem regimer, fem historier – en nordisk jämförelse [Five countries, five regimes, five histories – a Nordic comparison], in B. Bengtsson (ed.), E. Annaniassen, L. Jensen, H. Ruonavaara and J R. Sveinsson, *Varför så olika? Nordisk bostadspolitik i jämförande historiskt ljus* [*Why so Different? Nordic Housing Policies in Comparative Historical Light*], Malmö: Égalite.

Bengtsson, B. (2006c) Varför så olika? Om en nordisk gåta och hur den kan lösas [Why so different? Of a Nordic puzzle and ways to solve it], in B. Bengtsson (ed.), E. Annaniassen, L. Jensen, H. Ruonavaara and J.R. Sveinsson, *Varför så olika? Nordisk bostadspolitik i jämförande historiskt ljus* [*Why so Different? Nordic Housing Policies in Comparative Historical Light*], Malmö: Égalite.

Bengtsson, B. and Ruonavaara, H. (2010) Introduction to the special issue: path dependence in housing, *Housing, Theory and Society*, 27, 193–203.

Bengtsson, B. (ed.), Annaniassen, E., Jensen, L., Ruonavaara, H. and Sveinsson, J.R. (2006) *Varför så olika? Nordisk bostadspolitik i jämförande historiskt ljus* [*Why so Different? Nordic Housing Policies in Comparative Historical Light*], Malmö: Égalite.

Esping-Andersen, G. (1990) *The Three Worlds of Welfare Capitalism*, Cambridge: Polity Press.

Gomez Nielsen, B. (2010) Is breaking up still hard to do? Policy retrenchment and housing policy change in a path dependent context, *Housing, Theory and Society*, 27(3), 241–257.

Gulbrandsen, L. (2004) Home ownership and social inequality in Norway, in K. Kurz and H.-P. Blossfeld (eds) *Home Ownership and Social Inequality in Comparative Perspective*, Stanford, CA: Stanford University Press.

Jensen, L. (1995) Udviklingstræk ved det almennyttige beboerdemokrati i Danmark 1900–1990 [Development traits of tenant democracy in non-profit rental housing in Denmark, 1900–1990], in M. Madsen, H.-J. Nielsen and G. Sjöblom (eds) *Demokratiets mangfoldighed: Tendenser i dansk politik* [*The Diversity of Democracy: Tendencies in Danish Politics*], Copenhagen: Forlaget Politiske Studier.

Jensen, L. (2006a) Danmark – lokal boendedemokrati och nationell korporatism [Denmark – local housing democracy and national corporatism], in B. Bengtsson (ed.), E. Annaniassen, L. Jensen, H. Ruonavaara and J.R. Sveinsson, *Varför så olika? Nordisk bostadspolitik i jämförande historiskt ljus* [*Why so Different? Nordic Housing Policies in Comparative Historical Light*], Malmö: Égalite.

Jensen, L. (2006b) Bostadspolitiska regimer, förändringstryck och stigberoendets mekanismer [Housing policy regimes, pressure for change and the mechanisms of path dependence], in B. Bengtsson (ed.), E. Annaniassen, L. Jensen, H. Ruonavaara and J.R. Sveinsson, *Varför så olika? Nordisk bostadspolitik i jämförande historiskt ljus* [*Why so Different? Nordic Housing Policies in Comparative Historical Light*], Malmö: Égalite.

Karlberg, B. and Victorin, A. (2004) Housing tenures in the Nordic countries, in M. Lujanen (ed) *Housing and Housing Policy in the Nordic Countries*, Copenhagen: Nordic Council of Ministers.

Kemeny, J. (1981) *The Myth of Home Ownership*, London: Routledge & Kegan Paul.

Kemeny, J. (2006) Corporatism and housing regimes, *Housing, Theory and Society*, 23, 1–18.

Kvist, J. (1999) Welfare reform in the Nordic countries in the 1990s: using fuzzy-set theory to assess conformity to ideal types, *Journal of European Social Policy*, 9, 231–252.

Lujanen, M. (ed.) (2004) *Housing and Housing Policy in the Nordic Countries*, Copenhagen: Nordic Council of Ministers.

Mahoney, J. and Rueschemeyer, D. (eds) (2003) *Comparative Historical Analysis in the Social Sciences*, Cambridge: Cambridge University Press.

Niva, M. (1986) *The Development of the Housing Provision in Sweden and Finland in the Postwar Period.* Meddelande 1986:3, Nordiska institutet för samhällsplanering.

Ruonavaara, H. (1993) Types and forms of housing tenure: towards solving the comparison/translation problem, *Scandinavian Housing and Planning Research*, 10, 3–20.

Ruonavaara, H. (2005) How divergent housing institutions evolve: a comparison of Swedish tenant co-operative and Finnish shareholders' housing company, *Housing, Theory and Society*, 22, 213–236.

Ruonavaara, H. (2006) Den dualistiska bostadsregimen och jakten på det sociala [Finland – the dualist housing regime and the quest for the 'social'], in B. Bengtsson (ed.), E. Annaniassen, L. Jensen, H. Ruonavaara and J.R. Sveinsson, *Varför så olika?*

Nordisk bostadspolitik i jämförande historiskt ljus [*Why so Different? Nordic Housing Policies in Comparative Historical Light*], Malmö: Égalite.

Sveinsson, J.R. (2006) Island – självägande och fackligt inflytande [Iceland – self-building and union power], in B. Bengtsson (ed.), E. Annaniassen, L. Jensen, H. Ruonavaara and J.R. Sveinsson, *Varför så olika? Nordisk bostadspolitik i jämförande historiskt ljus* [*Why so Different? Nordic Housing Policies in Comparative Historical Light*], Malmö: Égalite.

Thelen, K. (2003) How institutions evolve. Insights from comparative historical analysis, in J. Mahoney and D. Rueschemeyer (eds) *Comparative Historical Analysis in the Social Sciences*, Cambridge: Cambridge University Press.

6

OWNER-OCCUPATION IN AN INCREASINGLY UNCERTAIN WORLD

The English experience

Christine Whitehead

Introduction

The size of the owner-occupied sector in any country will depend upon the attributes of this tenure and the costs and benefits of these attributes for different groups of households compared with those of the other tenures available. Countries where the housing stock includes a high proportion of houses, where access to mortgage funding is easy and the transaction costs are low and in particular where the regulatory environment and government policy support owner-occupation compared with rental tenures can be expected to have high owner-occupation rates. Those where most dwellings are flats, funding is highly constrained, transaction costs are high and rental tenures are favoured by government will have much lower rates. Thus, owner-occupation rates can in principle vary enormously between countries and there is no particular reason to expect any consistency. There is no such thing as an optimal rate. Rather, how the specific attributes, incentives and constraints play out will determine what is likely to be the sustainable owner-occupation rate into the longer term.

In this chapter we use these fundamentals of tenure choice to examine both the sources of growth in owner-occupation in England over the last 30 years and the potential for changes in this rate, given the current more uncertain environment. In particular we examine the reasons for government interest in continuing to expand owner-occupation and the challenges that such a policy is likely to face.

Until the financial crisis, government policy in England had continued to stress the potential for expanding owner-occupation to at least 75 per cent of all households. To this end, the government committed itself to increasing the number of homeowners by 1 million in Labour's third term (2005–10) (Labour Party, 2005). This would have put England into the highest group of industrialised nations with respect to owner-occupation along with, for example, Spain, Ireland and Norway – a very long way from the position in the 1960s when only half of all households were owner-occupied.

By 2010, however, owner-occupation levels had actually declined and the government had changed its position, with the Labour minister saying that 'home ownership has been dropping since 2005 and I'm not sure that's such a bad thing' (Healey, 2010). On the other hand, the Conservative shadow minister stated that 'Only Conservatives will stand up for the hard-working people who want to get on the housing ladder and own a home of their own' (Shapps, 2010).

Thus, by 2010 owner-occupation was still very much a matter of political debate even though, in the face of financial crisis, the numbers game is no longer central to the argument. Instead, there is arguably greater concern with evaluating the costs and benefits both to individual households and to the government.

In the first part of the chapter we examine how the move to much higher levels of owner-occupation was achieved, significantly as an outcome of government policy. Next we look at the rationale behind such a proactive policy stance as this helps to explain government objectives. We then turn to the question of the long-run viability of maintaining high levels of owner-occupation in the more uncertain environment of the twenty-first century. To address this question we look first at the earlier crisis in the late 1980s and early 1990s and how the market adjusted thereafter, and then at the specifics of the latest crisis starting in 2007. Finally we return to the fundamentals of tenure choice in order to assess future scenarios.

Moving to high levels of owner-occupation

General trends

In the post-war era up to the 1970s, England's tenure structure was particularly differentiated, with owner-occupation restricted to those with the capacity to borrow in a highly regulated market; social rented housing provided almost entirely by local authorities with rents well below market levels; and a private rented sector in which the majority of tenants had long-term security and controlled rents, and only a very small element provided easy-access accommodation. Table 6.1 shows the tenure structure in 1971 when just over half of households were owner-occupied.

The table also shows how the number of owner-occupied dwellings increased by almost 75 per cent up to 2001, stabilising at around 70 per cent of the total stock in England. This growth was at the expense of both social and private renting, both of which fell in absolute as well as proportional terms. It is also worth noting that growth was concentrated in the 1970s and 1980s and slowed in the 1990s.

TABLE 6.1 Dwelling stock and tenure, England, 1971–2007

	Owner-occupied		Private rented		Rented from HA		Rented from LA		Total
	Thousands	%	Thousands	%	Thousands	%	Thousands	%	Millions
1971	8,503	53	3,122	19			4,530	28	16.1
1979	10,019	57	2,168	12	368	2	5,140	29	17.7
1981	10,773	60	2,044	11	410	2	4,798	27	18.0
1991	13,237	67	1,927	10	608	3	3,899	20	19.7
2001	14,818	70	2,152	10	1,424	7	2,812	13	21.2
2007	15,420	70	2,611	12	1,850	8	2,068	9	22.0

Source: Department for Communities and Local Government Housing Statistics Live Table 104
(http://www.communities.gov.uk/documents/housing/xls/table-104.xls).
HA, housing association; LA, local authority.

The main sources of growth

Five main drivers lay behind the expansion of owner-occupation:

1. The relatively rapid growth in real incomes, with the associated increase in housing demand for higher-quality options concentrated in owner-occupation.
2. The increasing availability of housing finance from the mid-1970s through the integration of housing finance within the more general deregulation of global finance markets.
3. The tax benefits available to owner-occupiers, notably with respect to exemption from capital gains tax but also through mortgage tax relief up to the year 2000 (although with increasing limitations from the early 1970s).
4. Limited access to the rented sectors. The private rented sector, which was constrained by rent controls and lifetime security of tenure, was in decline until 1988 and had only just started to expand its role in the twenty-first century. At the same time, access to the social rented sector became more and more concentrated on those with priority needs.
5. Specific government policies to expand owner-occupation, notably the right to buy and low-cost home ownership (LCHO) initiatives.

Thus, in terms of the fundamentals demand increased, the real cost of purchase fell, funding constraints became less important, government became more active in helping marginal buyers and alternative tenure became more difficult to access. In this environment it was hardly surprising that the sector grew rapidly in the 1970s and 1980s.

A study in the late 1980s, reflecting on these pressures, suggested that around one-third of the growth in owner-occupation could be associated with financial deregulation, which enabled households who could afford owner-occupation to buy; one-third with income growth; and one-third with specific government initiatives (Kleinman and Whitehead, 1988).

Since that time the relative importance of these three factors has shifted more towards financial innovation and the benefits of owner-occupation as an asset, while the impact of specific government policies has, if anything, declined. Moreover, by 2000, tax benefits had been much reduced while funding for private renting had improved. So the cost–benefit story was beginning to look very different, especially for new entrants.

Government policy initiatives

During the period to 1979, government support for owner-occupation was mainly an outcome of the general tax structure, by which the principal home has always been exempt from capital gains tax as were mortgage and interest payments. In addition, the revenue from imputed income tax declined over time and the tax was finally removed in the mid-1960s. The importance of these benefits grew as the finance market opened up and inflation, especially in house prices, increased (Odling-Smee, 1975; Department of the Environment, 1977). As a result the first, very limited, moves to restrict these benefits were introduced in the early 1970s.

Although there was considerable growth in owner-occupation in the 1970s, by the end of the decade England was still in the middle group of countries with respect to owner-occupation, well below most other Anglo-Saxon countries – notably Australia, Canada and the United States (Freeman *et al.*, 1996). It was in this context that the Conservative government developed specific policies to expand owner-occupation.

There were relatively few policy options that could make big structural change possible, given the ownership of the existing housing stock. Large-scale increases in owner-occupation could come only from the local authority sector, in which there were significant numbers of households that could afford a mortgage and that lived mainly in houses in which they wished to remain (Holmans, 1970). Thus, the right to buy became the core policy instrument for expanding owner-occupation.

Since 1980 over 1.8 million dwellings in England have been sold to sitting tenants, with sales concentrated in the 1980s but still running at between 30,000 and 70,000 per annum through the 1990s and early 2000s. Thereafter, sales fell to an historic low of under 3,000 in 2008–9, mainly as a result of lower discounts, rapidly rising house prices and worsening affordability, especially in the south of the country.

The outcome of this policy was initially to enable many households to buy who had been excluded by the highly regulated finance market prevailing before the mid-1970s. To this extent it was a 'catch-up' exercise, although, as markets were liberalised and the benefits of owning grew with further house price increases and larger discounts, owner-occupation was spread further down the income scale (Munro *et al.*, 2005a).

A second initiative was to expand partial ownership options, first through shared ownership introduced in 1980 and then HomeBuy in the late 1990s. Shared ownership has enabled the household to purchase a proportion of a new dwelling provided by a housing association, and rent the rest from that association but with the right to staircase up to full ownership. HomeBuy was a shared equity product in which households could buy 75 per cent of the value of the property with the help of a traditional mortgage and 25 per cent with a zero interest equity mortgage (ODPM, 2005a). These initiatives and later versions of these basic forms have provided a niche element aimed at those who need only shallow subsidy to enter owner-occupation. The number of households assisted by these schemes since 1980 is around a quarter of a million (Munro *et al.*, 2005a; Monk and Whitehead, 2010).

The third source of expansion was through a massive shift in the tenure of new building. Government limited the capacity of the local authority sector to develop, expecting private development to fill the gap. As a result private sector output rose to almost 90 per cent of the total. Even so, there has been little appetite to increase output to levels above around 150,000 units per annum, unless some form of subsidy is available (Table 6.2). This is seen as one of the main reasons for the difficulties experienced in achieving adequate supply into the longer term and thus in curbing house price increases (Barker, 2003, 2004; Stephens *et al*, 2005).

Finally, the transfer of stock from private renting to owner-occupation, which had been occurring since the 1950s (at the same time as the sector was declining

TABLE 6.2 Housing completions by tenure

	Private		Housing associations (RSLs)		Local authorities		Total
	Thousands	*%*	*Thousands*	*%*	*Thousands*	*%*	*Thousands*
1971	170.8	58	10.2	3	113.7	39	294.7
[1979	118.4	57	16.3	8	74.8	36	209.5]
1981	99.0	58	16.8	10	54.9	32	170.6
1991	131.2	85	15.3	10	8.1	5	154.6
2001	114.6	89	14.6	11	0.2	0	129.3
2005	141.7	89	17.5	11	0.2	0	159.4
2007/8	144.7	86	23.1	14	0.3	0	168.1
2008/9	107.7	80	25.5	19	0.6	0	133.9

Source: Department for Communities and Local Government Housing Statistics Live Table 244 (http://www.communities.gov.uk/documents/housing/xls/1473581.xls).
RSL, registered social landlord.

as a result of large-scale slum clearance), continued, although at a lower rate, throughout the 1980s until well after rent deregulation in 1988 (Whitehead and Kleinman, 1985; Stephens *et al.*, 2005). This reflected the relative rates of return on owning versus renting, significantly a result of the differential tax treatment of the two sectors. This process was only reversed by the growth of investment based on buy-to-let mortgages available from the late 1990s, which improved access to finance and reduced the cost for individual owners (Rhodes and Bevan, 2003). Thereafter, private renting has grown by some half a million units – an expansion that has been strongly associated with the slowdown in the growth of owner-occupation.

To summarise, policies to expand owner-occupation that were first introduced on a national scale by the Conservative government in 1980, but which continue until the present time, have been mainly in the form of (1) providing incentives for both dwellings and households to transfer from social housing to owner-occupation; and (2) subsidies for a subset of lower-income employed households to enable them to enter owner-occupation. Together these two policies account directly for almost 40 per cent of the growth in owner-occupation of 5.4 million observed between 1979 and 2007 (although some proportion of these households would have transferred anyway without subsidy). Even so, the majority of the growth came more from increasing affluence and easier credit on the one hand and restrictions on what has been available in the rented sector on the other.

Government rationales for expanding owner-occupation

Given the obvious importance of policy in expanding owner-occupation, it is appropriate to ask why the UK government has traditionally put such an emphasis on owner-occupation.

The main reason given by the UK government has always been that it helps to meet household aspirations. Up to 90 per cent of individuals consistently state that they wish to own their own homes, either now or within a few years (Williams and Pannell, 2007). In this context the right to buy was a very popular policy, even among those who could not expect to benefit directly (Jones and Murie, 2006; King, 2010)

There are, however, other important economic, social and political reasons for expanding home ownership, many of which reflect the more general benefits of privatisation (Whitehead, 1993). These include immediate and longer-term benefits to public finances; benefits to the dwellings, the neighbourhood and the community; and benefits to the stability of the economy and society, including political benefits from voting behaviour.

The core issues for government relate to its own finances and to its future commitments. First, owner-occupation enables the substitution of private for public debt and helps ensure that people able to pay for their own homes actually do so. Second, in the context of asset transfer, it enables capital value to be realised and public debt to be reduced. Third, when people pay off their mortgages before retirement, owner-occupation puts households in a financially stronger position when their employment income disappears. In particular their outgoings fall, so pensions go further. Equally important from the government point of view is that in the UK only tenants are eligible for significant income-related housing assistance so owner-occupiers have to be more self-reliant. Also relevant is that owner-occupier households can vary the timing of repairs and improvements – ultimately putting them off to the next generation. Finally, housing assets can be realised and used to pay for other necessities, such as health care, again potentially reducing government expenditure (Whitehead, 1979; Saunders, 1990; Smith and Searle, 2010)

The second group of benefits relates to the impact of ownership on maintaining and improving dwellings. The evidence shows that people will both treat the property better and do more for themselves if they own the property – generating cost-effective maintenance at least into old age. Owners also have an incentive to maintain and improve the quality of the neighbourhood to ensure the value of their assets – and because many are 'aspiring' householders they also tend to support community activity, notably education (Whitehead, 1998; Rohe *et al.*, 2001; Dietz and Haurin, 2003).

The third group of benefits relates to the government's understanding that owner-occupation supports social stability through greater commitment of mortgagors to their jobs; greater commitment to the family environment for their children; general involvement in society because of their stake in that society; and ultimately their voting behaviour in a property-owning democracy (Whitehead, 1993; DiPasquale and Glaeser, 1999; Rohe *et al.*, 2001).

How many of these benefits are an outcome of owner-occupation as opposed to self-selection by better-off and more stable households is unclear (Wilkinson, 1996; Whitehead, 1998). There have been many attempts to measure aspects of these spill-over benefits. Most conclude that those specifically associated with owner-occupation are quite limited but are strongly related to lower mobility rates (Rohe *et al.*, 2001; Hilber, 2010). However, these perceptions are also reflected in consumer attitudes and satisfaction with owner-occupation (Elsinga and Hoekstra, 2005). In particular it can be readily shown that better-off households live in higher-quality homes and neighbourhoods, so it is problematic to untangle tenure from other factors.

Of course there are costs and risks to owner-occupation, especially if householders are overstretched; they borrow excessively against housing equity; household circumstances change for the worse; or the neighbourhood starts to decline (Maclennan *et al.*, 1997). Equally, owner-occupation reduces mobility and therefore the capacity to adjust to labour market changes, although the relevance of this has possibly been overstated as long as there is also a flourishing private rented market (Oswald, 1996).

More fundamentally, investment in physical assets is inherently a risky undertaking. Housing can in principle be expected to be in a relatively low-risk, utility-type class because in equilibrium the stream of rents, whether actual or imputed, can be expected to rise with economic growth. However, owner-occupation carries with it an important element of specific risk for the household associated with the attributes of the dwelling as well as uncertainties about the security of the income stream. The first suggests that, sensibly, people should diversify their portfolios with respect to housing; the second that they should insure against loss of income. Both processes are subject to significant market failures – and particularly because of the nature of housing many of the other benefits of owner-occupation discussed above may be thought to be lost by this risk transfer (Caplin *et al.*, 1997; Whitehead and Yates, 2010).

Some of these negativities are particularly relevant at the present time. Arguably, the housing finance crisis in the United States was exacerbated by the government's emphasis on expanding owner-occupation to those on lower incomes and facing higher risks, especially among minority groups. It was also strongly related to the rapid growth in the subprime market, which enabled credit-impaired households to borrow, as well as to the more general tax incentives for established homeowners to increase their borrowing. Something of the same can be said of the United Kingdom where limited alternatives helped push people into owner-occupation and cheap debt has supported over-consumption (Girouard *et al.*, 2006; Whitehead and Gaus, 2007).

Most importantly, the benefits to government, society and the individual can be realised only if owner-occupation can be maintained into the longer term. The fundamentals discussed in this section suggest that this will be the case only if households feel that they achieve the benefits of ownership; that they can afford the outgoings over their lifetime; that they will not want to move rapidly; that capital value and credit risk are reasonably under control; and that opportunities in other tenures do not better meet their needs. Since 1989 there have been two periods when these conditions have not held.

Evidence from the last economic cycle

The long-run viability of any particular level of owner-occupation depends on the attributes and circumstances of marginal purchasers. This is often related more to the extent of volatility in the housing market and the economy than to the more fundamental attributes (Stephens *et al.*, 2008; JRF Housing Market Taskforce, 2009). The question is then whether households are able to support themselves in owner-occupation if house prices fall, interest rates vary and their own incomes are reduced as a result of economic recession (as opposed to changes in household circumstances unrelated to the external environment, such as divorce).

Concern about long-run viability in this context comes from two main sources: the inherent volatility in a market in which housing demand can change much more rapidly than supply; and the interaction between the housing market and the economy as a whole, particularly with respect to changes in house prices, interest rates and expectations. Because of these relationships, when there are major shocks to the UK economy these tend to generate particularly extreme volatility in the housing market with the probability of over-adjustment in terms of prices, transactions and supply (Barker, 2003).

The UK housing market and its finance system have to some extent evolved to take account of this volatile environment. With respect to house prices, the mortgage finance market has dealt reasonably directly with negative equity issues, in that people cannot walk away from their debts but sales have been enabled. On the other hand, interest rate variations are clearly a major issue because the market is made up of variable and tracker-rate or short-term fixed-rate mortgages. The most important factor is the capacity to reschedule payments in the light of individual circumstances (Whitehead and Gaus, 2007; Ford and Wallace, 2009).

Equally, although the safety net of Income Support for Mortgage Interest (ISMI) was much reduced over the last decade, some government support remains, together with Mortgage Payment Protection Insurance (Stephens *et al.*, 2005; JRF Housing Market Taskforce, 2009). Indeed, it has been increased again in the current crisis (Scanlon *et al.*, 2011).

The extent to which these responses can address issues of volatility in a way that enables those who can afford owner-occupation into the longer term to remain as owners, but others without that capacity to not be drawn into an investment they cannot afford, is a core question for the future of owner-occupation in a more uncertain world. To examine this question we look at three stages in the latest economic cycle – the downturn of the late 1980s; the long period of expansion between the mid-1990s and the mid-2000s; and the current recession.

The crisis in the late 1980s/early 1990s

A major crisis occurred in the late 1980s when a particularly expansionary period was followed by sudden large interest rate increases and a rapid growth in unemployment. The crisis was further exacerbated by government tax changes, which helped to push many households, especially unrelated adults, into owner-occupation just before the economic environment worsened. At the same time, financial institutions were lending unprecedented multiples of income and loan-to-value ratios, as well as providing additional unsecured lending. As a result the numbers of mortgage transactions reached historic highs in 1988. When economic circumstances suddenly worsened, the results included rapid rises in arrears, a slowdown in transactions, almost 2 million households in negative equity and a large increase in mortgage possessions. These reached a peak of over 75,000 per annum in 1991. Thereafter possessions declined, but arrears of more than 12 months continued to rise, took some seven years to stabilise and did not start to fall until 1994. Overall the housing market did not pick up again until the mid-1990s.

The period from 1989 to 1995 represented the largest stress test to date for the housing finance market in the United Kingdom (Megbolugbe and Whitehead, 1994). The market overall passed the test reasonably well, in that lenders all survived and there was no evidence of financial crisis. The government made no direct formal intervention to bale out institutions or individuals. Instead, the industry was strongly advised to restructure mortgagor debt and to develop insurance in the form of Mortgage Payment Protection Insurance, to enable mortgagors to cover payments in the face of unemployment, sickness or injury (Holmans and Whitehead, 1999; Ford, 2001).

On the other hand, the position for many individual mortgagors who found themselves unemployed or otherwise unable either to pay the mortgage or to sell their home at a price that would cover the mortgage was clearly very difficult (Figure 6.1). Those who were most likely to suffer were people who had purchased in the two or three years before the sudden downturn and those who depended on multiple incomes to pay the mortgage. In the end, however, most of those who found themselves in negative equity were able to wait until the housing market improved. More importantly the approach by which banks and building societies rescheduled payments paid off for both the institutions and the vast majority of individuals.

Thus, the crisis from 1989 was mainly the result of unexpected changes in the economic environment together with some inappropriate changes in taxation policy. The outcome was to slow the longer-term growth in owner-occupation but not to reverse it. Moreover, the markets learned certain lessons on how best to adjust to sudden change and so improved the potential for long-run viability.

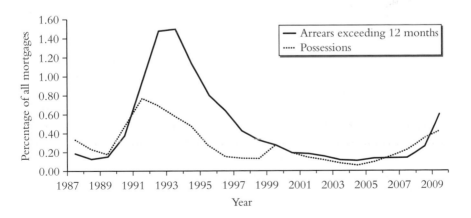

FIGURE 6.1 Mortgage arrears and possessions, 1987–2009.
Source: Adapted from CML Statistics (n.d., Tables AP1 and AP4).

The expansion and boom from the mid-1990s to the mid-2000s

From 1995 up to and including 2007 the economic environment for the housing market was particularly benign. Unemployment and inflation declined to historically low levels, as did nominal and real interest rates, reducing repayment costs. Although mortgage tax relief was removed in 2000, almost no mortgagor had actually to increase their repayments because of the background of generally falling interest rates (Gibb and Whitehead, 2007). All of this fuelled demand for housing but supply was not able to respond effectively (Table 6.2). At the same time, financial markets expanded the range of products available and housing finance became increasingly a means of investing in housing rather than simply enabling owner-occupation. Households could, as a result of this liberalisation, restructure their overall debt into a package secured against the value of the home – and so borrow against increases in house prices as well as against their value at the time of purchase (Scanlon *et al.*, 2008).

Subprime lending

The UK housing finance market was traditionally one based on individual assessment of both the potential mortgagor and the dwelling they wished to buy. During the 1980s and 1990s there was increasing use of standardised assessment using credit-rating approaches and computer-based valuations. The subprime market became a rapidly growing part of the mortgage market for those who did not meet increasingly formal criteria (Munro *et al.*, 2005b). In this context, Datamonitor.com (n.d.) suggested that some 20 per cent of adults had been refused credit by mainstream lenders in 2005. Although only a rough assessment, it suggested that there was a large potential market for lending to those with blemished credit records excluded by stringent credit-scoring requirements, as well as to those with irregular or uncertain incomes. A growing part of this market was for self-certified loans in which the borrower provides no independent evidence of their circumstances (often because they are self-employed) and pays a higher interest rate in consequence.

The second major reason for accessing the subprime market was credit impairment. Probably the largest proportion of the market – the Financial Services Authority (FSA) (the regulator) found up to 60 per cent in a small sample in 2005 – had been associated with remortgaging in circumstances in which the mortgagor had fallen behind with their payments or had other expensive debt, but had housing equity available.

Industry estimates, quoted by the Council of Mortgage Lenders (CML) and using the FSA definition, suggested that subprime lending accounted for perhaps 5–6 per cent of total industry gross advances, that is, some £15–16 billion in 2005 (Burton *et al.*, 2004). The proportion grew over the following two years but had started to decline before the credit crunch actually hit.

A rather different issue has been the extent to which risks were properly assessed and priced. The vast majority of subprime loans were sold through intermediaries, whose incentives were to maximise their own fees and therefore sales. The incentive for agents to suggest higher-cost and possibly higher-risk options was therefore significant, especially as fees were paid immediately. Moreover, these loans tended to be securitised, which transferred the majority of the risk to those who purchased the securitised instruments rather than the issuer (see Bratt, this volume).

Even so, the majority of loans were made to those with relatively low levels of credit adversity – often labelled 'near-prime' lending and providing a cheaper source of debt finance than other available sources, such as credit cards or unsecured loans. Moreover, the loans themselves included within them reassessment of risks and interest rates in the light of the mortgagor's repayment record. This in principle encouraged better debt management by the individual and transfer to the mainstream market – but it also meant that any signs of stress showed up more rapidly in the subprime than in the prime market. There is also evidence of greater use of more risky mortgage products and a greater probability of actions for possession among subprime borrowers (Collard and Kempson, 2005; Scanlon et al., 2008).

The changing menu of mortgage products

The range of products available in the United Kingdom at any one time in the new century until 2008 numbered in the thousands. Figures 6.2 and 6.3 show

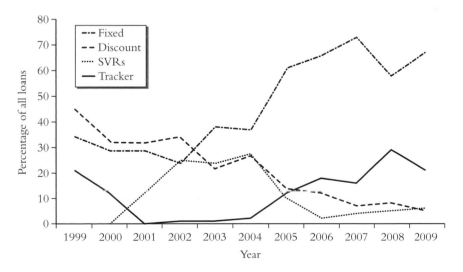

FIGURE 6.2 Types of loans taken out, 1999–2009.
SVR, standard variable rate.
Source: Adapted from CML Statistics (n.d., Table ML5).

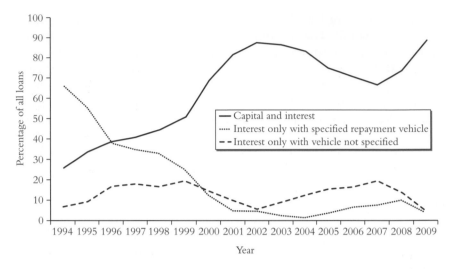

FIGURE 6.3 Types of loans taken out by first-time buyers, 1994–2009.
Source: Adapted from CML Statistics (n.d., Table ML6).

how the pattern of take-up of different types of mortgages changed over the decade.

Remortgaging was an increasingly important part of the growth in mortgage lending based on the consolidation of debt and the realisation of capital gains. It reached its peak in 2007 when it accounted for more than one-third of total approvals (CML Statistics, n.d., Table HP3). Most mortgages involved short-term discounts and fixed rates but there was also a growing role for longer-term index-linked mortgages. Interest-only mortgages – with or without an identified means of repayment – also grew (especially for remortgaging, where the proportion rose to 25 per cent in 2007).

There were continuing concerns about whether mortgagors could cope with rising interest rates and more fundamentally about the sophistication necessary to deal with the increasingly complex market. Insurance products were also poor value for most people (Whitehead and Gaus, 2007; Scanlon *et al.*, 2008).

Partially as a result of these innovations, debt increased significantly and the sector continued to expand in terms of numbers (although not in relation to asset values). Even so, the proportion of households in the owner-occupied sector started to fall in 2005. Among those under 30 the proportion had in fact fallen very much earlier – from around 50 per cent at its peak in 1993–4 to 36 per cent in 2007–8 (Department for Communities and Local Government, 2009; Whitehead, 2010). This reflected increasing affordability problems associated with the fundamentals of demand and supply as well as the growing availability of adequate private rented accommodation as much as changes in the cost and availability of debt finance.

Affordability and the changing position of first-time buyers

At the beginning of the twenty-first century, issues of access and affordability dominated discussion in the market, as house prices rose faster than incomes and both payments and deposits increased as a proportion of income (Table 6.3). Moreover, while rents rose relatively slowly, even in the private rented sector, weekly expenditure by owner-occupiers at the bottom end of the market increased very rapidly indeed (Figure 6.4).

The proportion of first-time buyer mortgages declined significantly, particularly from 2003. Those without access to funds from parents and family have been heavily disadvantaged by having to take out large loans on lower priced housing (Table 6.3). Those who succeeded in purchasing were relatively much better off than they had been a decade before – so younger, lower-income households were being excluded.

Evidence on the income distribution of borrowers supports this picture and suggests that the median nominal income of borrowers doubled in the 15 years between 1990 and 2005 – a rate of growth far in excess of average incomes (CML Statistics, n.d., Table HL4). Thus, mortgage borrowing went 'up market' in spite of the greater availability of debt finance. This reflected both the impact of rising house prices and the importance of multiple incomes in mortgagor households. Those on single incomes, and particularly those who could not call on family or other sources of funding for the deposit, were much more likely to be excluded from owner-occupation and therefore to remain in the private rented sector – or indeed to live at home – for much longer than in the past.

TABLE 6.3 Changing patterns of affordability

	Real house price increases, year on year % change	Repayments as % of income	Deposit as % of income, first-time buyers
2000	10.4	19.4	16.4
2001	4.3	18.8	16.7
2002	15.1	18.1	19.0
2003	11.2	19.9	23.0
2004	7.9	22.0	21.1
2005	3.5	22.5	19.3
2006	1.5	21.5	16.4
2007	6.5	23.5	17.2
2008	–4.9	22.8	21.8
2009	–0.7	18.4	27.7

Sources: CML Statistics (n.d., Table HP3); Department for Communities and Local Government (n.d.).

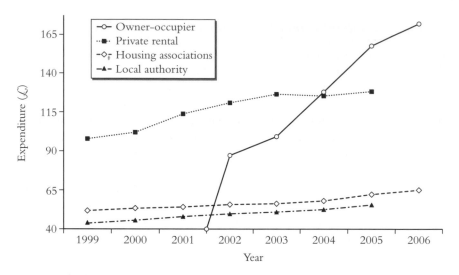

FIGURE 6.4 Weekly expenditure of poorer households, by tenure, England.
Note: Owner-occupiers: first-time buyers in bottom 25 per cent of the market; private rents for those on housing benefit.
Source: Adapted from Dataspring (http://www.dataspring.org.uk).

Moreover, the pattern of decline was very different from that of the earlier period of crisis between 1988 and 1992 when all types of households were holding off purchasing and the *proportion* of first-time buyers remained fairly constant. This time, with the overall market still expanding, first-time buyer mortgages fell in proportional terms from the turn of the century, and in terms of numbers since 2003, mainly because of affordability issues (Pannell, 2010).

One possible reason for these changes is that new generations of households are less interested in becoming owner-occupiers than their parents because there is a wider range of housing options available. However, what evidence there is (e.g. from the regular survey of tenure aspirations) suggests that the numbers wanting and expecting to be homeowners have not changed over the last few years (Williams and Pannell, 2007). What is true on the other hand is that increasing numbers of buy-to-let landlords entered the market and were able to outbid first-time buyers within the same segment of the market.

With respect to affordability, price-to-income ratios rose fairly steadily from the late 1990s, but interest payments fell so significantly in the earlier part of the new decade that, on average, they presented little problem. Even at the end of 2007 mortgage payments were lower as a proportion of income than in the late 1980s. Loan-to-value ratios were similarly lower. Average deposits, however, doubled from 5 per cent of the purchase price to 10 per cent over the decade and this proportion was significantly higher in London and the South East (CML Statistics, n.d., Table ML2). This suggests some element of self-regulation:

first-time buyers who felt that they could not afford the repayments tended to either put down a larger deposit or stay out of the market.

Averages of course hide very different personal experiences. More detailed work by the CML split first-time buyers into three groups: 'returnees', that is, those who had owned at some time before this purchase; those who appeared to be receiving help with their deposit; and those 'going it alone' (Tatch, 2006). The first group made up perhaps 20 per cent of the total and usually had a lump sum available and so borrowed less. The second group accounted for about 50 per cent of first-time buyers under 30. They took out lower loan-to-value mortgages even though they faced significant income multiples and relatively low incomes. Among the third group, those without capital, first-time buyers appeared to have higher incomes but were buying the cheapest properties and had particularly high loan-to-value ratios. The risks of negative equity were thus seen as mainly confined to the third group, but with risks of earnings loss and increasing interest rates applying to all.

Further evidence on whether people were overstretched related to the proportion of first-time buyers who had borrowed over 100 per cent of the purchase price. Clearly this group was most at risk if house prices were to fall and they needed to sell, as they had no equity buffer. At the height of the earlier lending boom in 1989, over one-third of first-time buyers borrowed 100 per cent or more. In 2006 that figure was only 4.7 per cent and falling.

The evidence on first-time buyer mortgages suggested that, in the mid-2000s, affordability, based on declared incomes, among those who actually managed to purchase was not a significant problem in a normal economic environment. It also suggested that where people were putting down larger deposits this was not only because of constraints imposed by financial institutions but also because of their own views on affordability. Even so, the Expenditure and Food Survey showed that over 40 per cent of those buying with a mortgage in 2004–5 were spending 30 per cent or more of their income on housing-related expenditure, including taxation, water sewerage and insurance, but excluding utilities, and that the average for those buying with a mortgage was 26 per cent (Office for National Statistics, 2008).

Finally, with respect to household assets, in the late 1980s an average loan of perhaps 95 per cent of value masked the fact that, taking account of unsecured loans from the same institutions, perhaps one-fifth of first-time buyers were borrowing over 120 per cent of value. House price declines therefore generated massive issues of negative equity (Bank of England, 1992). In the mid-2000s the situation appeared rather less frightening – in part because levels of transactions had been lower over the previous few years, people were borrowing lower proportions of value and prices were still going up. The Bank of England, for instance, found a very low incidence of households without at least £20,000 of housing equity in 2006 (Waldron and Young, 2006).

Analysis of this expansionary stage suggests that it was the fundamentals that were excluding people from owner-occupation and that the vast majority of those in the market could maintain that position in normal markets. But it also suggested that cohort effects could start to reduce the proportions of owner-occupiers, even in a buoyant market in which most households still wanted to buy.

The credit crunch and financial crisis

The situation since 2007 has undoubtedly been extremely frightening, with many commentators suggesting that prices would fall by anything up to 50 per cent, leaving large proportions of households in negative equity. Equally, many households were in the position of having to remortgage in a tightly constrained market because they were on short-term fixed-rate mortgages.

In itself negative equity may not matter if people do not need to move and can continue to pay the mortgage. But would they be able to do so? This raised three distinct issues: would households be able to find refinancing when their existing mortgage came to an end?; would mortgage repayments rise above their capacity to pay?; and would large numbers of households lose one or more incomes as the economy turned down?

In practice the outcome has not been anything like as cataclysmic as expected. First, although house prices fell by an average of 16 per cent they soon rebounded by nearly 10 per cent – so although there are households in negative equity the numbers are far smaller than expected. Second, most of those households who needed to remortgage were able to do so unless they were already credit impaired.

Third, although arrears and possessions rose rapidly in 2008, neither reached levels anywhere near as high as in the early 1990s, and possessions in particular are far below predictions (see Figure 6.1). This is partly because unemployment has not risen as expected and partly because of institutional forbearance. As importantly, repayments have gone down for large numbers of existing mortgagors as a result of the decline in interest rates. Were interest rates to rise again, the situation might be very different.

The major problems have been in terms of the availability of new mortgages and the increase in the deposits required (Scanlon et al., 2011). The numbers of mortgage approvals more than halved from 1.4 million in 2006 to 516,000 in 2008, turning up a little but only to around 600,000 in 2009 (CML Statistics, n.d., Table MM1). The number of property transactions similarly halved between 2006 and 2008. Moreover, the secondary mortgage market almost closed. Thus, the housing market ground almost to a halt. Those who were still able to obtain a mortgage had to do so under much more difficult terms and conditions. In particular, the deposits required by first-time buyers rose from around 16 per cent in 2006 to an average of over 27 per cent in 2009 (Department for Communities and Local Government, n.d., Table 540) while potential mortgagors were expected to have clean credit histories.

The impact of the credit crunch has clearly been to reduce access to funding for owner-occupation. Second-round effects have reduced demand as confidence declined and incomes became more uncertain. Most importantly, there have been alternatives available in the private rented sector, providing a way out for those who cannot sell as well as adequate housing for households who cannot or do not want to enter owner-occupation at this time.

Conclusions: home ownership in an increasingly uncertain world?

The starting point for looking to the future in England is that owner-occupation in proportional terms has actually declined since the early 2000s. This is in spite of all the emphasis on owner-occupation as 'the only tenure for those who succeed' and ever-available credit. Instead, what was happening was that private renting was growing at the expense of owner-occupation and, in particular, younger households were remaining as tenants for much longer than in the immediate past.

Since 2007, owner-occupation has fallen in absolute terms in the face of the financial crisis. It is suggested by CML and others that some 1 million households who would, on past trends, have become owner-occupiers by 2010 have been unable to do so and are presumably now either renters or living with friends and family. These downward pressures will be reinforced by increased costs of entering owner-occupation as regulation is tightened and the shortage of funds continues for the foreseeable future. Deposit requirements in particular will remain high. Owner-occupation rates could therefore continue to fall for some years and might not return to pre-crunch highs, unless there are further structural changes.

Looking into a world where the immediate issues of the credit crunch and the recession have been overcome, there are still many reasons for people to choose owner-occupation. Social housing is available to only a very few households who are able to afford owner-occupation for themselves. The private rented sector is a much better option than it was, but without further reforms, particularly with respect to contractual conditions, it will continue to provide mainly shorter-term solutions. Into the long term owner-occupation will remain the best option for a large proportion of households, especially while owner-occupation remains favoured in fiscal terms. However, the move to owner-occupation is likely to occur later in life when households are looking for a settled home, rather than chasing capital gains.

Equally, there are still good reasons for government to support owner-occupation because it can limit its own expenditures as well as help meet social and political goals. Moreover, there are considerable pressures to reduce the assistance available to tenants; to sweat social housing assets more effectively; and to lever in private equity into new development. The core constraint remains that of affordability, which, even with lower prices and low interest rates, is a major problem for large proportions of potential first-time buyers. In this environment government may introduce specific policies to support first-time buyers, as has happened in a number of other countries. These are likely to include further intermediate housing initiatives (Monk and Whitehead, 2010) and maybe stamp duty allowances and financial assistance to first time buyers (Conservative Party, 2009; HCA, 2011).

A more fundamental unresolved problem is the lack of balance between demand and supply, and this could get worse. If the flow of funds is brought back to some sort of normality, there is a large-scale potential housing demand from both existing owners who want to move and those who want to buy for the first time. So when and if the broader economic crisis begins to be resolved, the concern is that another boom/bust situation will emerge (Williams and Whitehead, 2011 forthcoming). The long-term tensions are even stronger because household formation is set to continue to expand against low levels of new supply.

Finally, in terms of numbers – or more accurately proportions – of owner-occupiers, although owner-occupation rates may fall for some time, the fundamentals of tenure choice point to continued demand for owner-occupation, even in a more uncertain world. The fact that the UK housing finance system has developed in ways that make it relatively easy to adjust to a volatile environment makes this scenario more likely. The two greatest uncertainties remain how the finance market will readjust over the next few years and how government modifies tenure-specific incentives.

References

Bank of England (1992) Negative equity in the housing market, *Bank of England Quarterly*, August.

Barker K (2003) *Review of Housing Supply: Securing our Future Needs – Interim Report – Analysis*, London: ODPM.

Barker K (2004) *Review of Housing Supply: Securing our Future Needs – Final Report*, London: ODPM.

Burton, D., Knights, D., Leyshon, A., Alferoff, C. and Signoretta, P. (2004) Making a market: the UK retail financial services industry and the rise of the complex sub-prime credit market, *Competition and Change,* 8(1).

Caplin, A., Chan, S., Freeman, C. and Tracy, J. (1997) *Housing Partnerships: A New Approach to a Market at a Crossroads*, Cambridge, MA: MIT Press.

Collard, S. and Kempson, E. (2005) *Affordable Credit: The Way Forward*, York: Joseph Rowntree Foundation.

Conservative Party (2009) *Strong Foundation Building*, Homes and Communities Policy Green Paper No 10, London: Conservative Party.

Council of Mortgage Lenders Statistics (CML) (n.d.) Online. Available at http://www.cml.org.uk/cml/statistics (accessed 4 October 2010).

Datamonitor.com (n.d.) UK consumer credit outlook, quarterly, Datamonitor Research Store. Online. Available at http://www.datamonitor.com.

Department for Communities and Local Government (2009) *Survey of English Housing Prelimiary Results 2007/08*, London: DCLG.

Department for Communities and Local Government (n.d.) Online. Available at http://www.communities.gov.uk/housing/housingresearch/housingstatistics/livetables/ (accessed 4 October 2010).

Department of the Environment (1977) *Housing Policy: A Consultation Document*, Cmnd 6851, London: HMSO.

Dietz, R. and Haurin, D. (2003) The social and private micro-level consequences of homeownership, *Journal of Urban Economics*, 54(3), 401–450.

DiPasquale, D. and Glaeser, E. (1999) Incentives and social capital: are homeowners better citizens? *Journal of Urban Economics*, 45(2), 354–384.

Elsinga, M. and Hoekstra, J. (2005) Homeownership and housing satisfaction, *Journal of Housing and the Built Environment*, 20(4), 401–424.

Freeman, A., Holmans, A. and Whitehead, C. (1996) *International Comparisons of Tenure Expenditure and Subsidy*, London: Council of Mortgage Lenders.

Ford, J. (2001) Failing home owners? The effectiveness of public and private safety nets, *Housing Studies*, 16(2), 147–162.

Ford, J. and Wallace, A. (2009) *Uncharted Territory? Managing Mortgage Arrears and Possessions*, London: Shelter.

Gibb, K. and Whitehead, C. (2007) Towards a more effective use of housing finance and subsidy, *Housing Studies*, 22, 183–200.

Girouard, N., Kennedy, M. and André, C. (2006) *Has the Rise in Debt Made Households More Vulnerable?*, Economics Department Working Paper No. 535, Paris: OECD.

Healey, J. (2010) Election 2010: Labour's Housing Agenda Lecture delivered to Smith Institute, March, London Smith Institute. Online. Available at http://www.smith-institute.org.uk/johnhealy (accessed 4 October 2010).

Hilber, C.A.L. (2010) New housing supply and the dilution of social capital, *Journal of Urban Economics*, 67(3), 419–437.

Holmans, A.E. (1970) A forecast of effective demand for housing in Great Britain in the 1970s, *Social Trends*, 33–45, London: HMSO.

Holmans, A. and Whitehead, C. (1999) Who should buy MPPI? *Housing Finance*, 42, 22–27.

Homes and Communities Agency (2011) FirstBuy. Online. Available at http://www.homesandcommunities.co.uk/firstbuy (accessed 1 September 2011).

Jones, C. and Murie, A. (2006) *The Right to Buy: Analysis and Evaluation of a Housing Policy*, Oxford: Blackwell.

JRF Housing Market Taskforce (2009) *How Can We Achieve Long-Term Stability in the Housing Market for Vulnerable Households?* Online. Available at http://www.jrf.org.uk/publications/housing-market-stability (accessed 4 October 2010).

King, P (2010) *The Right to Buy and the Desire to Own*, Bristol: Policy Press.

Kleinman, M.P. and Whitehead, C.M.E. (1988) British housing since 1979: has the system changed? *Housing Studies*, 3(1), 3–19.

Labour Party (2005) *Labour Party Manifesto: Looking Forward, Not Back*, London: Labour Party.

Maclennan, D., Meen, G., Gibb, K. and Stephens, M. (1997) *Fixed Commitments, Uncertain Incomes: Sustainable Owner-Occupation and the Economy*, York: Joseph Rowntree Foundation.

Megbolugbe, I. and Whitehead, C. (1994) Editors introduction/Introduction and update, *Housing Policy Debate*, 5(3).

Monk, S. and Whitehead, C.M.E. (2010) *Making Housing More Affordable: The Growth of Intermediate Tenures*, Oxford: Wiley Blackwell.

Munro, M., Pawson, H. and Monk, S. (2005a) *Evaluation of English Housing Policy 1995–2000. Theme 4: Widening Choice*, London: ODPM.

Munro, M., Leishman, C., Karley, N.K. and Ford, J. (2005) *Lending to Higher Risk Borrowers: Sub-Prime Credit and Sustainable Home Ownership*, York: Joseph Rowntree Foundation.

Odling-Smee, J.C. (1975) *The Impact of the Fiscal System on Different Tenure Sectors*, in *Housing Finance*, IFS Publications No. 12, London: Institute of Fiscal Studies.

ODPM (Office of the Deputy Prime Minister) (2005) *Sustainable Communities: Homes for All*, London: ODPM.

ODPM (Office of the Deputy Prime Minister) (2005a) *HomeBuy: Expanding the Opportunity to Own*, London: ODPM.

Office for National Statistics (2008) *Expenditure and Food Survey 2004/5*, London: ONS.

Oswald, A. (1996) *A Conjecture on the Explanation for High Unemployment in the Industrialised Nations: Part 1*, Economic Research Paper 475, Warwick: Department of Economics, University of Warwick.

Pannell, B. (2006) *Adverse Credit Mortgages*, CML *Housing Finance,* Issue 10, London: CML.

Pannell, B. (2010) *Affordability and First-Time Buyers*, CML *Housing Finance*, Issue 1, London: CML.

Rhodes, D. and Bevan, M. (2003) *Private Landlords and Buy-to-Let*, York: York Centre for Housing Policy, University of York.

Rohe, W., Van Zandt, S. and McCarthy, G. (2001) *The Social Benefits and Costs of Homeownership: A Cultural Assessment of Research*, LIHO-01.12, Joint Centre for Housing Studies, Cambridge, MA: Harvard University Press.

Saunders, P. (1990) *A Nation of Home Owners*, London: Unwin Hyman.

Scanlon, K., Lunde, J. and Whitehead, C. (2008) Mortgage product innovation in advanced economies: more choice, more risk, *European Journal of Housing Research*, 8(2), 109–131.

Scanlon, K., Lunde, J. and Whitehead, C. (2011) Mortgage products and government policies to help troubled mortgagors: responses to the credit crisis, *International Journal of Housing Policy*, 11(1), 23–49.

Shapps, G. (2010) Labour gives up on its pledge to increase home ownership, 23 April. Online. Available at http://www.conservatives.com/news/news_stories/2010/04/labour_gives_up_on_its_pledge_to_increase_home_ownership.aspx (accessed 4 October 2010).

Smith, S. and Searle, B. (eds) (2010) *The Housing Wealth of Nations, a Blackwell Companion to the Economics of Housing*, Oxford: Blackwell.

Stephens, M., Whitehead, C. and Munro, M. (2005) *Lessons from the Past, Challenges for the Future for Housing Policy: An Evaluation of English Housing Policy 1975–2000*, London: ODPM.

Stephens, M., Ford, J., Spencer, P., Wallace, A., Wilcox, S. and Williams, P. (eds) (2008) *Housing Market Recessions and Sustainable Home-Ownership*, York: Joseph Rowntree Foundation.

Tatch, J. (2006) *Interest Only – Why All the Interest?*, CML *Housing Finance*, Issue 11, London: CML.

Waldron, M. and Young, G. (2006) The state of British household finances: results from the 2006 NMG research survey, *Bank of England Quarterly Bulletin*, 46(4), 397–403.

Whitehead, C. (1979) Why owner-occupation? *CES Review*, 6, 33–41.

Whitehead, C. (1993) Privatising housing: an assessment of UK experience, *Housing Policy Debate*, 4(1), 104–139.

Whitehead, C. (1998) *The Benefit of Better Homes*, London: Shelter.

Whitehead, C. (2010) International trends in owner-occupation in light of the financial crisis, *Housing Finance International*, Winter.

Whitehead, C. and Kleinman, M. (1985) The private rented sector: a characteristic approach, *Urban Studies*, 22(6), 507–520.

Whitehead, C. and Gaus, K. (2007) *Policy Discussion Paper. At Any Cost? Access to Housing in a Changing Market Place*, London: Shelter.

Whitehead, C. and Yates, J. (2010) Is there a role for shared equity products in twenty-first century housing? Experience in Australia and the UK, in S. Smith and B. Searle (eds) *The Housing Wealth of Nations, a Blackwell Companion to the Economics of Housing*, Oxford: Blackwell.

Wilkinson, R.G. (1996) *Unhealthy Societies: The Affliction of Inequalities*, Oxford: Routledge.

Williams, P. and Pannell, B. (2007) *Homeownership at the Crossroads*, CML *Housing Finance*, Issue 2, London: CML.

Williams, P. and Whitehead, C. (2011 forthcoming) Causes and consequences? The shape and direction of the UK housing system after the financial crisis, *Housing Studies*.

7

HOME OWNERSHIP AS PUBLIC POLICY IN THE UNITED STATES

Rachel G. Bratt

Introduction

Home ownership in the United States has been used as a vehicle to promote diverse political, economic, and social goals and has been a focus of a wide variety of public policy initiatives. The goals of these policies have included, more or less explicitly and with varying emphasis over time, giving people a stake in society by enhancing financial and personal well-being; promoting confidence in the government; stabilizing and stimulating the economy; quelling social unrest and racial tensions; providing opportunities to non-white and low-income households to participate in the "American Dream"; stabilizing and rejuvenating deteriorated neighborhoods; and promoting wealth accumulation as a way to reduce economic inequality. Although these goals have been apparent in policy interventions, the evidence demonstrating that housing tenure status is responsible for attaining these diverse outcomes is somewhat equivocal.

Several investigations have explored the extent to which various goals and assumptions about home ownership do, in fact, materialize. One comprehensive review of the literature concluded that there is "considerable evidence . . . that homeowners are more likely to be satisfied with their homes and neighborhoods, more likely to participate in voluntary and political activities, and more likely to stay in their homes longer periods of time" (Rohe *et al.*, 2002, p. 400) the last purportedly contributing to neighborhood stability. Evidence on several other frequently cited positive impacts is sparse and inconsistent. For example, there is some evidence that home ownership can (but does not always) lead to increased self-esteem and promote life satisfaction and health (Rohe *et al.*, 2002, p. 400; see also Rohe and Stewart, 1996).

In another review examining the home ownership experiences of low-income and minority households, the authors concluded that there is evidence, some modest and some quite convincing, that owners enjoy fairly significant wealth accumulation and improved psychological and physical health. Children of owner-occupier families have greater educational success, have greater success in labor markets, are less likely to have behavioral problems, and are more likely to become homeowners themselves (Herbert and Belsky, 2008, p. 49). Home ownership has also been found to have positive impacts on the property values of homes within the immediate neighborhood (Rohe and Stewart, 1996; Ellen *et al.*, 2002). This measure is viewed as part of the overall positive connection between home ownership and neighborhood stability.

All studies that explore the benefits of home ownership are, however, saddled with the problem of establishing causality. To what extent do households with various characteristics become homeowners or does the fact of ownership produce the desired outcomes? In short, 'most of the studies do not adequately account for the self-selection of households to owner and renter occupancy' (Rohe *et al.*, 2002, p. 400). Indeed, home ownership does not necessarily produce better citizens, but, rather, middle-class people tend to buy their homes, congregate in better neighborhoods, and stay in their homes longer, becoming more embedded in the community than other types of residents (see Ronald, 2008).

Whether one views the research findings on the benefits of home ownership as robust or modest, support for this form of tenure has been long evident throughout the history of public policies in the United States. The government's promotion of home ownership has often been at the expense of rental housing programs, which typically have been viewed as a less desirable form of housing tenure. Although issues pertaining to rental housing are beyond the scope of this chapter, suffice to say that the United States has had a home ownership-centric housing policy, to the detriment of the approximately one-third of U.S. households who rent their homes. Home ownership is not ideal for all households; economic and personal circumstances and preferences make rental housing (or some hybrid form of tenure) far preferable for many households.

As the mortgage crisis began to unfold in mid-2007, it became clear that many of the deeply ingrained objectives associated with home ownership were being undermined. This chapter begins by reviewing how these objectives were expressed during key phases of U.S history through a range of public policy interventions that focused on political, economic, and social concerns. It goes on to assesses how the multiple goals of home ownership have suffered as a result of the mortgage crisis of the late 2000s.

The political, economic, and social goals of home ownership

Throughout the history of the United States, a variety of political, economic, and social objectives associated with home ownership have been evident. Housing policy has not simply been concerned with sheltering the population, which would be no small accomplishment in itself. Instead, the various public interventions related to home ownership have had a number of desirable and, over time, increasingly diverse objectives. In view of the many non-shelter roles that home ownership is assumed to play, it is not surprising that this policy approach has enjoyed significant support from Democratic as well as Republican administrations.

Pre-20th century to President Roosevelt

From the founding of the United States until the Depression era, home ownership was most closely related to the social goals of giving people a stake in society and promoting confidence in the government. It is not clear when the phrase "the American Dream" was coined[1] and when, exactly, it became associated with the goal of home ownership. In any case, a key principle of the young country was that property ownership and good citizenship were intertwined. At the time that the Declaration of Independence was signed, in 1776, only white men with property had the right to vote.[2]

During the nineteenth century, promoting property ownership became an important vehicle for settling the vast lands of the West. The Homestead Act of 1862 provided free land to settlers. Fulfilling a national economic need, this strategy was viewed as the "only means of building up in a wilderness great and prosperous communities" (quoted in Hibbard, 1924, p. 354). In addition, providing free land was intended to instill patriotism, since the 'affections of good citizens are always mingled with their homes and placed upon the country which contains their fields and gardens' (quoted in Hibbard, 1924, p. 352). At the same time, the government's desire to create a strong presence in areas occupied by Native American communities was a compelling political motivation.

In the early 1920s, the Department of Commerce strongly supported the "Better Homes for America" movement, which encouraged households to save for home purchase and to become informed about the home-buying process (Dean, 1945). Underlying this initiative was a desire to ensure that residents would have a stake in society and to promote confidence in the government. It contrasted the American way of life and the opportunity to own a home of one's own with communal styles of living under socialist or communist regimes. Indeed, a prevailing view was that "socialism and communism do not take root in the ranks of those who have their feet firmly embedded in the soil of America through home ownership" (cited in Dean, 1945, p. 4). At the same time, the National Association of Real Estate Boards underscored both the financial gains to be achieved through home ownership, and the sense that homeowners achieved a higher level of morality than renters, and were able to become "completely self-reliant and dominant" (cited in Vale, 2007, p. 26).

In 1931, President Herbert Hoover convened a conference on Home Building and Home Ownership at which he noted that "every one of you here is impelled by the high ideal and aspiration that each family may pass their days in the home which they own" (quoted in Dean, 1945, p. 44; also see Vale, 2007). Individuals were sure to benefit by becoming homeowners: "It makes for happier married life, it makes for better children, it makes for confidence and security . . . it makes for better citizenship . . . [Moreover, for society at large, home owner- ship] penetrates the heart of our national well-being' (cited in Vale, 2007, p. 32). The flowery rhetoric notwithstanding, it was insufficient to address the escalating rate of home foreclosures and the stagnation in the building industry during the early 1930s.

President Roosevelt to the 1960s

As the Great Depression took hold, radically undermining conditions that had supported home ownership, a new activist president, Franklin D. Roosevelt, created a series of agencies and programs to help homeowners. These assisted defaulting homeowners, promoted more affordable home loans through federal mortgage insurance, and more generally stimulated the construction industry and supported the banking and mortgage finance system through a new set of regulatory protections and institutions. Thus, home ownership was viewed as a key vehicle for stabilizing and stimulating the economy. In addition, the implicit and explicit goals of home ownership during the eighteenth and nineteenth centuries—to help households develop a stake in society and to promote confi- dence in the government—were also prominent during this period.

In proposing the creation of a new Home Owners' Loan Corporation (HOLC), which eventually helped about 800,000 defaulting homeowners to refinance and save their homes from foreclosure, President Franklin D. Roosevelt told the U.S. Congress that "the broad interests of the nation require that special safeguards should be thrown around home ownership as a guar- antee of social and economic stability" (Home Owners' Loan Act, 1933). The strategy appeared to work. The new program contributed to social stability as well as to presidential power. "By enabling thousands of Americans to save their homes, it [HOLC] strengthened their stake both in the existing order and in the New Deal. Probably no single measure consolidated so much middle-class support for the administration" (Schlesinger, 1959, p. 24).

The Depression era also saw the creation of the Federal Housing Administration (FHA), which provided mortgage insurance for lenders, as a way to stimulate the banking and home-building industries and, at the same time, promote home ownership for moderate-income people. Commenting on the motivations behind this legislation, one observer noted that: "it was primar- ily sold politically as a program to unfreeze the home building industry and thereby stimulate employment and the economy" (Keith, 1973, p. 24). Reflecting on the broader set of post-Depression initiatives, which included both the FHA and HOLC, as well as other new programs, another analyst stated that: "Each new housing bill was advocated as a means of stimulating the durable goods industries or putting men to work. Housing thus was looked upon as a remedy for general economic ills rather than a problem in itself" (Colean, 1944, pp. 261–262).

Another key intervention of this period was the creation of the Federal National Mortgage Association, whose role was to provide a source of liquidity for mortgage originators, as a further inducement to encourage lending. Originally known by its acronym, FNMA, and later as Fannie Mae, it was created in 1938 and has been the largest government-sponsored secondary mortgage market entity in the United States (The agency was privatized in 1968, but was placed under federal control in September 2008, in the wake of the mortgage crisis; see Bratt, Chapter 8.)

Thus, the Depression era saw a number of interventions aimed at preserving home ownership for those who could be helped through the HOLC, promoting new home ownership opportunities through the FHA, making mortgage lending more attractive to lenders, and, at the same time, priming the economic pump.

The 1960s to the 1970s

A new wave of congressional enthusiasm for home ownership surfaced in the 1960s. Similar to the Depression era, there was a strong desire to stimulate the economy. However, a variety of other political and social objectives were also compelling. In particular, the policies of this period also aimed at quelling social unrest and racial tensions and providing opportunities to non-white and low-income households to become part of the "American Dream."

In 1968, the Secretary of the U.S. Department of Housing and Urban Development (HUD) referred to home ownership with familiar rhetoric: "To own one's own home is to have a sense of place and purpose. Home ownership creates a pride of possession, engenders responsibility and stability" (Weaver, 1967, p. 7). But home ownership was also grasped as the means to quiet the unrest among blacks and to help rejuvenate the cities. A noted urbanist opined: "There is no question that the chance of riots in Newark or for that matter any other major core area would have been substantially lower with more Negro ownership" (Sternlieb, 1968, p. 1607). And echoing the arguments of earlier years – that home ownership is good for the social well-being of the nation – the *Report of the National Advisory Commission on Civil Disorders* (Kerner Commission, 1968) stated: "The ambition to own one's own home is shared by virtually all Americans, and we believe it is in the interest of the nation to permit all who share such a goal to realize it" (p. 477).

Also in 1968, Congress enacted the first major federal home ownership program for the non-rural poor.[3] Known as Section 235, this interest rate subsidy initiative was aimed at expanding the number of people who could own their own homes, particularly inner-city residents, members of racial minority groups, and those with low and moderate incomes. Between 1969 and 1979, the Section

235 program enabled some 500,000 households to achieve home ownership (Hays, 1995, p. 117; Martinez, 2000). But the program was short-lived, with major scandals and defects in its operations surfacing less than five years after its creation: shoddy construction and rehabilitation standards; inflated property appraisals; inadequate assessments of the ability of borrowers to cover the costs of the loan; very low down-payment requirements; inadequate counseling for homebuyers; rampant greed and speculation; and inadequate regulatory oversight by government officials. Forty years later, there was an eerie repetition of these problems, which contributed to the mortgage crisis (see Bratt, Chapter 8). The Nixon administration froze funding for the Section 235 program in early 1973 as part of a moratorium on virtually all federal housing subsidy programs.

A smaller Section 235 program reappeared in 1976, only to die in 1987 (Carliner, 1998, pp. 313–314). Congressional interest in a major federal home ownership subsidy program for the non-rural poor evaporated, with bad memories of the Section 235 program tainting the possibility of any such initiative.

This period also saw significant growth in the federally supported secondary mortgage market institutions. The Government National Mortgage Association, or GNMA (and later known as Ginnie Mae), was created in 1968 with the mission to purchase mortgages on federally subsidized housing developments and below market interest rate loans. It has, since the 1960s, remained under federal control. Another government-sponsored secondary mortgage market entity, the Federal Home Loan Mortgage Corporation, FHLMC, was created in 1970 as a private corporation and is commonly known as Freddie Mac (as with Fannie Mae, it was placed under federal control in September 2008).

All three institutions comprising the government-sponsored secondary mortgage market were created to purchase loans originated by primary mortgage market lenders, with the goal of increasing the availability of credit and thereby expanding opportunities for households to purchase homes. As discussed in Chapter 8, Fannie Mae and Freddie Mac played increasingly dominant roles in the mortgage market from the mid-1970s through most of the first decade of the twenty-first century.

The 1980s to the new millennium

Although the previous historic goals of state-promoted home ownership have persisted through to the current period, new ones have been added. However, the whole range of goals associated with home ownership has been threatened by the mortgage crisis, as discussed in the following section.

In 1990, President George H.W. Bush's HUD Secretary, Jack Kemp, revived interest in low-income home ownership. In introducing new legislation to create the HOPE program (Home ownership and Opportunity for People Everywhere), he stated that a key goal was "Expanding home ownership and affordable housing opportunities for low- and moderate-income families and young families just starting out" (Kemp, 1990, p. 40).

The rhetoric and reality of home ownership flourished under the Clinton administration. In 1994 President Clinton reaffirmed the multiple goals of home ownership: "More Americans should own their own homes, for reasons that are economic and tangible, and reasons that are emotional and intangible, but go to the heart of what it means to harbor, to nourish [and] to expand the American Dream" (HUD, 1995). This was to be achieved, in part, by reducing down-payment requirements, making terms more flexible, thereby reducing the cost of interest, and increasing the availability of alternative mortgage financing products. Lenders and homeowners responded and the home ownership rate, which had stagnated in the 1980s, increased several percentage points to reach 67.7 percent of U.S. households by the end of the Clinton administration.[4]

Home ownership retained its popularity throughout the George W. Bush administration. His first HUD Secretary, Mel Martinez, articulated strong positive feelings about home ownership by noting

> the pride my dad and mom had when they bought their first home in America with the help of FHA. Owning your own home is the American Dream and I intend to fight for those who do not yet own a home, so they can live the American Dream and experience the transformation that can happen in a life through home ownership.
>
> (Martinez, 2001)

Despite this enthusiasm and the overall gains in home ownership rates, only a relatively small number of low-income homeowner households received direct federal housing assistance[5] and there were large disparities in relative numbers of low-income and higher-income homeowners, as well as between white and minority homeowners.[6]

A key way that home ownership is supported in the United States is through the federal tax advantages provided to homeowners. Nearly 1 million home-owners who earn $30,000 or less receive federal assistance indirectly – through the income tax system's provision that allows the deduction of mortgage interest and property tax payments when calculating their tax liability. This is, in fact, a subsidy, but it predominantly and overwhelmingly advantages those with the highest incomes. In terms of dollar volume, households with incomes of less than $30,000 per annum receive only about $400 million in tax relief, compared with over $65 billion for those earning more than $30,000 (Joint Committee on Taxation, 2007).

In June 2002, President George W. Bush committed to increase minority home ownership by 5.5 million households by the end of the decade, thereby helping to close the gap between white and minority home ownership (HUD, 2002a). Four months later, HUD released a report supporting this agenda (HUD, 2002b), but it did not recommend a new deep subsidy to promote low-income home ownership. After outlining the economic benefits that would be realized if the minority home ownership gap were reduced, the HUD

report recommended modest increases in or new funding for home ownership education, increasing the supply of affordable homes, providing assistance
with down-payment and closing costs, and offering financing options, thereby
making home ownership more accessible to a wider range of households (HUD,
2002b). Specifically, concerning down-payment assistance, the American
Dream Home Ownership Act was enacted in December 2003 and provided
funding to assist first-time homebuyers cover down-payment and closing costs.[7]

Toward the end of the Bush administration, in the midst of rising home
foreclosures, the president proclaimed June 2008 as "National Homeownership
Month" and noted his commitment to "helping Americans achieve their dreams
of home ownership."[8] One month later, the president signed into law a major
housing bill that (among a number of initiatives) attempted to provide relief for
homeowners in serious mortgage default and promoted home ownership for
first-time buyers, by offering a new tax credit of up to $7,500 to be used toward
the down payment.[9]

A new era for home ownership policy

Despite the shock of the mortgage crisis and fundamental failures in the tenure
system, there has been continuing presidential support for home ownership.
President Obama nominated his new HUD secretary, Shaun Donovan, stating
that he "knows that we can put the dream of owning a home within reach for
more families, so long as we're making loans in the right way, and so long as
those who buy a home are prepared for the responsibilities of home ownership"
(Obama, 2008). Troubled by the high number of homeowners in mortgage
distress, Obama further noted several of the multiple goals and roles of home
ownership: "It not only shakes the foundation of our economy, but the foundation of the American Dream. There is nothing more fundamental than having
a home to call your own. It's not just a place to live or raise your children or
return after a hard day's work – it's the cornerstone of a family's financial security" (Obama, 2008). This commitment to home ownership was demonstrated
during the first year of the Obama administration when the first-time homebuyer tax credit was increased to $8,000. Although this program may have been
valuable to some homebuyers and had certain symbolic importance, it did not
target the numerous defects arising from significant changes in the mortgage
finance system over the previous four decades.

Thus, in the most recent era, as with previous periods in the history of the
United States, there has been enthusiastic, bipartisan support for home ownership. In addition to all the previously articulated reasons for supporting home
ownership, two new goals have become particularly prominent. First, recent
public policies aimed at promoting home ownership are often explicitly focused
on this tenure form's ability to promote more stable and revitalized neighborhoods. This relationship has been both viewed as "conventional wisdom"
(Rohe and Stewart, 1996) and fueled by academic research. As noted earlier,

homeowners are less likely to move than renters and home ownership appears to have positive impacts on the property values within the immediate neighborhood. The second contemporary goal of home ownership, assisting people to build assets, embraces home ownership as a means to contribute to family well-being by enhancing their economic position. This goal is an expansion of the social goal espoused earlier – to promote a family's financial well-being— but, in recent years, there has been an explicit focus on lower-income households.

It is hardly surprising that home ownership as a vehicle for wealth accumulation is particularly important for low-income and minority households. Nevertheless, home ownership does not guarantee positive financial outcomes, as demonstrated in a number of studies (see Stone, 1993; Stegman *et al.*, 2007). Particularly noteworthy is that for low-income households with subprime mortgages the financial gains of home ownership are far less than for other households (Belsky *et al.*, 2007). But as non-housing wealth accumulation for low-income households is typically negligible or non-existent, "housing wealth is synonymous with total wealth" (Boehm and Schlottmann, 2008, p. 250).

Along with the view that home ownership is beneficial to lower-income households, it is also looked to as a vehicle for decreasing the dramatic levels of economic inequality that are so characteristic of the United States and which have become more severe since the late 1980s (Bernstein *et al.*, 2008).

Former Federal Reserve Board chairman Alan Greenspan (2002) has articulated the importance of home ownership for neighborhood stability and wealth accumulation – the newer goals for home ownership – while also repeating several of the classic arguments:

> The choice to buy a home is a decision to plant a family's roots in a community with all the implicit incentives to make that community thrive. Where home ownership flourishes, it is no surprise to find increased neighborhood stability, more civic-minded residents, better school systems, and reduced crime rates. Just as important is the effect of home ownership on a household's ability to accumulate assets. For most households, home ownership represents a significant financial milestone and is an important vehicle for ongoing savings . . . [As of 1998] home ownership represented 44 percent of gross assets for families earning $50,000 or less annually.
>
> (p. 1)

Essentially, since the founding of the United States, various public policies concerning home ownership have focused on critical political, economic, and social objectives. Many of these objectives have persisted through the centuries, while new ones have been added. The simple desire for households to secure a place to live, and for governments to provide decent housing for its residents, have been joined by goals that are farther removed from the role of housing as shelter. At the same time, the compelling personal motivations underlying the quest for home ownership have provided fertile ground for abuse and greed to flourish on the part of many key actors engaged in mortgage finance (see Bratt, Chapter 8).

The multiple goals of home ownership and the role of the mortgage crisis

The mortgage crisis began to surface in mid-2007. Since then, default and foreclosure rates have skyrocketed. By July 2009, over 1.5 million properties were in some stage of mortgage distress, which represented a 9 percent increase from the previous six months and a nearly 15 percent increase compared with the first six months of 2008 (RealtyTrac, 2009a). By the end of 2009, the rate at which properties were defaulting or being foreclosed started to slow, but it was still much higher than the previous year (RealtyTrac, 2009b). Various analysts have predicted that there will be between 8 and 13 million foreclosures by 2014 (Congressional Oversight Panel, 2009). Clearly, this dire situation is undermining the ways in which home ownership has been seen in the United States as a vehicle to fulfill an array of political, economic, and social goals.

Arguably, most homeowners aspire to gain economic security and to provide their families with a stable living environment by way of their housing choice. A foreclosure, however, produces the opposite effect. It diminishes the opportunity of households to set down roots and for them to feel connected to the broader community. Households lose not only their shelter, but also whatever financial investment they had, while almost certainly experiencing a sense of personal failure. An example of a worst-case scenario unfolded recently in Massachusetts, when a woman committed suicide because her house was about to be taken by the bank. She faxed a chilling note to her mortgage company saying that, "by the time they foreclose on the house today" she would be dead. In another note to her family she said, "Take the [life] insurance money and pay for the house" (Levenson, 2008). Although we can hope that few people take this drastic step, at the very least we know that there will be many more people whose "dreams are foreclosed" (Ballou, 2008). Of course, with so many people losing their homes, the relatively recently articulated goal of home ownership – to promote wealth accumulation as a way to reduce economic inequality – is also being severely undermined as a result of the mortgage crisis.

An earlier section of this chapter discussed the ways in which home ownership has been used to quell social unrest and racial tensions. This does not appear to have been a key goal in recent years, nor does social unrest appear to have been exacerbated by the current situation surrounding home ownership. Not only are thousands of people losing their homes through foreclosure, but also countless others have been unable to buy, since mortgages have become so difficult to obtain. Even for those who would be considered highly credit-worthy borrowers – people with good credit scores, a solid income, and an adequate down-payment – mortgage lenders are often saying "no" (Streitfeld,

2009). Thus, what appears to be an over-reaction to the mortgage crisis on the part of many lenders is further preventing the attainment of home ownership for many Americans.

Although there was a high level of frustration over the general weak economic conditions in the United States through the last years of the 2000s, this did not translate into the kind of social upheavals common in the 1960s. The deep concerns around home ownership might have predicted a far stronger civic response.

Several home ownership initiatives, starting in the 1960s, also embraced the specific goal of opening opportunities to non-white and low-income households to enable them to gain a stake in the "American Dream." We now know that the mortgage crisis is having a particularly negative impact on this population. Although subprime borrowers are not necessarily lower income and can, in fact, have a wide range of income levels, non-white households comprise a disproportionate number of subprime borrowers. According to Fishbein (2007), over 55 percent of African American and 46 percent of Latino households financed in 2006 received subprime loans compared with fewer than 20 percent of white borrowers (p. 2).[10]

The more implicit expectation that home ownership promotes confidence in the government is certain to be thwarted as families lose their homes through foreclosure. Where, one might ask, was the safety net to help people overcome temporary difficulties? Although it is still too soon to fully understand the extent to which various government initiatives will assist homeowners facing foreclosure, early reports were mostly negative (see, for example, *Huffington Post*, 2009). One respected source labeled the foreclosure prevention plan as "flawed from the start," as it did not include a mechanism to require lender participation (*New York Times*, 2009).

In addition to confidence in the federal government likely being undermined as a result of the mortgage crisis, many states also are encountering serious financial problems, with California probably presenting the most extreme case. Although only a portion of California's fiscal difficulties can be blamed on the mortgage crisis, these problems are likely to worsen as revenues from real estate transactions decline (Archibold, 2008).

Another key goal of home ownership, helping to stimulate and stabilize the economy, has been profoundly affected by the mortgage crisis. The national and international dislocations in credit markets are concrete indicators of how the mortgage crisis has de-stabilized the full breadth of the financial sector. In the United States, in the last half of 2008, two giant investment houses, Bear Stearns and Merrill Lynch, were purchased by other banks and a third, Lehman Brothers, went bankrupt;[11] financial institutions posted huge loses; and the federal government was forced to bail out Fannie Mae and Freddie Mac. In view of these events, it is hard to imagine that earlier home ownership initiatives not only were aimed at stimulating or stabilizing the economy, but also were actually able do so.

Home ownership programs are typically viewed as generally good for a community, and they also have been used to stabilize and rejuvenate deteriorated neighborhoods. But the increase in foreclosures is already having a damaging, if not devastating effect on communities across the country, especially in neighborhoods with large percentages of non-white households, which experience particularly high rates of foreclosure (Ludwig, 2007). Here is one account of a neighborhood in South Jamaica, Queens, New York, with a large African American and immigrant non-white population:

> More than two years ago, most homes here were occupied and the neighborhood was making strides against the drugs, violence and abandonment that had plagued it in the past . . . But today [residents and merchants] mostly talk about decreasing property values, increasing crime, struggling small businesses and fraying community bonds.
>
> (Fernandez, 2008)

When there are a large numbers of foreclosures in a given neighborhood, these vacant and unsold homes depress the overall local housing market and also create shortfalls in property tax revenues (Joint Economic Committee, 2007; Immergluck, 2008). In Los Banos, California, for example, the bust has become apparent throughout the town: "Storefronts in its older strip malls are empty. Citywide, sales-tax revenue is down 15% from initial projections and the city is also bracing for big declines in property tax revenue" (Corkery and Karp, 2008). In another California town, Perris, about 1 out of 53 houses has received notices of default, the first step toward foreclosure. This means that whole blocks are becoming abandoned as foreclosed homes sit vacant waiting for a buyer (Streitfeld, 2007).

The Midwest has, perhaps, been hit even more profoundly than the east and west coasts. In Cleveland, Ohio, for example, the mortgage crisis is having ripple effects throughout the entire city, creating a major downward spiral that has implications for the merchants as well as for the property owners in a given area. As foreclosures mount, business declines and property values of non-foreclosed homes fall. Here is a rather gloomy picture of the situation:

> Livable homes can be had for as little as $6,000 or $7,000, while many others have tumbled into complete disrepair, leaving city officials in a desperate battle against the resultant blight. In [one area] alone, more than 50 arson fires have been set this year, while many of the vacant homes are ravaged by scavengers, looking to cash in on the copper wiring and plumbing and aluminum siding that they sell as scrap metal. It is a stunning decline that is sure to shrink the city's property tax base for years to come.
>
> Jackson, the mayor, said the collapse is rippling across the region, with declining property values hurting even residents of more affluent neighborhoods . . . The demand for goods and services are negatively impacted and

the city has avoided deficits only by making across-the-board spending cuts in the past two years.

(Fletcher, 2008)

To make matters worse, the structure of the contemporary mortgage finance system makes it more difficult for mortgage servicers to dispose of properties in a way that would be advantageous to the surrounding community, as "properties in a particular neighborhood may be held in many disparate trusts with different rules regarding any ability to sell the properties at a discount" (Immergluck, 2009, p. 218).

In addition to home ownership being viewed as a mechanism for promoting community development, as noted earlier, there is evidence that, in comparison with renters, homeowners tend to participate more in civic activities and that the greater length of time that they stay in their homes contributes to neighborhood stability. Yet all these goals are being undermined as families lose their homes to foreclosure.

In foreclosed homes with tenants, another set of problems occurs. Foreclosures typically mean that tenants are evicted, as banks usually require that houses be vacant before they assume ownership, thereby dislocating completely innocent victims in the mortgage crisis and further contributing to neighborhood instability (Leland, 2007; Harris, 2008).

Clearly, the mortgage crisis has created personal tragedies and community, citywide and statewide problems, as well as national and international economic upheavals. At the core of the problems is the new set of relationships within the mortgage lending industry that has reallocated traditional roles involving risk and responsibility on the part of homebuyers as well as other key actors in the mortgage finance system.[12] This is the focus of the following chapter.

Acknowledgments

Thanks to Dan Immergluck, Langley Keyes, and James Jennings for reading an earlier version of this manuscript and for offering many helpful comments, as well as to the editors of this book, Richard Ronald and Marja Elsinga.

References

Archibold, R.C. (2008) California leaders seek answers to credit crunch, *New York Times*, 9 October. Online. Available at http://www.nytimes.com/2008/10/09/us/09calif.html?sq=california%20subprime%20crisis&st=cse&scp=1&pagewanted=print (accessed 14 October 2008).

Ballou, B.R. (2008) In Roslindale, a dream foreclosed, *Boston Globe*, 26 September. Online. Available at http://www.boston.com/news/local/articles/2008/09/26/in_roslindale_a_dream_foreclosed/ (accessed 14 October 2008).

Belsky, E.S., Retsinas, N. and Duda, M. (2007) The financial returns to low-income home ownership, in W.M. Rohe and H.L. Watson (eds) *Chasing the American Dream: New Perspectives on Affordable Home ownership*, Ithaca, NY: Cornell University Press.

Bernstein, J., McNichol, E. and Nicholas, A. (2008) *Pulling Apart: A State-by-State Analysis of Income Trends*, Washington, DC: Center on Budget and Policy Priorities and Economic Policy Institute.

Boehm, T.P. and Schlottmann, A.M. (2008) Wealth accumulation and home owner-ship: evidence for low-income households, *Cityscape*, 10(2), 225–256.

Carliner, M.S. (1998) Development of federal home ownership policy, *Housing Policy Debate*, 9(2), 299–321.

Colean, M.L. (1944) *American Housing*, New York: 20th Century Fund.

Congressional Oversight Panel. (2009) *Taking Stock: What Has the Trouble Asset Relief Program Achieved?*, Washington, DC: Government Printing Office.

Corkery, M. and Karp, J. (2008) California home sales revive, but not without intense pain, *The Wall Street Journal*, 22 October. Online. Available at http://sbk.online.wsj.com/article/SB122462963345656289.html (accessed 25 October 2008).

Dean, J.P. (1945) *Home ownership: Is It Sound?*, New York: Harper and Row.

Decker, J.L. (1992) *Made in America: Self-styled Success from Horatio Alger to Oprah Winfrey*, Minneapolis: University of Minnesota Press.

Ellen, I.G., Schill, M.H., Susin, S. and Schwartz, A.E. (2002) Building homes: reviving neighborhoods: spillovers from subsidized construction of owner-occupied hous-ing in New York City, in Nicolas P. Retsinas and Eric S. Belsky (eds) *Low-Income Home Ownership: Examining the Unexamined Goal*, Cambridge, MA: Joint Center for Housing Studies and Brookings Institution Press.

Fernandez, M. (2008) Door to door, foreclosure knocks here, *New York Times*, 19 October. Online. Available at http://www.nytimes.com/2008/10/19/nyregion/19block.html?partner=rssnyt&emc=rss (accessed 21 October 2008).

Fishbein, A. (2007) The foreclosure epidemic: the costs to families and communities of the predictable mortgage meltdown, *Multinational Monitor*, 28(3), May/June. Online. Available at http://www.multinationalmonitor.org/mm2007/052007/interview-fishbein.html (accessed 29 October 2008).

Fletcher, M.A. (2008) Takeover by PNC heralds fall of a Cleveland institution, *Washington Post*, 25 October. Online. Available at http://www.washingtonpost.com/wp-dyn/content/article/2008/10/24/AR2008102401327_pf.html (accessed 29 October 2008).

Greenspan, A. (2002) *Economic Development and Financial Literacy*, remarks at the Ninth Annual Economic Development Summit, Greenlining Institute, Oakland, CA, 10 January.

Harris, E.A. (2008) Even renters aren't safe, *New York Times*, 13 April. Online. Available at http://www.nytimes.com/2008/04/13/realestate/13cover.html (accessed 29 August 2008).

Hays, R.A. (1995) *The Federal Government and Urban Housing: Ideology and Change in Public Policy*, Albany: State University of New York Press.

Herbert, C.E. and Belsky, E.S. (2008) The home ownership experience of low-income and minority households: a review and synthesis of the literature, *Cityscape*, 10(2), 5–59.

Hibbard, B.H. (1924) *A History of the Public Land Policies*, New York: MacMillan.

Home Owners' Loan Act (1933) Public Law No. 43, 73rd Congress, H.R. 5240.

HUD. See U.S. Department of Housing and Urban Development.

Huffington Post. (2009) Bailout watchdog: Obama foreclosure plan inadequate, new direction needed, 9 December. Online. Available at http://www.huffington-post.com/2009/12/09/bailout-watchdog-obama-fo_n_385199.html (accessed 20 December 2009).

Immergluck, D. (2008) From the subprime to the exotic: excessive mortgage market risk and foreclosures, *Journal of the American Planning Association*, 74(1), 59–76.

Immergluck, D. (2009) *Foreclosed! High-Risk Lending, Deregulation, and the Undermining of America's Mortgage Market*, Ithaca, NY: Cornell University Press.

Joint Center for Housing Studies (2004) *The State of the Nation's Housing*, Cambridge, MA: Harvard University Press.

Joint Committee on Taxation. (2007) *Estimates of Federal Tax Expenditures for Fiscal Years 2007–20011*. Prepared for the House Committee on Ways and Means and the Senate Committee on Finance, 24 September, Washington, DC: US Government Printing Office.

Joint Economic Committee (2007) *The Subprime Lending Crisis: The Economic Impact on Wealth, Property Values and Tax Revenues, and How We Got Here*. Report and Recommendations of the Majority Staff, Washington, DC: U.S. Congress..

Keith, N.S. (1973) *Politics and the Housing Crisis Since 1930*, New York: Universe Books.

Kemp, J. (1990) *Joint Hearings before the Committee on Banking, Housing, and Urban Affairs and the Subcommittee on Housing and Urban Affairs*, U.S. Senate, 101st Congress, 2nd Session, 20 March.

Kerner Commission (1968) *Report of the National Advisory Commission on Civil Disorders*, New York: Bantam Books.

Leland, J. (2007) As owners feel mortgage pain, so do renters, *New York Times*, 18 November. Online. Available at http://www.nytimes.com/2007/11/18/us/18renters.html?ei=5088&emc=rss&en=ac0867fa0effebf5&ex=1353042000&partner=rssnyt (accessed 20 September 2008).

Leland, J. (2008) Baltimore finds subprime crisis snags women, *New York Times*, 15 January. Online. Available at http://www.nytimes.com/2008/01/15/us/15mortgage.html (accessed 29 August 2008).

Levenson, M. (2008) The anguish of foreclosure, *Boston Globe*, 24 July. Online. Available at http://www.boston.com/news/local/articles/2008/07/24/the_anguish_of_foreclosure?mode=PF (accessed 14 October).

Ludwig, S. (2007) Losing ground, *Shelterforce Online*, 150, Summer. Online. Available at http://www.nhi.org/online/issues/150/losingground.html (accessed 29 August 2008).

Martinez, M. (2001) Hearing on the nomination of the Honorable Mel Martinez, of Florida, to be the Secretary of Housing and Urban Development, Senate Banking Committee, 17 January. Online. Available at http://www.hud.gov/about/secretary/martineztestimony.cfm (accessed 29 August 2008).

Martinez, S.C. (2000) The Housing Act of 1949: its place in the realization of the American Dream of home ownership, *Housing Policy Debate*, 11(2), 467–487.

Millennial Housing Commission. (2002) *Meeting Our Nation's Housing Challenges*, Washington, DC: MHC.

National Low Income Housing Coalition (2001) Low income housing profile. Online. Available at http://www.nlihc.org/pubs/profile/profile.pdf (accessed 3 September 2008).

New York Times. (2009) More foreclosures to come, 12 November. Online. Available at http://www.nytimes.com/2009/11/12/opinion/12thu2.html, 12 November (accessed 20 December 2009).

Obama, B. (2008) Text of Obama's radio address for 13 December. Online. Available at http://thepage.time.com/text-of-obamas-radio-address-for-dec-13/ (accessed date).

RealtyTrac. (2009a) 1.9 million foreclosure filings reported on more than 1.5 million U.S. properties in first half of 2009. Online. Available at http://www.realtytrac.com/ContentManagement/PressRelease.aspx?ItemID=6802 (accessed 20 December 2009).

RealtyTrac. (2009b) U.S. foreclosure activity decreases 8 percent in November. Online. Available at http://www.realtytrac.com/contentmanagement/pressrelease.aspx?chanelid=9&accnt=0&itemid=8116 (accessed 20 December 2009).

Rohe, W.M. and Stewart, L.S. (1996) Home ownership and neighborhood stability, *Housing Policy Debate*, 7(1), 37–81.

Rohe, W.M., Van Zandt, S. and McCarthy, G. (2002) Social benefits and costs of home ownership, in N.P. Retsinas and E.S. Belsky (eds) *Low-Income Home Ownership: Examining the Unexamined Goal*, Cambridge, MA: Joint Center for Housing Studies and Brookings Institution Press.

Ronald, R. (2008) *The Ideology of Home Ownership: Homeowner Societies and the Role of Housing*, Basingstoke, Palgrave Macmillan.

Schlesinger, A.M., Jr (1959) *The Coming of the New Deal*, Boston: Houghton-Mifflin.

Stegman, M.A., Quercia R.G. and Davis, W. (2007) The wealth-creating potential of home ownership: a preliminary assessment of price appreciation among low-income homebuyers, in W.M. Rohe and H.L. Watson (eds) *Chasing the American Dream: New Perspectives on Affordable Home ownership*. Ithaca, NY: Cornell University Press.

Sternlieb, G. (1968) *Housing and Urban Development Act of 1968. Hearings before the Subcommittee on Housing and Urban Affairs*, U.S. Senate, 90th Congress, 2nd Session, Part 1, March.

Stone, M.E. (1993) *Shelter Poverty: New Ideas on Housing Affordability*, Philadelphia: Temple University Press.

Streitfeld, D. (2007) A town right on the default line, *Los Angeles Times*. Online. Available at http://www.latimes.com/business/la-fi-perris16mar16,0,5883478,print.story (accessed 14 October 2008).

Streitfeld, D. (2009) Tight mortgage rules exclude even good risks, *New York Times*, 11 July. Online. Available at http://www.nytimes.com/2009/07/11/business/11housing.html (accessed 12 July 2008).

U.S. Commission on Civil Rights. (1971) *Home Ownership for Lower Income Families: A Report on the Racial and Ethnic Impact of the Section 235 Program*, Washington, DC: U.S. Commission on Civil Rights.

U.S. Department of Housing and Urban Development (1995) Home Ownership and its Benefits, Urban Policy Brief, Number 2, August. Online. Available at http:www.hudser.org/publications/txt/hdbrf2.txt (accessed 3 September 2008).

U.S. Department of Housing and Urban Development (2002a) *Blueprint for the American Dream*, Washington, DC: HUD.

U.S. Department of Housing and Urban Development (2002b) *Economic Benefits of Increasing Minority Home ownership*, Washington, DC: HUD.

Vale, L. (2007) The ideological origins of affordable home ownership efforts, in W.M. Rohe and H.L. Watson (eds) *Chasing the American Dream: New Perspectives on Affordable Home ownership*, Ithaca, NY: Cornell University Press.

Weaver, R. (1967) *Housing Legislation of 1967. Hearings before the Subcommittee on Housing and Urban Affairs of the Committee on Banking and Currency*, U.S. Senate, 90th Congress, 1st Session, July–August.

8

HOME OWNERSHIP RISK AND RESPONSIBILITY BEFORE AND AFTER THE U.S. MORTGAGE CRISIS

Rachel G. Bratt

Introduction

Problems in the United States surrounding home ownership, specifically the mortgage crisis, have had global repercussions. In September 2008 stock exchanges across the world were in an apparent free fall (*New York Times*, 2008). Global subprime-related credit losses have since been estimated at more than $400 billion and total worldwide losses for all loans and securities connected to the U.S. financial system could exceed $945 billion (Joint Economic Committee, 2008a). Although international and U.S. markets began to rebound in 2009, various analysts have predicted between 8 and 13 million foreclosures by 2014 (Congressional Oversight Panel, 2009).

Fueled in part by the United States' long-standing commitment to promote home ownership (see Bratt, Chapter 7), a complex web of actors and relationships emerged during the latter quarter of the twentieth century and in the early years of the new millennium. This chapter underscores the extent to which the United States has created a mortgage finance system that has shifted the risk inherent in mortgage lending away from the originator of the loan to other investors who are far removed from the lending decision. This has resulted in a system with altered conceptualizations of how risks and responsibilities should be carried by homeowners and lenders and which is poorly attuned to the needs of homebuyers. Many of the problems associated with the recent mortgage crisis were first noticed decades ago. This chapter presents the lessons that could or should have been learned.

The chapter also discusses how the financial regulatory framework has failed to sufficiently safeguard borrowers, giving enormous latitude to lenders and investors. Although there have been a number of federal efforts aimed at promoting home ownership, particularly for lower-income and non-white households, these efforts have not fully met the desired goals. Weak federal oversight of private market actors has prevailed, providing the latter with lucrative opportunities that have trumped historic concerns for prudence in mortgage lending. The chapter further addresses how the mortgage crisis unravelled and how the federal government has responded, and makes observations about the types of risks and responsibilities that both lenders and homeowners must assume if mortgage lending transactions are to be successful. In particular, in order to achieve the multiple goals of home ownership, specific interventions and safeguards must be instituted that will counter the de-personalized, risk-shifting, and baroquely complex nature of the contemporary mortgage finance system. At the same time, more rigorous oversight of financial entities and instruments is needed to promote transparency and prevent the kinds of inappropriate incentives and opportunities that contributed to the mortgage crisis. Hopefully, changes in the financial regulatory system will, finally, heed the lessons from the past, as well as from the current era.

Mortgage finance before and after the 1970s

Throughout the nineteenth century and the first half of the twentieth century, the United States had a "conventional" mortgage finance system. This typically involved lenders, primarily savings and loan associations (S&Ls), originating loans to borrowers, servicing the loan on a monthly basis, and holding the mortgage until the loan was repaid. It was a fairly straightforward transaction, with lenders generally familiar with their clients and with the neighborhoods in which they did business. Beginning in the 1960s, mortgage finance started to become more complex. Although the changes have produced many advantages (e.g. an overall increase in credit availability and the smoothing out of economic cycles, making the flow of credit more constant), they also paved the way for the mortgage crisis of the late 2000s.

The roots of the second system of mortgage finance date back to 1934 when the federal government created the Federal Housing Administration (FHA). The FHA offered mortgage insurance on loans originated by a wide range of financial institutions. However, S&Ls and other conventional lenders were never active participants in this program, providing an opportunity for a new type of loan originator to emerge, the mortgage company. By 1972, mortgage companies originated 74.3 percent of all FHA-insured loans while S&Ls and savings banks (together known as thrift institutions) were responsible for only 13.1 percent (HUD, 1973a, pp. 173, 161).

During the second half of the twentieth century, the overall share of home mortgages (including both FHA and conventional loans) held by thrift institutions declined significantly, from about 56 percent in the 1970s to less than 10 percent in 2003. In their place, secondary mortgage market entities, notably Fannie Mae and Freddie Mac (see Bratt, Chapter 7), which purchased loans from the originators, emerged as the dominant holders of mortgages.

By the 1970s, then, two distinct mortgage systems were operating. First, the conventional mortgage market dominated by S&Ls continued to offer (primarily) non-FHA-insured loans. Second, mortgage companies offered FHA-insured mortgages, which were then sold to a federally supported secondary mortgage market entity, particularly Fannie Mae and other long-term investors. Although S&Ls and other depository institutions have responsibilities to safeguard the assets of their depositors, and have tended to be cautious whether or not using FHA mortgage insurance (Bacheller, 1971, p. 277), mortgage companies, whose risk is limited, have often been far less careful in their lending decisions – inadequately ascertaining the ability of potential homebuyers to pay the loan or not properly assessing the quality of the property (see U.S. House of Representatives, 1972).

Lax lending practices on the part of mortgage companies came to the fore in the 1970s, in part because, unlike depository institutions, which are monitored by one of the federal regulatory agencies, mortgage companies were (and still are) very lightly regulated. In addition, the Department of Housing and Urban Development (HUD), as the overseer of the FHA insurance fund, and as the risk taker in these transactions, should have safeguarded interests through diligent oversight of mortgage companies and with assurances that accurate underwriting and property appraisals had been performed. However, this often did not occur as the agency succumbed to pressure to approve as many loans as possible, particularly for lower-income subsidized homebuyers. To compound the problems, scores of HUD employees, as well as others hired by the agency on a fee-for-service basis, were indicted for fraud (HUD, 1973b). Thousands of pages of congressional testimony revealed that, at least through the early 1970s, the government often abdicated its role and refused to act as though it was carrying the risk (Bratt, 1976)

The laissez-faire attitude toward approving mortgagors and properties was also fueled by the many opportunities for private sector actors to make significant profits. Many real estate agents purchased properties for cash at low prices and quickly re-sold them to lower-income borrowers carrying FHA insurance. Mortgage companies, in turn, realized profits from origination fees and from bulk sales of mortgages to secondary mortgage market entities. The ultimate investors in these subsidized loans also failed to assure the integrity and creditworthiness of the lending transaction.

The experiences with low-income home ownership during the 1970s revealed similar problems and abuses as those connected with the current mortgage crisis: unprepared borrowers often with weak income or credit profiles, unscrupulous lenders, a weak regulatory environment, and the ability of the financial sector to shift the risk onto others. In both periods, high rates of default and foreclosure were an outcome. However, the events of the 1970s did not hint at the range of ripple effects caused by the new mortgage derivative instruments, which came much later. Also, the problems of that earlier era impacted individual borrowers; they did not undermine the U.S. economy, let alone cause havoc with global capital markets.

Homeowners in default in the 1970s

The extent to which defaulting homeowners in the 1970s encountered serious problems foreshadowed the events of the recent mortgage crisis. In addition to playing a weak role at the point of loan origination, HUD also failed to enforce its own rules stipulating how lenders should provide relief to families in default. Although congressional hearings documented many of the defects of the low-income home ownership program, HUD's unwillingness to require mortgagees to extend forbearance to defaulting homeowners was barely acknowledged. HUD's guidelines in the 1970s explicitly described foreclosure as a last resort, but mortgagees consistently failed to follow those guidelines and HUD failed to intervene on behalf of homeowners. A Fannie Mae report published in 1973 disclosed that only 3.3 percent of 26,575 delinquent but eligible FHA loans were receiving forbearance (Federal National Mortgage Association, 2003). Reports from HUD personnel confirmed that the agency rarely followed its own guidelines and seldom gave relief to defaulting mortgagors (Bratt, 1976; HUD, 1996). At least part of the problem related to the difficulties that lower-income homeowners in default had in renegotiating the terms of their loans. This was due, to some extent, to the disconnection between mortgage originators and long-term investors (Bratt, 1976).

In 1992, Congress finally required HUD to determine how to avoid foreclosures. Within four years, the agency had reportedly changed its operation significantly. It was apparently "moving forward in a proactive way to develop a full menu of options for assisting borrowers with financial difficulties," although there were still many initiatives needed to assist homeowners in avoiding foreclosure (HUD, 1996, p. 91).

The ability of borrowers to renegotiate the terms of their loans is still difficult: determining who owns the mortgage and how a new repayment schedule can be instituted is even more challenging today than in the 1970s. In both periods, the entity that has responsibility for the mortgage lending decision assumes little risk in the transaction and, at the same time, the risk-taker, in the form of the ultimate investor, is far removed from the actual processes of assessing the property, income, and creditworthiness of the borrower. Although the seeds for this situation were sown between the 1930s and 1970s, the federal deregulation of financial institutions that began in the 1980s was a critical contributor to the late 2000s upheavals in the mortgage market.

Regulatory changes in the financial system in the 1980s

A prevailing feeling during the 1980s was that the private sector should be liberated from federal regulation. Republican president Ronald Reagan's 1982 Commission on Housing emphasized that "the genius of the market economy, freed of the distortions forced by government housing policies and regulations . . . can provide for housing far better than Federal programs" (Report of the

President's Commission on Housing, 1982, p. vxii). And discussing the broad changes needed in housing finance, it stated that "the nation can no longer rely so completely on a system of highly regulated and specialized mortgage investors and a single type of mortgage instrument if the strong underlying demand for housing credit is to be met" (p. 120) Arguing for "a new legal and regulatory structure" and a "broader-based, more resilient system of housing finance," it called for "unrestricted access of all mortgage lenders and borrowers to the money and capital markets . . . [and for] sweeping policy measures to change the structure of the housing finance system" (ibid., p. 120).

Although it is beyond the scope of this chapter to detail the deregulation story, the outcome was a lax regulatory environment. As S&Ls moved away from the familiar turf of mortgage lending, they often entered into high-risk, speculative commercial ventures. However, S&L personnel were typically ill-equipped to prudently assess these new transactions, due to their historical focus on mortgage lending. By the late 1980s, the problems facing S&Ls emerged as a full-blown crisis. The entity set up to insure the deposits in these institutions became insolvent and over 1,000 thrift institutions eventually collapsed. In response, the Financial Institutions Reform, Recovery, and Enforcement Act (FIRREA) of 1989 bailed out the S&Ls, safeguarded depositors' accounts, and instituted other remedial steps (Stone, 2006; Immergluck, 2009).

A free market ideology shaped federal thinking for the following 25 years, during both Democratic and Republican administrations, and turned out to be one of the key factors leading to the mortgage crisis. Perhaps the most important step deregulating the financial industry during President Clinton's Democrat administration was the repeal of the Glass–Steagall Act, which removed the requirement that commercial and investment banking activities be conducted by separate entities. This invited large commercial banks to become involved with various types of financial instruments such as residential mortgage-backed securities (RMBS) and collateralized debt obligations (discussed later). The repeal of Glass–Steagall also allowed commercial banks to form new entities called structured investment (or special purpose) vehicles, which served as conduits for these new types of securities as they were bought and sold on the financial markets.

At the close of the 1980s, the mortgage finance system was unrecognizable from its historic roots. The relationships formed during that period have accelerated over the past two decades, with the mortgage finance system becoming intertwined with national, as well as global, capital markets. No longer are mortgage loans originated by local lenders who have a deep knowledge of the neighborhoods in which they operate and who hold the loans as long-term investments in their portfolios. Today, mortgage loan originators are most often mortgage companies who sell the "paper" to a host of investors through a variety of investment vehicles. The layers of securitization and the complexity and opaqueness of these transactions are fundamental to understanding the mortgage crisis of the late 2000s.

The mortgage system of the 2000s – part I: regulatory environment

Many factors contributed to the mortgage crisis and a considerable literature has emerged concerning its causes. As a backdrop, it is important to highlight that the aggressive investment during much of the 2000s was fueled by low short-term interest rates provided by the Federal Reserve Bank. With easy credit and attractive loan terms, inflation in housing costs followed leading to the so-called "housing bubble" (Joint Economic Committee, 2008b). Low interest rates drove many investors to seek higher-yielding opportunities and encouraged the origination of subprime loans, in which the higher risks were accompanied by higher rates of return.

The lax federal regulatory environment permitted mortgage abuses to flourish. As Federal Reserve Board chairman Ben Bernanke acknowledged, it was regulatory failure, rather than low interest rates, that fueled the housing bubble and the subsequent financial crisis (Rampell, 2010). Although a law prohibiting abusive and deceptive lending by all originators was passed in 1994, the Federal Reserve Board neglected to exercise its regulatory responsibilities, or to implement the law in a way that would have prevented the kinds of abuses that proliferated. It was not until July 2008 that Chairman Bernanke issued a strong rule implementing the Home Ownership and Equity Protection Act (HOEPA). Stein (2008) argues that, "had these rules been issued just three years earlier, countless foreclosures could have been prevented" (p. 20).

In hindsight, even former Federal Reserve Board chairman Alan Greenspan has acknowledged that he made mistakes in opposing greater federal regulation and stated: "Those of us who have looked to the self-interest of lending institutions to protect shareholder's equity (myself especially) are in a state of shocked disbelief" (Scannell and Reddy, 2008).

In addition to the laxity of the Federal Reserve, there were at least four additional major regulatory lapses, oversights, or possible misinterpretations of federal mandates. First, in contrast to other Fortune 500 companies, all of which have publicly traded stock, neither Fannie Mae nor Freddie Mac (the government-sponsored enterprises, or GSEs) was regulated by the Securities and Exchange Commission (SEC). Instead, they were overseen by an independent entity within HUD, the Office of Federal Housing Enterprise Oversight, which provided relatively less stringent oversight of the financial dealings of the GSEs. This arrangement may have contributed to the problems that auditors discovered in each of the GSE's accounting procedures. Eventually, federal investigations were launched, which revealed serious improprieties and resulted in significant fines (Associated Press, 2007; Bajaj, 2008a).

In 2005, led by Republican Senator Chuck Hagel, a bill was introduced that would have provided a greater level of federal oversight of the GSEs by creating a new independent regulatory agency. A partisan fight ensued with

Democrats opposing the bill, accompanied by vigorous lobbying by a consulting firm retained by Freddie Mac (Associated Press, 2008). The bill, the Federal Housing Enterprise Regulatory Reform Act of 2005 (S. 190) died with the 109th Congress.

A second major regulatory lapse is that mortgage companies have never had to meet the requirements of any federal regulatory agency. Instead, they have been loosely regulated by the individual states. Moreover, "The federal agency with principal authority over enforcing consumer protection laws regarding the fast-growing set of subprime mortgage companies was the Federal Trade Commission, an agency that was not at all equipped for such levels of activity" (Immergluck, 2009, p. 13). Unhampered by the kinds of restrictions imposed on depository institutions, mortgage companies have been allowed to operate on a more or less laissez-faire basis. Although they take very little risk in mortgage lending transactions, because they sell the loans they originate to Fannie Mae, Freddie Mac, or other investors, mortgage companies are responsible for the decision of whether to lend and on what terms. However, as discussed previously, we know that as early as the 1970s, and continuing to the 2000s, this responsibility often was neglected.

Third, by 1994 there were clear signals that financial derivatives, which were being issued by investment firms, needed much greater federal scrutiny. In an accurate foreshadowing of the mortgage crisis, a government General Accounting Office (GAO) report noted the lack of adequate requirements to ensure that derivatives dealers follow "good risk-management practices." Further, it highlighted the extreme concentration of derivative activity and that, if any one of these investors faced serious problems, the financial system as a whole could be threatened. It further warned that this situation could require federal intervention and involve "industry loans or a financial bailout paid for by taxpayers" (U.S. General Accounting Office, 1994, p. 7).

Although the GAO report called for firms dealing in derivatives to be regulated by the SEC, its recommendations were either never fully followed or poorly monitored. Opposing these types of recommendations, Alan Greenspan staunchly supported the derivatives market operating in an environment unfettered by government regulation.

Under pressure from the big investment banks, in 2004 the SEC changed a key rule that allowed these entities to assume significantly higher levels of debt, for every dollar of assets. This change freed up billions of dollars of reserves that could be put into new types of investments (Labaton, 2008). In doing this, the SEC allowed the firms to rely on their own computer models for determining the riskiness of investments.

The fourth and last key regulatory concern revolves around the extent to which the GSEs misinterpreted Congress' affordable housing goals. Under the Federal Housing Enterprises Financial Safety and Soundness Act of 1992, both Fannie Mae and Freddie Mac were obligated to target a certain percentage of their lending activity to very-low-, low-, and moderate-income households, as well as to buyers of homes located in census tracts with high levels of low-income and minority households. Thus, in an effort to counter well-documented discriminatory mortgage lending practices, during the 1990s and 2000s, the GSEs were encouraged to buy mortgages on homes purchased by low- and moderate-income people, even if their credit records were too weak for conventional loans.

Despite allegedly being alerted that Freddie Mac's underwriting standards had declined and that this was exposing the company to losses, the former chairman and CEO of Freddie Mac stated that: "we couldn't say no to anyone" (Duhigg, 2008a). Furthermore, as Fannie Mae was losing business to Wall Street firms, it came under increased pressure to lower its standards. A Fannie Mae senior executive allegedly stated: "Everybody understood that we were now buying loans that we would have previously rejected . . . But our mandate was to stay relevant and to serve low-income borrowers. So that's what we did" (Duhigg, 2008b).[1]

According to one observer, GSEs made "wrongheaded investments in loans that did not document income," but the GSEs also were successful in moderating the credit crunch and their investments in "low-income and low-wealth communities ha[ve] substantially improved the lives of hundreds of thousands of American families" (Stein, 2008). On balance, according to economist Paul Krugman (2008), Fannie Mae and Freddie Mac "aren't responsible for the mess we're in . . . [they] had nothing to do with the explosion of high-risk lending a few years ago."

Although the extent to which the GSEs may have misinterpreted congressional affordable housing goals and contributed to the mortgage crisis may be debatable, this discussion highlights a fundamental policy issue: how can the needs of low-income but creditworthy borrowers be combined with a disciplined approach to underwriting? This question was probably confronted more directly by the GSEs than by any other set of actors.

The mortgage system of the 2000s – part II: key actors and practices

Given the regulatory context and economic environment of the 2000s, private mortgage market actors were able to engage in a virtual "feeding frenzy." The overall story is one of aggressive lending and intricate investment schemes (all of which sought to maximize profits), with each entity carefully managing risk by shifting exposure from itself onto another, and with inadequate regulatory oversight. Thus, the contemporary mortgage finance system is characterized by lenders that have a great deal of responsibility when the loan is originated (whether or not they exercise it), but which carry virtually no risk once the loan is sold. A schematic overview of how the mortgage crisis came together can be seen in Figure 8.1. By necessity, many details have been omitted that are provided elsewhere (see, for example, Immergluck, 2009; Zandi, 2009).

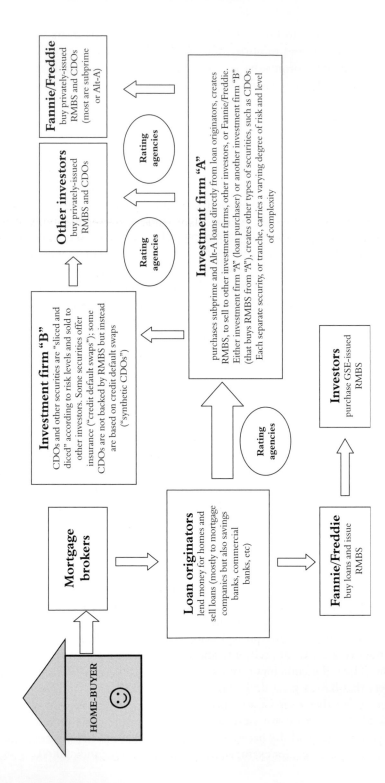

FIGURE 8.1 Schematic overview of the contemporary mortgage finance system.

Attractive loan terms and aggressive lending

With capital plentiful, lenders vigorously pursued potential borrowers, attracting them with low initial teaser interest rates and mortgages with very high loan-to-value ratios. Homes were often purchased with very low down-payments or even no down-payment at all. This meant that in a market downturn, such as the one that unfolded in 2007, homeowners had minimal equity to cushion price declines.

Adjustable or variable interest rate loans also made home purchases more feasible. Although there were often very low initial interest rates, these rates were scheduled to reset at some point in the future, generally one to three years from the time of mortgage origination. Many lenders assessed the ability of borrowers to pay the loan based on the initial interest rate only, not the interest rate on the reset mortgage. So long as incomes rose or home values were constant or going up, the owner could either cover the new debt payments or sell the home. But, as has become apparent, many owners could do neither.

With "subprime" loans, households may be approved for mortgages with weaker credit histories or income qualifications than typically would be permissible. At least some of the households who bought homes should never have been approved for loans in the first place, as they could not afford the mortgage payments over the short or the long term. The term "predatory lending" describes loans that are based on the value of the asset, with little consideration of whether the borrower is able to cover the debt. Subprime loans, whether predatory or not, also carry significant prepayment penalties. If a homeowner wants to sell or refinance their home during the period of restriction, one to three years or longer, thousands of dollars of prepayment fees may be added to the transaction, thereby reducing or eliminating any equity that may have accrued. Many homeowners may lapse into mortgage default and foreclosure, because of the financial disincentive associated with prepayment penalties (Quercia *et al.*, 2005). Similar to subprime loans are "Alt-A" loans, which typically were extended to people with good credit scores who did not provide proof of income or assets. Alt-A borrowers also experienced a high rate of default (Bajaj, 2008b).

Many mortgage lenders have blamed their aggressive lending on their interpretation of the federal Community Reinvestment Act (CRA), enacted in 1977. In an effort to counter long-standing patterns of discriminatory lending practices, the CRA requires banks to meet the credit needs of their local communities, with a particular emphasis on the needs of low-income areas and non-white borrowers. The "stick" for non-compliance is the ability of a federal regulatory agency to reject a bank's application to change some form of its operations, such as merging with another institution or opening or closing a branch.

Critics of CRA have argued that, with lenders seeking to comply with the law, they excessively loosened underwriting criteria. In short, affirmative-action policies trumped sound business practices (Jacoby, 2008). This argument notwithstanding, the great majority of poor lending decisions were made by mortgage companies, which were not subject to CRA. Those lenders failed to distinguish between shoddy loans that should not have been made, and those that were warranted based on the borrower's credit history, income, and value of the property. Indeed, one study found that banks covered by CRA were "substantially less likely than other lenders to make the kinds of risky home purchase loans that helped fuel the foreclosure crisis" (Traiger & Hinckley, 2008, p. 1).

Thus, blaming the CRA for the aggressive mortgage lending is a weak attempt to shift responsibility from those that should bear it – the lenders and investors. Pointing the finger at the federal government for excessive regulation in the form of CRA gets the story backwards: it was not too much regulation, it was too little.

Mortgage companies

Repeating the problems that arose in the 1970s, many mortgage originators, mostly mortgage companies, abandoned the basic responsibility of verifying borrower incomes, assets, and debt, and many loans were provided with no income documentation required (Stein, 2008). With virtually no risk once the mortgage was sold, many originators also explicitly falsified income data in order to help homeowners qualify for loans. At the same time, property inspections were sometimes inadequate, resulting in households assuming ownership without accurate information about the cost of repairs required.

Mortgage companies have been particularly interested in originating subprime loans, because of the profit potential upon the sale of the notes. Since the demand on Wall Street for higher-yielding subprime loans was so intense, "it encouraged subprime lenders to abandon reasonable qualifying standards, to forget about standard documentation requirements, and to ignore whether borrowers could actually afford the loan" (Stein, 2008, p. 17). Indeed, they often managed to get borrowers to accept less favorable terms (in terms of penalties, interest rates, etc.), even if they could qualify for a better loan. As of 2005, "30 percent of [subprime] loans [were] made by subsidiaries of banks and thrifts, less supervised than their parent company, and 50 percent [were] made by independent mortgage companies" (Joint Economic Committee, 2007, p. 17).

Mortgage brokers

Mortgage brokers often work in tandem with mortgage companies. Brokers serve an intermediary function: they work with homebuyers to gather the necessary paperwork and then place the loan with a lender. Although seemingly working in the buyer's interest they do not, in fact, have any explicit responsibility to do so. Playing a "particularly destructive role in the subprime market," loans originated through mortgage brokers typically end up costing the homeowner thousands of dollars more than loans originated directly through a lender (Stein, 2008, p. 19).

Because mortgage brokers receive a fee for their services from the mortgage lender once the loan has closed, they have a strong incentive to qualify as many borrowers as possible and to place a high volume of loans. In fact, they may even receive extra payments for brokering high-interest loans or ones that carry prepayment penalties. Mortgage brokers operate in a virtually risk-free environment as there are no financial implications for them whether or not loans succeed. In 2006, some 63 percent of the subprime loan originations and more than 29 percent of *all* mortgage originations were placed by mortgage brokers (Joint Economic Committee, 2007).

Securitization and the creation of derivative mortgage products

Mortgages were often packaged as RMBS by one of the GSEs, such as Fannie Mae or Freddie Mac; purchased by an investment firm; repackaged and sorted based on specific loan characteristics and assessments of risk levels; and resold to other investors as collateralized debt obligations (CDOs). RMBS provide an income stream to investors, which is generated from interest and principal payments generated from a pool of mortgages. The first RMBS were actually issued by Ginnie Mae in 1970 and represented the opening wedge of the securitization process. However, the early generation of RMBS tended to be relatively simple investment instruments.

Leading up to the mortgage crisis, many of the problematic RMBS had been issued by private investment firms (private label securities) and not by one of the federally supported secondary mortgage market entities. CDOs are securities based on other securities, such as RMBS. Bonds derived from these securities could be pooled, based on relative degrees of risk, providing varying yields. Each layer of the security or "tranche" represented a "unique combination of interest rates, term to maturity, rate of repayment of principal and risk" that could appeal to varying kinds of investors (Stone, 2006, p. 91). Some securities offered a special kind of insurance, known as "credit default swaps." Other CDOs were not backed by mortgages at all and could be based solely on credit default swaps and were known as "synthetic CDOs." Still other CDOs were based on other CDOs and known as "CDOs squared" (Schwartz, 2010).

High-level tranches, which would carry AAA investment ratings, could (completely miraculously) be created out of lower-level (meaning high-risk) assets of the original security. By creating new investment opportunities, "silk purses" could be made out of a much lower-valued asset, or a "sow's ear" (Immergluck, 2009, p. 96).

Rating agencies

Before an investor buys a block of mortgages, securities that are backed by mortgages, or any other derivative product, rating agencies assess the credit-worthiness of the asset backing the investment. This is an important step in the overall mortgage lending system, as federal regulatory agencies require banks, insurance companies, and pension managers to purchase only high-quality debt with the quality judged by rating agencies (Rosner, 2007). However, the rating agencies are neither passive nor disinterested parties in transactions involving the sale of mortgage securities: a great deal of their business during the 2000s was dependent on the ratings they gave these assets. Moreover, rating agencies are paid by the entities issuing the securities and "actively advise issuers of these securities on how to achieve their desired ratings" (Rosner, 2007). This created an incentive for rating agencies to provide as favorable ratings as possible in an effort to win contracts from major investment banks (Joint Economic Committee, 2008a). Furthermore, rating agencies gave the highest AAA rating to CDOs far more frequently than to other types of investments (Rosner, 2007). Thus, rating agencies occupy another level of risk shifting, with investors apparently having relegated too much authority to these agencies rather than carrying out their own analyses about the level of risk and creditworthiness of a given security (Forbes.com, 2007).

Investors

The ratings agencies were clearly culpable, but they were only middlemen. Fueling their activities were investors seeking the highest yielding investments. Although the front-line mortgage originators stood to gain a great deal by making loans, profits depended on a ready market for these mortgages. Hedge funds and other investors looking for high-yielding investments created an "all but insatiable demand" that had been "unmet as a result of low, long-term interest rates worldwide on traditional investment vehicles" (Mallach, 2008, p. 2). As long as housing prices continued to rise, "the underlying quality of the mortgages was of no particular interest to the investment firms. Bonuses depended on short-term revenue, which trumped any incentives to worry about what would happen if the market changed" (Stein, 2008, p. 19).

Credit default swaps

Many issuers of CDOs (such as the large Wall Street investment firms) sought to decrease the risk to investors further by purchasing a specialized type of insurance known as "credit default swaps," which covered about 15–20 percent of a given security. But by giving this insurance product a new name, rather than calling it what it was, "insurance," the normal regulatory structure governing insurance products was bypassed. American International Group (AIG), the largest insurer of this type of debt, amassed a credit default swap portfolio of some $527 billion, but ended up being unable to meet all of its obligations. This type of insurance created a further layer of risk shifting with yet another opportunity for lenders (albeit those that were far removed from originating the mortgages) to create the illusion of a secure debt instrument (Goldstein, 2008). And, as noted above, new "synthetic CDOs" could be issued based on assets carrying credit default swaps.

Thus, the mortgage crisis evolved from a set of complex institutional relationships and rather bizarre, manufactured financial instruments (which were often not based on real assessments of risk) that were intertwined and difficult to trace. At the same time, federal oversight of this new world of finance was virtually absent.

The role of homebuyers

Of course, the actions of private mortgage lending and investment communities would not have been problematic without willing buyers. Many people who bought or refinanced homes in the early 2000s, particularly those who received subprime loans, were ill prepared for the responsibilities of home ownership and/or they assumed their new debts with a limited understanding of their legal obligations. These problems should have been prevented by proper enforcement of the Home Ownership and Equity Protection Act of 1994, which directed lenders to disclose the details of financial products as a way to protect consumers. Nevertheless:

> HOEPA did little to actually proscribe abusive or unsound lending practices for the vast majority of mortgages – even the majority of high-risk or high-cost mortgages – because it only had any real teeth for loans priced over very high fee and rate thresholds.
>
> (Immergluck, 2009, p. 11)

In addition to HOEPA, borrowers can become more informed by participating in a home ownership/mortgage finance counseling program. However, participation in such programs has not been a prerequisite for loan approval (Hirad and Zorn, 2002). With little knowledge about the home-buying process, and with the widespread availability of mortgage products with low down payments and interest rates, many people jumped at the opportunity to become homeowners. To make matters worse, many homeowners were not truthful about their income or assets. A review of 100 loans found that 90 percent of borrowers had overstated their incomes by 5 percent or more. In almost 60 percent of cases, borrowers inflated their incomes by more than half (Morgenson, 2007a).

But how did so many people come to believe that they could manage the challenges of home ownership with, perhaps, minimal savings and an unstable or low-paying job? By the late twentieth century, there was a huge shift from the basic fiscal conservatism of the U.S. population. Debt was being assumed at record levels for at least two reasons. People generally believed in a robust future, with house prices continuing to rise, and home refinancing offered a mechanism to raise needed cash. As housing prices rose much more steeply than incomes through the 1980s and 1990s, it became virtually impossible to close the gap. More and more families had to borrow money to cover the basic necessities of living and many were trying to stabilize their housing costs through home ownership (as opposed to fast-increasing rental costs), or by borrowing against the equity in their homes. Whatever the explanation for why families took on more debt than they could manage, it is clear that the events leading up to the mortgage crisis fueled and reinforced the sense that assuming an unaffordable mortgage was, perhaps, a good bet.

Borrowers in default, redux

One of the most vexing aspects of the mortgage finance system is that, for a borrower in default, locating the lender with a stake in the loan, working out a forbearance agreement, and setting up a new payment schedule often have become an extremely difficult set of tasks (as noted above, this was first observed in the 1970s). Mortgage servicers often cannot advise a defaulting homeowner whom they should contact to work out a new payment arrangement. For example, "because of the way mortgages are packaged into pools and sold to investors, it is still not clear who owns the faltering loans" (Morgenson, 2007b). The agreements governing securities may limit the number or percent of loans in any given pool of mortgages that can be modified, or they may state that "any modifications to loans in or near default should be in the best interests of those who hold the securities" (Morgenson, 2007c) – clearly a situation that runs exactly counter to the needs of distressed borrowers.

Loan modifications can be very helpful in assisting defaulting homeowners keep their homes, if done properly (e.g. fundamentally changing the terms of the loan by reducing the amount of principal owed or significantly lowering the interest rate) (Cutts and Green, 2004). Recognizing the importance of providing creative mechanisms for assisting homeowners in default, some lenders have extended forbearance, with positive results. By altering repayment schedules, rather than initiating foreclosure, lenders have been able to repossess homes less often (Leonhardt, 2002). However, from the perspective of investors, loan modifications may not always be financially beneficial (Adelino *et al.*, 2009).

Beyond the issue of whether or not lenders provide opportunities for defaulting borrowers to renegotiate their loans, it is clear that the numerous actors involved in the contemporary mortgage finance system, and the complexity of the financial instruments developed, created an unstable system in which risk was shifted from one entity to another. Layers of transactions, complex financial derivatives, and computer models that obscured the underlying risk were critical components behind the mortgage crisis.

The mortgage system unravels and the government responds

Many observers have noted that they had no warning that a mortgage crisis was looming or that it would create such chaos in the United States and global economies (Frank, 2007; Ryan, 2007). Nevertheless, as discussed above, a government report written in 1994 predicted the precariousness of the institutions and arrangements that were being devised (U.S. General Accounting Office, 2008).[2]

Whether anticipated or not, defaults and foreclosures on subprime as well as conventional loans started to mount. Homebuyers had little equity in their homes, the economy was spiraling down, and the "housing bubble" burst. As foreclosures increased, investors were required to mark down the value of various investment vehicles – the assets whose ultimate value rested on the subprime and conventional mortgage loans. With the balance sheets of these investors weakening, it became difficult or impossible for these entities to raise additional credit on the capital markets, both to cover the widening asset-capital spread and to raise new funds. At the same time, investors in subprime loans began to disappear and mortgage companies and other originators were unable to sell already negotiated loans, thereby making these entities financially vulnerable. Meanwhile, Fannie Mae and Freddie Mac, although not major investors in subprime mortgages, started to experience defaults throughout their portfolios and also encountered difficulty raising funds on the capital markets. This reduced the pass-through payments on RMBS and, ultimately, on derivative products such as CDOs. Concurrently, issuers of privately issued CDOs (investment firms) and insurers of derivative products began to receive claims on defaulting assets, which they were unable to cover with their own reserves or borrowed funds (Morgenson, 2008).

Banks became wary of lending to anyone, including other banks, with investors scared about the quality of mortgages (and other assets) backing up new loans. Credit dried up and the markets began to shut down. Meanwhile, businesses started to contract and unemployment skyrocketed, further exacerbating the problems faced by millions of homeowners.

The U.S. government attempted to reverse the decline through various initiatives. The HOPE for Homeowners program, contained within the massive Housing and Economic Recovery Act of 2008, and revised in 2009, provides a mechanism for lenders to voluntarily modify the principal of defaulting mortgages using FHA insurance. In addition, the Federal Reserve Board issued new rules to protect consumers from unfair or deceptive mortgage lending practices (Ben Bernanke, quoted in Board of Governors of the Federal Reserve System, 2008).

The major bailout bill, formally known as the Emergency Economic Stabilization Act of 2008, authorized $700 billion for the federal government to purchase distressed assets from financial institutions, thereby providing investors and the credit markets with renewed confidence in the financial system (the Troubled Asset Relief Program, or TARP). So-called "toxic investments" were based on the underlying defaulting or likely-to-default mortgages, many of which had been sold and then recollateralized.

In the last months of the Bush administration and in the midst of a growing financial crisis, numerous proposals were made to more aggressively assist homeowners in distress, as opposed to indirectly pumping money into financial institutions and the credit markets. Less than one month after President Obama took office, in February 2009, two foreclosure mitigation initiatives were launched under an umbrella program known as Making Home Affordable. The Home Refinancing Program (HARP) assists homeowners who are not in default and whose loans are owned by Fannie Mae or Freddie Mac to refinance their mortgages, thereby making them more affordable. Although no federal funds are used in this initiative, the Home Affordable Modification Program (HAMP) was targeted to receive $75 billion to facilitate the modification of delinquent mortgages.[3]

In September 2008, with Fannie Mae and Freddie Mac experiencing huge losses, the U.S. Treasury activated measures, authorized by the Housing and Economic Recovery Act, to provide a line of credit to Fannie Mae and Freddie Mac, enabling them to maintain liquidity and continue operating. Shortly thereafter, they were placed under federal control. Also that month, in recognition of AIG's pivotal role in the economy, the government orchestrated a bailout of AIG in the form of an $85 billion federal loan, with the government acquiring about an 80 percent share of the company. That September, Lehman Brothers filed for bankruptcy, following the demise of another prominent investment bank, Bear Stearns, just six months earlier.

As the chaos surrounding the mortgage crisis has continued to unfold, it has become clear that, in addition to the broad-scale economic implications and outcomes, many of the long-standing social goals associated with home ownership have been undermined (see Bratt, Chapter 7).

Reinstituting risk and responsibility in mortgage finance

The early reports on the extent to which the government's interventions to assist homeowners in default were disappointing; there was little expectation that the HARP and HAMP programs would substantially reduce the rate of foreclosures (Congressional Oversight Panel, 2009, pp. 62–63). In view of mounting foreclosures, proposals have been made to provide additional assistance. For homeowners who owe more than their homes are worth – an estimated 11 million U.S. mortgaged homeowners (Streitfeld, 2010) – simply lowering monthly payments does not eliminate the risk of default, as there is no equity cushion to fall back on.

In March 2010 the Obama administration launched a new initiative, which, among other provisions, encouraged lenders to reduce the principal balance of the loan for owners in default or whose homes are worth less than their mortgages. While lenders are likely to be resistant to this approach, some non-defaulting homeowners also oppose leniency as they have worked hard to stay current with their payments. In short, "if the lunch truly is free, the demand for free lunches will be large" (Streifeld, 2008).

Regardless of how successfully the various emergency initiatives will address the problems, it is important to try to understand the "big picture" in the hope that future crises will be averted. At the outset, it should be underscored that U.S. federal housing policy should be less focused on home ownership and rec-ognize that it is not, by any means, desired or appropriate for everyone. Rental housing, in particular, is a desirable form of tenure which fully meets the needs of many households. A renewed rental housing agenda is part of HUD's mis-sion under the Obama administration.

Risk and responsibility need to be reintroduced into the mortgage finance system and additional regulatory interventions are required. In the United States' existing mortgage finance system, the two sides that carry the risk may be ill prepared for this responsibility (especially in the case of many homeown-ers) or are cushioned by layers of investors and intermediaries (as with the lenders). At the same time, mortgage brokers and originators assume little or no risk and, although their role on the front-line of mortgage transactions would suggest that they should carry out their tasks with a sense of responsibility, they often fail to do so. The financial incentives for aggressive and even irresponsible lending have been substantial, while disincentives have been largely absent. It is necessary to recreate a mortgage lending system in which both borrowers and lenders also assume responsibility.[4]

To help would-be borrowers navigate the complexities of the home owner-ship experience, and understand their risk and responsibility, a support system needs to be put into place. The experiences with the Section 235 program of the late 1960s and early 1970s, as well as the problems that unfolded during the 2007–8 mortgage crisis, demonstrate that home ownership initiatives aimed either at low-income households or at households with poor credit histories must pay careful attention to the many possibilities for private market actors to take advantage of these generally inexperienced or vulnerable homebuyers. Non-profit organizations, in particular, have a critical role to play by providing counseling services before the mortgage is executed (Werwath, 1997; DiPetta et al., 2001; Rohe et al., 2002). Post-purchase counseling, which includes informa-tion on home maintenance, impacts of market changes, and mechanisms to avoid foreclosure, is also extremely important.

Beyond making sure that homebuyers understand the full set of responsibili-ties being assumed, homebuyers should also shoulder some measure of risk by having a financial or personal investment. For example, in low-income home ownership programs operated by the non-profit organizations Habitat for Humanity and Nehemiah, this issue is addressed head on. Nehemiah homeown-ers often make an initial investment of several thousand dollars and, although

Habitat homeowners may have a more limited financial investment, they are required to invest a significant amount of their time through "sweat equity" (Bratt, 2007). Whether investing time or money, or both, these and similar efforts promote a sense of responsibility on the part of the homeowner, and the outcomes, in terms of lowered foreclosure rates, are compelling (McGhee, 2008; Hagerty and Simon, 2009; National Community Land Trust Network, 2009).

To the extent that FHA insurance is involved in mortgage transactions, or if any other government-sponsored programs are being utilized, it is important for a revitalized HUD to accept its role as risk-taker and to play a much stronger role in protecting homeowners. In contrast, as the mortgage crisis unfolded, HUD was almost completely absent in helping to resolve the problems facing lower-income homeowners. As the nation's lead housing agency, the Obama administration's HUD is fully engaged in this agenda and, hopefully, will be able to play a significant and positive role.

The mortgage crisis has also demonstrated that lenders must be responsible for ascertaining the ability of borrowers to carry the loan payments. It is startling that a recommendation of the U.S. Congress' Joint Economic Committee (2007) contained the following self-apparent and common-sense statement:

> At a minimum, the federal government should require lenders to determine that the borrower has the ability to repay a loan at the fully-indexed rate[5] and assume fully amortized payments . . . Policymakers should also require lenders to verify a borrower's income using tax documents or other reasonable documentation.
>
> (p. 25)

At the same time, it is critical that lenders carry some level of risk and a mechanism is needed whereby all actors in the mortgage lending system are held accountable for the decisions they make. This would prevent "moral hazards," in which "individuals or organizations engage in riskier behavior, than they otherwise would, because of a tacit assumption that someone else will bear part or all of the costs and consequences if the incurred risk turns out badly" (Wolf, 2002, p. 19). Moral hazards have been rampant in recent years, as the risk associated with irresponsible lending and investment decisions was shifted to other entities. If insurance against risk is to be reintroduced into the financial marketplace, the problem of how to minimize negative repercussions must be addressed.

The mortgage crisis revealed a basic dilemma concerning home ownership programs. On the one hand, there is a desire to make the loan terms attractive and to set credit limits low enough to qualify as many households as possible. On the other, it is essential that lenders make realistic credit assessments to prevent households from purchasing when they are unlikely to do so successfully. The Section 235 program, nearly 40 years ago, should have taught us that inadequate credit checks and income verifications will result in approving people for loans who are ill-equipped financially for home ownership. Even worse, in the years preceding the mortgage crisis we knew that mortgage originators purposely overstated the incomes and assets of potential borrowers, responding to the incentives to make loans, and to move the "paper" through the financial system. To remove the potential for originators to perform either lax or intentionally false underwriting, new procedures and greater regulatory oversight are needed. This would ensure that all actors involved in underwriting a loan are assuming both the responsibility, and a degree of risk.[6]

First, there needs to be a much greater degree of regulation of all of the various actors who are involved with mortgage lending decisions – mortgage brokers, all types of mortgage companies, and rating agencies. All must be held accountable for responsible lending behavior. Although some states have regulations pertaining to these entities, and others have "tried to apply federal predatory lending advisories to all lenders or regulate brokers or lenders in their state . . . the resources that states have for oversight are far fewer than those of the federal government" (Joint Economic Committee, 2007, p. 18). The Housing and Economic Recovery Act of 2008 takes a step in this direction by including provisions requiring some regulatory control over mortgage companies, including new licensing requirements.

Second, the entire regulatory structure through which mortgage-backed securities are sold needs to be thoroughly reviewed and revamped. As part of this restructuring, much more transparency in the system is required. Not only will this make the task of regulation much easier, but also it is critical from the homeowner's standpoint. At the very least, each mortgage document must be traceable from origination to the final investor; the borrower should know, at all times, whom to contact if payment difficulties arise and if there is a need to request a renegotiation of the terms of the loan. In addition, the documents governing all transactions related to any future sales of the mortgage paper must allow for this type of renegotiation. In short:

> the banking system should be restored to its basic role of supplying credit to the real economy, with as few complications as possible. We need a system in which banks accept savings and make loans; where investment banks underwrite securities such as ordinary stocks and bonds; and where the complexity of bonds is strictly limited.
>
> (Kuttner, 2008)

Or, as Treasury Secretary Timothy Geithner succinctly stated: "We need a much simpler financial oversight structure" (Labaton and Calmes, 2009). Although such a system may be hard to imagine, the goal of greater transparency must be embraced, even if securitization of mortgage instruments continues to be a part of a re-structured mortgage finance system.

Third, whatever form Fannie Mae and Freddie Mac take in the future, as owners or backers of about half of the mortgage debt in the country, much

closer regulatory oversight will be required. Presumably, there will be a continued focus on monitoring these entities' housing goals, with particular attention
to interest rates charged to minority borrowers and to developing loan products
and flexible underwriting to facilitate secondary mortgage market purchases for
loans originated in underserved areas.

Over the long term we may see the development of a new mortgage and
home ownership system that puts homebuyer needs in the forefront of the lending decision. However, in the short term, we will continue to witness large
numbers of households losing their homes and *their* "American Dream" severely
interrupted, if not totally abandoned.

Acknowledgments

Thanks to Dan Immergluck, James Jennings, Langley Keyes, and Alex Schwartz
for offering many helpful comments, as well as to the editors of this book,
Richard Ronald and Marja Elsinga.

References

Adelino, M., Gerardi, K. and Willen, P.S. (2009) Why don't lenders renegotiate more
    home mortgages? Redefaults, self-cures, and securitization, Public Policy Discussion
    Paper No. 09–4, Federal Reserve Bank of Boston. Online. Available at http://www.
    bos.frb.org/economic/ppdp/2009/ppdp0904.pdf (accessed 7 July 2009).
Associated Press. (2007) Freddie Mac settles accounting-fraud charges, 28 September.
    Online. Available at http://www.msnbc.msn.com/id/21027918/#story (accessed 19
    September 2008).
Associated Press. (2008) Freddie Mac paid $2m to thwart regulation, *Boston Globe*, 20
    October. Online. Available at http://www.boston.com/business/articles/2008/10/20/
    freddie_mac_paid_2m_to_thwart_regulation/ (accessed 25 October 2008).
Bacheller, J.H., Jr (1971) *Competition in Real Estate and Mortgage Lending, Hearings Before
    the Subcommittee on Antitrust and Monopoly of the Committee on the Judiciary*, U.S. Senate,
    92nd Congress, 2nd Session, September.
Bajaj, V. (2008a) Fannie Mae won't face U.S. charges over its books, *New York
    Times*, 25 August. Online. Available at http://www.nytimes.com/2006/08/25/
    business/25fannie.html?_r=1&pagewanted=print&oref=slogin   (accessed   19
    September 2008).
Bajaj, V. (2008b) Housing lenders fear bigger wave of loan defaults, *New York Times*, 4
    August. Online. Available at http://www.nytimes.com/2008/08/04/business/04lend.
    html (accessed 3 September 2008).
Board of Governors of the Federal Reserve System. (2008) Press release, 14 July. Online.
    Available at http://www.federalreserve.gov/newsevents/press/bcreg/20080714a.htm
    (accessed 25 October 2008).
Bratt, R.G. (1976) *Federal Home Ownership Policy and Home Finance: A Study of Program
    Operations and Impacts on the Consumer*, PhD thesis, Massachusetts Institute of
    Technology.
Bratt, R.G. (2007) Housing for low-income households: a comparison of the Section
    235, Nehemiah and Habitat for Humanity Programs, in W.M. Rohe and H.L. Watson

(eds) *Chasing the American Dream: New Perspectives on Affordable Home Ownership*, Ithaca, NY: Cornell University Press.

Congressional Oversight Panel. (2009) *Taking Stock: What Has the Trouble Asset Relief Program Achieved?* Washington, DC: Government Printing Office.

Cutts, A.C. and Green, R.K. (2004) *Innovative Servicing Technology: Smart Enough to Keep People in Their Houses?*, Freddie Mae Working Paper #04–03, p. 21. McLean, VA: Freddie Mac.

DiPetta, A., Flanagan, E., Hamer, M., Schubert, M. and Tresher, A. (2001) *Winning Strategies: Best Practices in the Work of Home-Ownership Promotion*, Washington, DC: Neighborhood Reinvestment Corporation.

Duhigg, C. (2008a) At Freddie Mac, chief discarded warning signs, *New York Times*, 5 August. Online. Available at http://www.nytimes.com/2008/08/05/business/05freddie.html?hp (accessed 3 September 2008).

Duhigg, C. (2008b) Pressured to take more risk, Fannie reached tipping point, *New York Times*, 5 October. Online. Available at http://www.nytimes.com/2008/10/05/business/05fannie.html (accessed 21 October 2008).

Federal National Mortgage Association (2003) Monthly summary of delinquent mortgages, *Delinquency Reporting System*, 2 March, Washington, DC.

Forbes.com. (2007) Credit crisis hurts rating agencies. Online. Available at http://www.forbes.com/2007/08/13/credit-rating-crisis-oxford_0814oxfordanalytica_print.html (accessed 29 August 2008).

Frank, B. (2007) Lessons of the subprime crisis, *Boston Globe*, 14 September. Online. Available at http://www.boston.com/news/globe/editorial_opinion/oped/articles/2007/09/14/lessons_of_the_subprime_crisis/ (accessed 27 October 2008).

Goldstein, M. (2008) Merrill's AIG problem, *BusinessWeek*, 16 September. Online. Available at http://www.businessweek.com/investing/insights/blog/archives/2008/09/merrills_aig_pr.html (accessed 27 October 2008).

Hagerty, J.R. and Simon, R. (2009) Activist financier 'terrorizes' bankers in foreclosure fight, *The Wall Street Journal*, 20 May. Online. Available at http://online.wsj.com/article/SB124276441945635993.html (accessed 10 July 2009).

Hirad A. and Zorn, P. (2002) Prepurchase home ownership counseling: a little knowledge is a good thing, in N.P. Retsinas and E.S. Belsky (eds) *Low-Income Home Ownership: Examining the Unexamined Goal*, Cambridge, MA: Joint Center for Housing Studies and Brookings Institution Press.

HUD. See U.S. Department of Housing and Urban Development.

Immergluck, D. (2009) *Foreclosed! High-Risk Lending, Deregulation, and the Undermining of America's Mortgage Market*, Ithaca, NY: Cornell University Press.

Jacoby, J. (2008) Frank's fingerprints are all over the financial fiasco, *Boston Globe*, 28 September. Online. Available at http://www.boston.com/bostonglobe/editorial_opinion/oped/articles/2008/09/28/franks_fingerprints_are_all_over_the_financial_fiasco/ (accessed 30 September 2008).

Joint Economic Committee. (2007) *The Subprime Lending Crisis: The Economic Impact on Wealth, Property Values and Tax Revenues, and How We Got Here*. Report and Recommendations of the Majority Staff, U.S. Congress. Washington, DC: U.S. Congress.

Joint Economic Committee. (2008a) *The U.S. Housing Bubble and the Global Financial Crisis: Vulnerabilities of the Alternative Finance System*, Research Report #110–23, June 25, U.S. Congress. Washington, DC: U.S. Congress.

Joint Economic Committee. (2008b) *The U.S. Housing Bubble and the Global Financial Crisis: Housing and Housing-Related Finance*, U.S. Congress. Washington, DC: U.S. Congress.

Krugman, P. (2008) Fannie, Freddie and you, *New York Times*, 14 July. Online. Available at http://www.nytimes.com/2008/07/14/opinion/14krugman.html (accessed 22 October 2008).

Kuttner, R. (2008) Back-to-basics banking, *Boston Globe*, 11 October. Online. Available at http://www.boston.com/bostonglobe/editorial_opinion/oped/articles/2008/10/11/back_to_basics_banking/ (accessed 13 October 2008).

Labaton, S. (2008) Agency's '04 rule let banks pile up new debt, and risk, *New York Times*, 3 October. Online. Available at http://www.nytimes.com/2008/10/03/business/03sec.html (accessed 3 October 2008).

Labaton, S. and Calmes, J. (2009) Obama proposes a first overhaul of finance rules, *New York Times*, 14 May. Online. Available at http://www.nytimes.com/2009/05/14/business/14regs.html (accessed 11 July 2009).

Leonhardt, D. (2002) Lenders trying an alternative to foreclosure, *New York Times*, 4 May. Online. Available at http://query.nytimes.com/gst/fullpage.html?res=9C04EEDE1E31F937A35756C0A9649C8B63 (accessed 20 September 2008).

McGhee, T. (2008) Habitat succeeds as others sink, *Denver Post*. Online. Available at http://www.denverpost.com/ci_10910104?source=rss (accessed 26 June 2009).

Mallach, A. (2008) *Tackling the Mortgage Crisis: 10 Action Steps for State Government*, Washington, DC: Brookings Institute.

Morgenson, G. (2007a) Crisis looms in market for mortgages, *New York Times*, 11 March. Online. Available at http://www.nytimes.com/2007/03/11/business/11mortgage.html (accessed 20 September 2008).

Morgenson, G. (2007b) Mortgages' mystery: the losses, *New York Times*, 22 April. Online. Available at http://select.nytimes.com/2007/04/22/business/yourmoney/22gret.html?_r=1&oref=slogin (accessed 20 September 2008).

Morgenson, G. (2007c) Mortgage maze may increase foreclosures, *New York Times*, 6 August. Online. Available at http://www.nytimes.com/2007/08/06/business/06home.html (accessed 20 September 2008).

Morgenson, G. (2008) Behind insurer's crisis, blind eye to web of risk, *New York Times*, 28 September. Online. Available at http://www.nytimes.com/2008/09/28/business/28melt.html?partner=rssnyt&emc=rss (accessed 28 September 2008).

National Community Land Trust Network. (2009) Annual mortgage foreclosure survey shows community land trusts continues to beat the market, press release, 6 March.

New York Times. (2008) Global markets react to bank woes. Online. Available at http://www.nytimes.com/slideshow/2008/09/15/us/0915-MARKETS_index.html (accessed 20 September 2008).

Quercia, R.G., Stegman, M.A. and Davis, W.R. (2005) *The Impact of Predatory Loan Terms on Subprime Foreclosures: The Special Case of Prepayment Penalties and Balloon Payments*, Chapel Hill: Center for Community Capitalism, University of North Carolina.

Rampell, C. (2010) Lax oversight caused crisis, Bernanke says, *New York Times*, 3 January. Online. Available at http://www.nytimes.com/2010/01/04/business/economy/04fed.html (accessed 3 January 2010).

The Report of the President's Commission on Housing. (1982) Washington, DC: President's Commision on Housing.

Rohe, W.M., Quercia, R.G. and Van Zandt, S. (2002) *Supporting the American Dream of Home Ownership: An Assessment of Neighborhood Reinvestment's Home Ownership Pilot Program*, Chapel Hill: Center for Urban and Regional Studies, University of North Carolina.

Rosner, J. (2007) Stopping the subprime crisis, *New York Times*, 25 July. Online. Available at http://www.nytimes.com/2007/07/25/opinion/25rosner.html (accessed 27 October 2008).

Ryan, P. (2007) Subprime crisis hits alarming level, *ABC News* (Australia), 25 July. Online. Available at http://www.abc.net.au/news/stories/2007/07/25/1988319.htm (accessed 27 October 2008).

Scannell, K. and Reddy, S. (2008) Greenspan admits errors to hostile house panel, *The Wall Street Journal*, 24 October. Online. Available at http://sbk.online.wsj.com/article/SB122476545437862295.html (accessed 25 October 2008).

Schwartz, A.F. (2010) *Housing Policy in the United States: An Introduction* (2nd edn), New York: Routledge.

Stein, E. (2008) *Turmoil in the U.S. Credit Markets: The Genesis of the Current Economic Crisis*, Testimony of Eric Stein, Center for Responsible Lending before the U.S. Senate Committee on Banking, Housing and Urban Affairs, 16 October.

Stone, M.E. (1986) Housing and dynamics of U.S. capitalism, in R.G. Bratt, C. Hartman and A. Meyerson (eds) *Critical Perspectives on Housing*, Philadelphia: Temple University Press.

Stone, M.E. (2006) Pernicious problems of housing finance, in R.G. Bratt, M.E. Stone and C. Hartman (eds) *A Right to Housing: Foundation for a New Social Agenda*. Philadelphia: Temple University Press.

Streitfeld, D. (2008) Mortgage plan may irk those it doesn't help, *New York Times*, 31 October. Online. Available at http://www.nytimes.com/2008/10/31/business/31bailout.html?_r=1&hp=&oref=slogin&pagewanted=print (accessed 31 October 2008).

Streitfeld, D. (2010) A bold U.S. plan to help struggling homeowners, *New York Times*, 26 March. Online. Available at http://www.nytimes.com/2010/03/27/business/27modify.html (accessed 3 April 2010).

Traiger & Hinckley (2008) *The Community Reinvestment Act: A Welcome Anomaly in the Foreclosure Crisis*, 7 January, Washington, DC: Traigler & Hinckley LLP.

U.S. Department of Housing and Urban Development. (1973a) *Statistical Yearbook*, Place: Publisher.

U.S. Department of Housing and Urban Development. (1973b) *Office of Inspector General, Office of Audit. Report on Internal Audit of HUD Single Family Appraisal/Inspection Procedures and Mortgagees' Loan Processing Activities*, 05–2–4001–0000, 14 September. Washington, DC: HUD.

U.S. Department of Housing and Urban Development. (1996) *Providing Alternatives to Mortgage Foreclosure: A Report to Congress*, March, Washington, DC: HUD, p. 71.

U.S. General Accounting Office. (1994) *Financial Derivatives: Actions Needed to Protect the Financial System*, GGD-94–133, 18 May, Washington, DC: General Accouting Office.

U.S. House of Representatives. (1972) *Defaults on FHA-Insured Home Mortgages – Detroit, Mich.* Fifteenth Report by the Committee on Government Operations, 20 June. Washington, DC: House of Representatives.

Werwath, P. (1997) Helping families build assets, *Cost Cuts*, 14(1), March, the Enterprise Foundation.

Wolf, C., Jr (2002) *Straddling Economics and Politics: Cross-Cutting Issues in Asia, the United States, and the Global Economy*, Santa Monica, CA: RAND.

Zandi, M. 2009. *Financial Shock: Global Panic and Government Bailouts – How We Got Here and What Must Be Done to Fix It*. Upper Saddle River, NJ: FT Press.

Part III

Housing ladders and fading dreams

9

THE SHIFTING HOUSING OPPORTUNITIES OF YOUNGER PEOPLE IN JAPAN'S HOME-OWNING SOCIETY

Yosuke Hirayama

Introduction

A normative and pervasive life-course pattern has been embedded in the development of Japan's post-war homeowner society. In the past, many middle-class families have successively ascended the housing ladder, thus attaining home ownership (Hirayama, 2007). The private ownership of housing has provided a material basis for securing homes and accumulating assets, but has also been a key symbolic marker of membership in mainstream society. Since the middle of the 1990s, however, it has become increasingly difficult for younger generations to acquire a foothold on the rungs of the property ladder (Forrest and Hirayama, 2009; Hirayama, 2010; Hirayama and Ronald, 2008). The notable decrease in the number of young people following conventional life courses and housing careers has implied that the traditional organization of Japan's home-owning society is unravelling.

This chapter explores a decline in housing opportunities for young people in Japan. The focus is on the differentiation of housing trajectories between 'parental home dwellers', 'single people' and 'family-formers'. In this chapter, 'parental home dwellers' are defined as unmarried individuals living in their parents' home in which their parent is the head (main earner) of the household; 'single people' are defined as unmarried individuals who form one-person households; and 'family-formers' are defined as married individuals establishing their own independent households who are either the head of their household or the spouses of the head. Family-formers have, typically, climbed up the housing ladder towards home ownership relatively smoothly, but they have been on the decrease. Increasing numbers of parental home dwellers and single people have been living outside the housing ladder system. This chapter highlights the differentiation in young people's housing experiences that has facilitated transformations in Japan's homeowner society. Empirical evidence illustrating this differentiation is drawn from recalculations of micro data from the 2003 Housing and Land Survey as well as various other aggregate data sets.

Japan has long been experiencing an unstable economy, affecting young people's housing opportunities. The collapse of the bubble economy at the beginning of the 1990s marked a turning point and Japan entered a notably prolonged period of recession. Although the economy eventually began to recover in 2002, household economies did not improve. Moreover, Japan again entered a severe recession in 2008 with the onset of the global financial crisis triggered by the U.S. subprime mortgage meltdown. Since the early 1990s, increasing economic insecurity has provoked further generational fractures with regard to housing conditions.

However, it was not only economic stagnation but also changes in public policy practices related to family formation, employment protection and housing provision that encouraged realignment in young people's housing trajectories. In post-war Japan, the conservative nature of public policy has been maintained in the sense that it has continuously advantaged middle-class family households who purchase their own home and follow conventional life courses. With the global diffusion of neo-liberalism, however, since the middle of the 1990s the Japanese government has reoriented policy towards accentuating the role of the market in providing employment and housing. Public policy arrangements have thus become characterized by a combination of conservative and neo-liberal approaches (Hirayama, 2010). Young family-formers have been protected by conservative policy in accessing the owner-occupied housing sector. On the other hand, unmarried individuals, that is, parental home dwellers and single people who are neither the target of, nor protected by, conservative family-oriented policies, have been particularly affected by the implementation of neo-liberal policies, and found themselves excluded from the residential property ladder system.

This chapter demonstrates the important role played by public policy practices in reshaping young people's housing pathways. Japan constitutes one of the most mature home-owning societies among industrial and post-industrial societies. However, it has more recently been undergoing radical changes in the circumstances of home ownership (Hirayama and Ronald, 2007). As the expansion of the owner-occupied sector has been sustained in various countries, along with increasing attention focused on the varied social outcomes of home ownership systems (Doling and Ford, 2003; Forrest and Murie, 1995; Groves *et al.*, 2007; Ronald, 2008), generational differences have appeared as central variables that have differentiated housing situations (Forrest and Hirayama, 2009; Forrest and Lee, 2004; Hirayama, 2010; Hirayama and Ronald, 2008; Kurz and Blossfeld, 2004; Yip *et al.*, 2007). Japan is a mature but dynamic home-owning society in which the generation-based differentiation in housing opportunities can clearly be observed. Insights into the Japanese experience can thus more generally contribute to the understanding of new phases in the development of homeowner societies. This chapter begins by providing a framework to explain the way in which public policy has impacted on housing opportunities for younger generations. It then moves on to look at changes in young people's establishment of households to highlight the decrease in family-formers and the counter increase in parental home dwellers and single people. Finally, the chapter explores the fragmentation of housing trajectories among young individuals.

Policy developments and younger generations

The dual nature of public policy, which reflects both conservative and neo-liberal characteristics, is a key factor that has accounted for transformations in young people's housing opportunities. In post-war Japanese homeowner society, public policy has explicitly been conservative, focusing on maintaining conventional life-course patterns, in which middle-class families have benefited from advantageous positions in accessing home ownership. At the same time, with the growing influence of neo-liberalism, the government has begun to seek market solutions to addressing housing and social issues. It would be misleading to consider that neo-liberal policies are completely replacing conservative policies; the rise of neo-liberal policy has become more apparent while conservative policy has been deeply embedded in Japan's post-war society. This section investigates the organization of public policy measures, which has come to define young people's housing conditions.

Family policy

A particular set of policy measures, which constitutes the category of family policy, has promoted the establishment of conventional households, reflecting the conservative course of Japanese public policy. This has been intertwined with the development of the homeowner society. Nuclear family households that are at an advantage in terms of various family policy-related benefits have acquired firm footholds on the housing ladder to access home ownership. The close link between establishing a family and acquiring an owner-occupied home has been a central element in shaping the home-owning society. This in turn means that non-conventional households are at an apparent disadvantage in climbing up the ladder towards entering the owner-occupied housing sector.

Public policy in Japan has relied on families as welfare providers with the development of the 'male breadwinner family' model (Yokoyama, 2002). This has been assumed to be effective as a substitute for the minimal expansion of public welfare provision. In the Japanese labour market, the status of women has been much lower than that of men in terms of stable employment, promotion opportunities and remuneration. Marriage has thus been almost the only means for many women to obtain economic security. Tax and social security systems, which have been the main government interventions to facilitate the establishment of families, have prioritized the protection of conventional households. Married women who earn less than 1,300,000 yen (€10,000 [€1 = 130 yen,

April 2009]) are provided with an entitlement to a basic pension without having to make contributions while those whose incomes are 1,030,000 yen (€7,923) or less assist their husbands in qualifying for income tax deductions. This has effectively advantaged those who are married and has led many women to maintain the status of dependent wives to maximize their economic benefits (Nagase and Murao, 2005).

Japanese society has been referred to as a 'company society' in which the corporate sector has played a significant role in providing welfare based on a model of the 'company as a family' (Fujita and Shionoya, 1997). The government has also encouraged, in parallel with support of standard families, the provision of corporate-based welfare to avoid expanding the direct provision of public welfare. Within the framework of the company society, major companies have provided employees with a range of occupational welfare, including housing welfare (Sato, 2007). This has clearly coincided with the male breadwinner family model. Low-rent company housing has often been provided to male employees whose spouses are housewives or part-time workers, corresponding with the tax and social security systems. Male employees with their family members are able to utilize low-interest company loans to purchase houses. In terms of young unmarried employees, many companies provide men with company dwellings or rental subsidies. Young women are often employed on the condition that they commute from parental homes and they are then expected to quit working after marriage or childbirth.

Despite the fact that family policy has advantaged conventional households, there has been a noticeable increase in young people who have delayed marriage and thus the establishment of independent families. This means an increase in young individuals who are in disadvantageous positions and not protected by public policy. Between 1980 and 2005, the unmarried rates for the 30–34 age group rose from 21.5 per cent to 47.1 per cent for men, and from 9.1 per cent to 32.0 per cent for women (see Figure 9.1). Unlike some Western societies, cohabitation by non-married couples is uncommon in Japan, although such couples are on the increase. The unmarried rate is higher for men than for women for all age groups. The percentage of never-married people at the age of 50, who are defined as 'lifelong never-married persons' in Japanese statistics, increased to 15.4 per cent for men and 6.8 per cent for women by 2005. This figure is expected to rise further because the unmarried rate among current young people remains high.

The neo-liberalization of government policies has led to some changes in family policy, promoting the individualization of social security benefits. The introduction of a new pension system, which enables divorced couples to split their entitlement to the earnings-related portion of the former husband's pension, started in 2007. A research committee within the Council for Gender Equality (2002) recommended that the systems of taxation and social security be transformed towards a more individualized model. According to the committee, current systems based on the male breadwinner family model do not

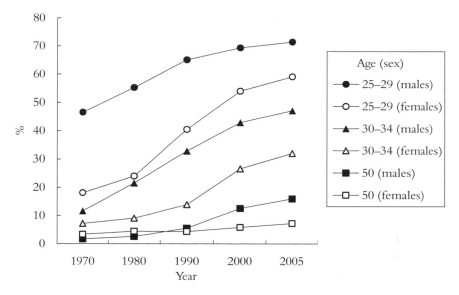

FIGURE 9.1 Unmarried rates by age and sex.
Source: Adapted from Statistics Bureau, Population Census.

support people's free choice in terms of forming households but have led many women to choose particular patterns of family life. However, the focus on individualization by social security policies has been minimal while the conservative characteristics of family policy have mostly been preserved.

Japan has one of the lowest fertility rates in the world. The total population began to decrease in 2004 because of falling fertility. This also led to an inevitable decline in the workforce. The government thus began to seek to improve women's working conditions, although male breadwinner families were still advantaged. This policy shift was due not only to increasing claims for equality by women but also to the necessity to address fertility and workforce issues. The government has encouraged companies to form childbirth-oriented environments for female employees, involving increased compensation for maternity and childcare leave. However, progress in implementing pro-childbirth policies has been slow and has not yet been effective in stimulating a recovery in fertility. Moreover, government concerns for women have concentrated on married women who may possibly contribute more to mitigating the decline in fertility rates. Increasing numbers of unmarried women are beyond public policy cover.

Labour policy

Compared with family policy, which has largely continued to be conservative, labour policy has more explicitly moved towards a neo-liberal course, which has accelerated the casualization of the workforce market. Until the economic bubble burst, many corporations in the company society operated a lifelong employment system and a seniority system for progressive wage rises and promotions. The immediate aftermath of the bursting of the bubble marked a turning point, however, as Japan entered a long, traumatic period of deep recession. In addition, the business environment has increasingly become more competitive with the expansion of the global economy. With the weakening of the company society system, an increasing number of corporations have abandoned the system of lifelong employment and introduced a performance-based system to replace the seniority system.

The government, which had protected security of employment with regulatory measures, began to liberalize the labour market in the 1990s. The major amendment to the Dispatched Labour Law in 1999 and 2003 played a key role in casualizing the labour market. As a result, there has been a decline in regular employment and instead an increase in non-regular, low-wage employment. More importantly, the impact of changes in employment practices has not been even across generations but, rather, is concentrated among younger generations. Although the 'company society' has been relatively well maintained for older cohorts, neo-liberal policies have particularly affected employment conditions for younger cohorts (Genda, 2001). This has led to more young people facing difficulties in securing employment and thus housing. Including all employees, the average rate of non-regular employment (part-time, temporary and dispatched employees) rose from 15.8 per cent in 1982 to 33.0 per cent in 2007. During the same period, the rate of non-regular employees aged 20–24 increased more sharply, from 11.4 per cent to 43.1 per cent (see Figure 9.2). The wage gap between regular and non-regular employees is noticeably larger in Japan than in other developed countries (Nagase, 2002). A new word, 'freeter', has appeared to describe non-regular workers aged 15–34, and more recently the word 'NEET' (Not in Employment, Education or Training) has been imported to describe the characteristics of the growing army of unemployed young people. According to the Labour Force Survey, the number of freeters increased from 0.5 million in 1982 to 1.01 million in 1992, and then to 2.17 million in 2003, although it slightly decreased to 2.01 million in 2005. The number of NEETs aged 15–34 rose from 440,000 in 2000 to 640,000 in 2005 (Ministry of Health, Labour and Welfare, 2006). Because of emerging employment conditions it has become almost impossible for an increasing number of young non-regular workers to obtain a foothold on the housing ladder.

Women have also been greatly disadvantaged in the labour market. There is thus a sharp contrast in terms of housing conditions between married and unmarried women (Hirayama and Izuhara, 2008). The Equal Opportunity Act enacted in 1986 and the major amendments to this in 1997 and 2006 provided an institutional framework for enhancing women's status in the labour market. This forced corporations to abandon explicit gender discrimination in employment practices. However, they developed new employment categories in which employees, who accepted company orders such as work-related moves and

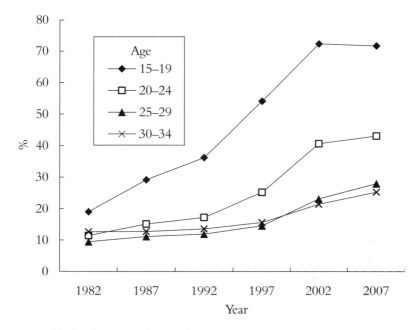

FIGURE 9.2 Ratio of non-regular employees by age.
 Note: non-regular employees: part-time, temporary and dispatched employees.
 Source: Adapted from Statistics Bureau, Employment Status Survey.

longer working hours with higher salaries and greater employment stability, were considered *de facto* men. This system has effectively maintained gender discrimination in employment. Moreover, the casualization of the workforce has impacted more on women than on men. The level of non-regular employees aged 25–29 in 2007 was 39.9 per cent among women and 18.3 per cent among men. Consequently, it has become more difficult for women to access the housing ladder unless they marry male breadwinners.

Housing policy

The government has, historically, systematized housing policy to take the initiative in promulgating a home ownership-oriented housing system (Hirayama and Ronald, 2007). The Government Housing Loan Corporation (GHLC) was established as a state agency in 1951 to provide middle-class households with long-term, low-interest mortgages for the acquisition or construction of their own homes. Of the various housing policy measures, the granting of GHLC mortgages was particularly emphasized to promote middle-class home ownership. Despite rapid urbanization, the level of owner-occupied housing has hovered at around 60 per cent because of the measures used to accelerate the acquisition of housing. The level of private rental housing has been the second highest at around a quarter of all housing. However, housing policy has not supported the supply of private rental housing; there has been little assistance for the construction of private rental housing and absolutely no provision of rental subsidy. Direct provision of rental housing by the public sector has been marginal. Public housing has been provided to low-income households and public corporations have constructed rental housing for urban middle-income households. However, the ratios of low-income public housing and public corporation housing to total housing have been very low, corresponding to around 5 per cent and 2 per cent respectively. The Japanese government has thus characteristically operated a tenure-discriminatory housing system as a conservative policy measure, and focused on supporting middle-class home ownership as a means of popularizing and preserving conventional life-course patterns.

Housing policy has paralleled family policy to advantage conventional households (Hirayama, 2003; Hirayama and Izuhara, 2008). One-person households have been excluded from most housing policy measures. Once singles became married, housing policy came into play. This played an important role in preserving conventional life-course patterns. The GHLC did not provide one-person households with mortgages until 1981. Of single-person households, GHLC mortgages were only available to those over 40 until 1988 and to those over 35 before the age restriction was removed in 1993. In addition, the GHLC did not provide mortgages to those who wished to purchase or build small houses. This was aimed at promoting the construction of spacious homes but implicitly excluded one-person households. Public corporations provided rental housing mainly to family households with a very limited number of dwellings for single-person households. The public housing system for low-income people excluded one-person households. In 1980, elderly singles qualified for public housing, but non-elderly single households are still excluded from low-income public housing.

The government began to undertake the neo-liberalization of housing policy in the middle of the 1990s, which expanded the market-based supply of housing and mortgages (Hirayama and Ronald, 2007). New starts in low-income public housing and public corporation housing have almost stopped and their roles in housing policy will become marginalized even more. The GHLC, which had been the core of post-war housing measures, was discontinued in 2007. This meant a particularly important watershed in the history of Japanese housing policy. The Housing Finance Agency, the successor of the GHLC, withdrew from the primary mortgage market and has thereafter only dealt with the secondary mortgage market.

The neo-liberalization of housing policy has affected the housing conditions of younger generations in particular. Unlike conservative housing policy, the housing and mortgage markets do not discriminate against non-conventional households including one-person households. However, the market economy inevitably excludes low-income people and those with poor credit. With the casualization of employment, an increasing number of young non-regular workers with low wages will undoubtedly be further excluded from the housing and mortgage markets. In addition, since the collapse of the bubble, the affordability of home ownership has been undermined (Hirayama, 2010). Although the post-bubble deflationary economy has led to a drop in housing prices, a decline in incomes has translated into smaller capacity to save for deposits and larger mortgage liabilities, resulting in heavier economic burdens for those seeking to purchase a house. Older generations have moved up the housing ladder towards home ownership, supported by government subsidies. Younger generations, however, will not be provided with the same level of support by the government to become members of the homeowner society. They are required to climb their own housing ladder by themselves within the framework of the market economy.

Changes in household formation

This section looks at changes in the rates of 'parental home dwellers', 'single people' and 'family-formers' to explore transformations in young people's household formation. It has been assumed that young individuals change from being parental home dwellers to independent singles and to family-formers, or from parental home dwellers directly to family-formers, in leading a conventional life course. However, young people's life courses have increasingly been fragmented. There has been a vigorous cycle in which successive generations have ascended the housing ladder towards attaining home ownership that has maintained Japan's home-owning society. However, the cycle is inevitably being eroded by increased differentiation in life courses among younger generations.

As shown in Figure 9.3, which was prepared from various data obtained from the population census, parental home dwellers and single people (but parental home dwellers in particular), have been increasing in number while family-formers have been in decline. This is primarily due to rising numbers of unmarried people. Between 1980 and 2005, the percentages of parental home dwellers and single people rose from 24.0 per cent and 12.1 per cent to 41.3 per cent and 19.3 per cent respectively for the 25–29 age group, and from 8.2 per cent and 5.6 per cent to 24.8 per cent and 13.5 per cent respectively for the 30–34 age group. Even among older individuals aged 35–39, during the same period the rate of parental home dwellers rose from 2.9 per cent to 16.0 per cent, and that of single people from 3.4 per cent to 8.9 per cent. On the other hand, the percentage of family-formers continuously dropped to 28.1 per cent for the 25–29 age group, 50.3 per cent for the 30–34 age group and 61.3 per cent for the 35–39 age group by 2005. This obvious decline in transitions into family-formers means a decline in conventional life-course patterns.

There are differences in the ways that households are established by men and women (see Figure 9.3). The numbers of family-formers are higher for women than for men. This coincides with the fact that there are more unmarried men than unmarried women. In 2005, the percentage of family-formers of those aged 30–34 was 44.8 per cent for men and 55.8 per cent for women. Of

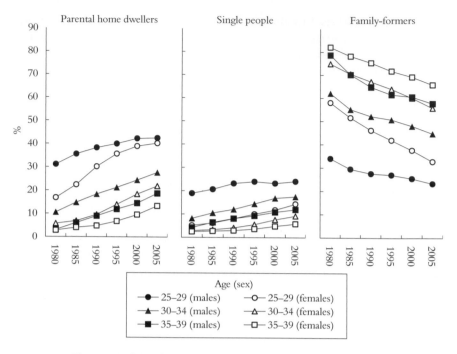

FIGURE 9.3 Changes in household type by age and sex.
Source: Author's calculations from the Population Census.

unmarried individuals, women are more likely to be parental home dwellers than men. In 2005, the ratio of parental home dwellers to single people for those aged 30–34 was 1.6:1 for men and 2.4:1 for women. This means that unmarried women tend to continue to live in their parents' homes and that they do not tend to leave home to become independent singles but only leave to get married. In addition, young women are more often employed if they agree to commute from their parental homes. This reflects and reinforces the tendency by unmarried women to remain as parental home dwellers.

Because the rapid increase in young adults living in their parents' homes has been a novel phenomenon, it has intensified not only academic but also popular debate. In 1991, Miyamoto, Iwagami and Yamada first began to conduct a series of surveys on parental home dwellers to highlight affluent parents' over-protection of their dependent adult children (Miyamoto et al., 1997). At that time, the aftermath of the bubble economy generated an image that young adults living in parental homes indulged themselves in the consumption of luxury goods without having to incur housing costs or food expenses. Yamada (1999), who called parental home dwellers 'parasite singles', more explicitly pointed out young people's dependent attitudes. This catchy term provided a trigger provoking a 'parasite bashing' phenomenon in popular discourses, in which the dependent behaviours of young adults were severely criticized (Kitamura, 2001).

Since the late 1990s, however, in the context of the post-bubble prolonged recession, many researchers have begun to emphasize the economic instability of parental home dwellers (Iwagami, 1999; Kitamura, 2001; Miyamoto, 2004; Nagase, 2002; Ohishi, 2004; Shirahase, 2005). A survey on young adults living in their parents' homes, conducted by the National Institute of Population and Social Security Research (2001), found that many parental home dwellers were not 'lazy' but rather, despite working, did not have sufficient income to leave home to establish an independent household. Yamada (2004) has also begun to shift his view on 'parasite singles' towards emphasizing the exacerbated economic circumstances surrounding the young generation. These arguments and research findings have suggested that the increase in parental home dwellers cannot necessarily be attributed to young people's dependent attitudes but to their own economically rational choices.

The neo-liberalization of labour policy and the consequent casualization of the employment market has accelerated the increase in the number of young non-regular workers and deprived them of opportunities to leave their parents' homes and to get married. The establishment of families in Japan has been based on the male breadwinner family model. This has been reflected in the clear correlation between the unmarried rate and economic status, particularly among men. The Employment Status Survey in 2002 revealed that the percentage of unmarried men aged 30–34 in regular employment was 41 per cent, while the figure for those in non-regular employment was notably higher at 70 per cent (Ministry of Health, Labour and Welfare, 2006). It is also important to look at the increase in marriages within the same social classes. The implication is that economic status has begun to determine the marriage rate not only among men but also among women (Nagase, 2002). Iwagami (1999), Miyamoto (2004) and Ohishi (2004), among others, carried out surveys on younger cohorts and found evidence that the rates of non-regular workers were substantially higher for parental home dwellers than for those who had left their parents' homes. Obviously, there are close links between the casualization of the labour force, the increase in unmarried young people and the increase in parental home dwellers.

Changes in people's attitudes towards marriage have led to a delay by young people in starting independent households. According to a survey periodically conducted by the NHK Broadcasting Culture Research Institute (2004), the rate of those who answered 'it is a matter of course to get married' and 'it is a matter of course to have children' decreased from 45 per cent and 54 per cent in 1993 to 36 per cent and 44 per cent in 2003 respectively. The younger the respondents were, the lower the rates were. Moreover, as younger people are spending longer in education, they are forming households later. It is, however, necessary to look at not only the change in people's attitudes towards marriage but also the apparent tendency of young people who have a lower employment status to more often remain unmarried. Regardless of young people's attitudes towards marriage, it is difficult for non-regular, low-wage employees to choose to get married and establish their own families.

Some commentators have attributed the 'parasite' phenomenon to a cultural tendency peculiar to Japan – parents who are overprotective of their children and the delay by young adults in becoming independent (Miura, 2005; Yamada, 1999). However, increases in parental home dwellers have been observed not only in Japan but also in many other societies (Ministry of Health, Labour and Welfare, 2003). The rates of young people living in parental homes in Southern European countries including Spain, Greece and Italy have been much higher than in Japan, and are increasing even more. In West European countries and Anglo-Saxon societies, there have traditionally been only a small number of parental home dwellers. In Britain, France, Germany and the United States, however, the numbers of those living in parental homes have recently begun to increase. This is largely as a result of the deregulation of employment markets, which has become a common tendency across many societies. It is therefore reasonable to regard the increase in parental home dwellers in Japan not only as a particularly domestic cultural phenomenon but also as a reflection of wider economic transformations.

Moreover, as Mandic (2008) and Mulder (2006) among others have suggested, home ownership-oriented housing systems tend to delay marriage and the establishment of families. It is most likely that young individuals who wish to leave home to form their own households need affordable rental housing before entering home ownership markets. However, housing systems that prioritize the promotion of home ownership tend not to support the supply of private rental housing. Social rental housing sectors are also marginal in property ownership-based societies. Of countries with a high level of owner-occupation, the shortage in affordable rental housing available to young people to establish their own households is a common feature.

In Japan, tenure-discriminating housing policy, which has concentrated on expanding home ownership, has accounted for the increase in parental home dwellers. A limited number of public rental dwellings available for young households, low-quality private rental housing in terms of floor space and amenities, and high rents for privately rented housing have effectively combined to discourage young people from establishing their own independent families. In addition, the neo-liberalization of housing policy has meant fewer public subsidies for younger cohorts to acquire housing. Many young people have been seeking to secure housing in the private rental market only to find it difficult to access adequate, affordable places to live in. This has in turn led to the increase in parental home dwellers. The housing policy system, along with the casualization of the workforce, has progressively been eroding young people's footholds on the housing ladder.

Differentiation of housing trajectories

In this section, we examine differences in housing trajectories between 'parental home dwellers', 'single people' and 'family-formers', drawing on recalculations of micro data taken from the 2003 Housing and Land Survey. In the majority of research on housing, there has been a tacit assumption that housing is an issue at the household level. Therefore, housing statistics often use 'households as a unit' base, in which the situation of the head of the household is assumed to represent that of the entire household. However, it is necessary to look at housing at the individual level to reveal young people's housing conditions because they are not necessarily the heads of households. Although single people and most male family-formers are the heads of households in census statistics, parental home dwellers and most female family-formers are not. As Japan's Housing and Land Survey uses a 'household as a unit' base, micro data from the survey were reorganized in terms of an 'individual unit' base in order to explore the housing situations that younger people experience.

Housing tenure

As illustrated in Figure 9.4, there are clear differences in housing tenure among young people. More than four-fifths of parental home dwellers live in owner-occupied housing (owned by their parents). This holds true for both men and women and from the 20–24 age group to the 35–39 age group. The increase in parental home dwellers can be understood within the context of public policy practices. Conservative family policy has promoted reciprocity within the family, which partly accounts for a particular form of intergenerational relationship producing parental home dwellers. The neo-liberalization of labour policy has accelerated the increase in young non-regular workers who have almost no choice but to continue to live in their parents' homes. Housing policy has encouraged the current generation of parents to move up the housing ladder towards acquiring their own spacious home. In Japan, there is a large disparity between owner-occupied housing and rented housing in terms of floor area – 124 square metres on average for an owner-occupied dwelling and 46 square metres for a rented dwelling in 2003. Therefore, parents' acquisition of an owner-occupied home has also helped enable younger generations to live with them. It can be assumed that many parental home dwellers occupy their own private rooms in the house. The combination of family, labour and housing policies has thus been responsible for the increase in young individuals who have lived in their parents' homes for longer periods.

In mature home-owning societies such as Japan, the inheritance of residential properties has become more significant in housing practices (Hirayama, 2007; Izuhara, 2005). Although it is difficult for many parental home dwellers, whose economic conditions have been exacerbated, to acquire their own homes, they are likely to inherit their parents' homes in the future. A decrease in the number of siblings combined with a high level of home ownership among the older generation means a rise in the possibility that offspring will inherit residential properties. Housing assets also tend to be passed down to those who live at home with their parents. Increased longevity, however, tends to delay

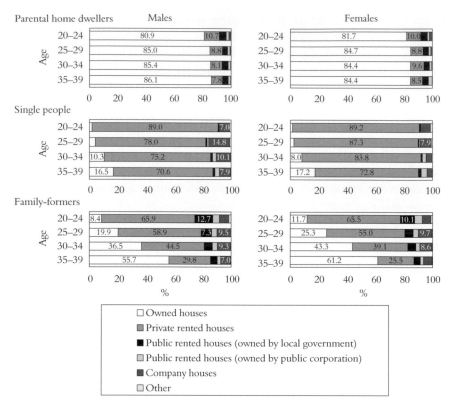

FIGURE 9.4 Housing tenure by household type, age and sex.
    Source: Author's calculations from micro data from the 2003 Housing
    and Land Survey of Japan.

succession. Therefore, parental home dwellers will be considerably older before they inherit housing properties.

Most single people who have left the natal home live in private rental housing. The rates of private rental dwelling for both men and women aged 20–24 are very high at approximately 90 per cent. The figures among older age groups are lower than those among younger age groups but are still considerably high, for example about 70 percent for those aged 35–39. Generally speaking, people who remain single are unlikely to be able to purchase their own dwelling; older age is correlated with a higher level of home ownership, although the home ownership rates for men and women aged 35–39 are still low: less than one in five. The percentage of those in company housing is higher for men (14.8 per cent for those aged 25–29) than for women (7.9 per cent for the same age group). This is due to the fact that many corporations have excluded unmarried women from company housing.

Unlike parental home dwellers and single people, family-formers have, more typically, climbed the housing ladder to become homeowners. Although the percentage in private rental housing at the age of 20–24 is high (65.9 per cent for men and 65.5 per cent for women), it is low at the age of 35–39 (29.8 per cent for men and 25.5 per cent for women). Accordingly, the levels of home ownership are much higher at age 35–39 (55.7 per cent for men and 61.2 per cent for women) than at the age of 20–24 (8.4 per cent for men and 11.7 per cent for women). The home ownership rate for women is higher than that of men among the same age groups. This is because women tend to marry men older than themselves. Family-formers at younger ages are also more likely to live in public rental housing than parental home dwellers and single people. The percentages in public housing (including both public housing for those with low incomes and public corporation housing) for the 20–24 age group are 17.4 per cent for male family-formers and 15.5 per cent for female family-formers. The public rental housing system has excluded young one-person households, as policy assumes that poorer young singles can remain parental home dwellers and do not need access to public rental housing. This has differentiated the rates of public rental housing among young people according to the type of household. Public rental housing has provided a foothold on the lower rungs of the housing ladder, but this has been provided only to households involving married couples.

Household income

Questionnaires administered by the Housing and Land Survey have included not individual incomes but household incomes. Here, differences in household income according to the type of household are examined (see Figure 9.5). It is important to note that the household incomes of older parental home dwellers are lower than those of younger parental home dwellers. About half of the households with either male or female parental home dwellers aged 20–24 have annual incomes of 7 million yen (€53,846) or more; this reduces to one-fifth for those aged 35–39. This difference is mostly caused by parents' retirement. The number of low-income households with an annual income of less than 3 million yen (€23,077) is relatively high at about one-third for both men and women aged 35–39. Regardless of whether or not parental home dwellers are 'parasitic', their parents' incomes, which they may rely on, decrease with advancing age. If parental home dwellers are in secure employment, an increase in their own incomes with advancing age is likely to compensate for the decrease in their parents' incomes. However, many parental home dwellers are also more likely to be non-regular workers on low wages. Parental home dwellers in the household are not heads of household but adult children, meaning that they are not the main earner in the household. Male parental home dwellers aged over 30 are thus likely to have a low level of income.

The annual incomes of single people increase with advancing age but remain low compared with those of married people. Moreover, it is important to look at the large income gap between men and women within the single person

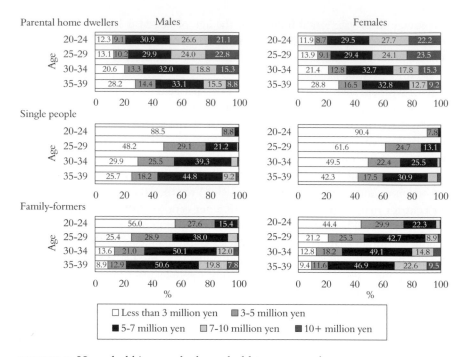

FIGURE 9.5 Household income by household type, age and sex.
Source: Author's calculations from micro data from the 2003 Housing and Land Survey of Japan.

category. The percentages of low-income single people aged 35–39 whose incomes are less than 3 million yen are 25.7 per cent for men and 42.3 per cent for women. This contrast is observed in all age groups. Women have been and continue to be disadvantaged in the labour market, which accounts for the noticeable income gap.

Family-formers have experienced a steady increase in their household incomes. Although the percentages of households with an annual income of 7 million yen or more for family-formers at the age of 20–24 are very low at 1.0 per cent for men and 3.4 per cent for women, the figures at the age of 35–39 are considerably higher at 27.6 per cent for men and 32.1 per cent for women. Annual incomes are higher for female family-formers than for male family-formers, which is due to the tendency of women to marry older men. Family-formers have moved up the housing ladder towards home ownership, which has been buttressed by the continual increase in their incomes.

Rental payments

Housing cost is an important element that has shaped housing conditions. Although the research items on the 2003 Housing and Land Survey did not include mortgage repayments, they did involve monthly rents. As there are very few renters among parental home dwellers, monthly rent payments by single people and family-formers are examined here (see Figure 9.6). Most incomes of single people are low but rise with age. This is reflected in higher rent payments by older tenants. The percentages of single men and women who spend 50,000 yen (€385) or more per month on rent payments are 39.5 per cent and 45.3 per cent for those aged 20–24, and 60.4 per cent and 65.7 per cent for those aged 35–39 respectively. Despite the fact that single women's incomes are lower than those for men (see Figure 9.5), women tend to live in rental housing paying higher rents than men. This suggests differences in housing preferences between men and women. According to Yui (2004), single women in urban areas in particular placed importance on short commuting times and thus central locations, anti-crime environments and high-quality amenities. This arguably accounts for single women's more expensive rent payments. In addition, more single men than single women live in company dwellings paying low rents, which leads to the differentiation in rent payments. As previously discussed, compared with unmarried men, unmarried women are more likely to be parental home dwellers. This is partly because they need high-cost housing despite their lower incomes.

There are mainly two groups in the family-former category in terms of rent payments. The first consists of those whose rent payments increase with age. This is because of the increase in income in line with advancing age. The second group comprises those whose rent payments are low regardless of age. This

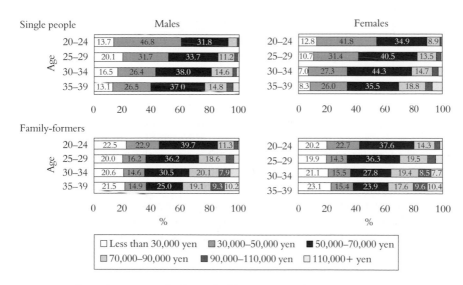

FIGURE 9.6 Rental payments by household type, age and sex.
Source: Author's calculations from micro data from the 2003 Housing and Land Survey of Japan.

includes family-formers who continue to live in company housing. A low level of rent payments makes it possible for family-formers to live in company housing for a long time and to accumulate savings before purchasing their own homes.

Conclusions

In post-war Japan, membership in mainstream society was defined by marriage and the establishment of a family, stable employment and income, and the private ownership of residential property, with the majority of middle-class households leading a conventional life course, moving up the housing ladder towards home ownership (Hirayama, 2003). Since the middle of the 1990s, however, an increasing number of young people have been confronted by difficulties in obtaining a foothold on the housing ladder. This chapter has explored the differentiation in housing trajectories between 'parental home dwellers', 'single people' and 'family-formers', finding that it is primarily family-formers who have climbed up the ladder towards home ownership. It is almost impossible for parental home dwellers and single people (who are drastically increasing in number) to achieve owner-occupation. The fragmentation of life courses among younger generations is now beginning to unravel the cycle of successive ascent up the housing ladder that has underpinned and sustained the home-owning society.

We demonstrated that public policy practices relating to family, employment and housing accounted for transformations in the housing conditions of young people. Family-formers have benefited from conservative policies to promote middle-class housing purchases. On the other hand, parental home dwellers and single people have been excluded from conservative policies because housing and family policies have not focused on unmarried people. In addition, the neo-liberalization of labour policy to facilitate casual employment has impacted on younger generations in particular, which has led to a rapid increase in parental home dwellers and single people. Many young casual workers on low wages have no choice but to continue to live in their parents' homes, while many low-income single people are living in low-quality private rental housing with almost no prospects of accessing the owner-occupied housing sector. The long-standing recession during the post-bubble period worsened young people's economic environments. This was followed by the occurrence of the global financial crisis, further undermining young people's housing opportunities. However, the nature and changing organization of public bodies have structurally affected housing trajectories among the younger cohort.

The term 'gap society' has recently not only spread through academia but also been used in popular discourse in describing the current condition of Japanese society (Shirahase, 2006; Tachibanaki, 2006). Social class-based inequalities have long been observed and analysed in Japan as well as in many other countries. However, the term 'gap society' is often used to emphasize the expansion of social inequalities with generations as a key variable. Japan's housing system was a mechanism that provided people with the 'promise' of entry into the homeowner society. Many renters who aimed at purchasing a house regarded themselves as potential homeowners, and young people on low incomes in the past, within the seniority system of predictable wage augmentation and promotion, were able to expect an increase in income. The older generations relied on the paternalistic company society and benefited from government subsidies in purchasing their own houses. In the emerging 'gap society', however, young people, particularly parental home dwellers and single people, are increasingly failing to accomplish the 'promise' of establishing a family, finding a career or acquiring a house.

In response to the global economic crisis, since 2008 the Japanese government has begun to intervene further in the housing market. Emergency housing measures, with the intention of stimulating economic recovery, have concentrated on encouraging middle-class families to purchase a house, mainly by means of reducing tax for homebuyers. This is likely to further widen cleavages among younger generations with regard to housing opportunities. Middle-class couples are more likely to be provided with government assistance to enter the home ownership market while unmarried people in unstable employment are excluded from the benefits of emergency housing measures.

It is likely that changes in the housing conditions of young people are eroding the traditional basis of post-war Japan's home-owning society with the compounding of social inequalities. Moreover, the increase in parental home dwellers and single people will inevitably undermine fertility even more, encouraging a decrease in the total population and the workforce. This will also be associated with an accelerated increase in the proportion of older people. In this context, the housing situation of younger generations is a key driver for future social changes. Examining home ownership transformations in Japan places young people's housing conditions into sharp focus. It is evident that not only Japan but also many other homeowner societies in the West and in the East Asian region are developing generational fractures in housing opportunities. A suggestion drawn from Japan's present experience is that housing for young people is an important policy issue not only in itself but also in shaping wider social processes.

References

Council for Gender Equality (2002) *Raifu Sutairu no Sentaku to Zeisei, Shakai Hosho Seido, Koyo Sisutemu ni Kansuru Hokokusho* [*Report on Lifestyle Choice and Systems of Taxation, Social Security and Employment*], Tokyo: Council for Gender Equality.

Doling, J. and Ford, J. (2003) *Globalization and Home Ownership: Experiences in Eight Member States of the European Union*, Delft: Delft University Press.

Forrest, R. and Murie, A. (eds) (1995) *Housing and Family Wealth: Comparative International Perspectives*, London: Routledge.

Forrest, R. and Lee, J. (2004) Cohort effects, differential accumulation and Hong Kong's volatile housing market, *Urban Studies*, 41(11), 2181–2196.

Forrest, R. and Hirayama, Y. (2009) The uneven impact of neo-liberalism on housing opportunities, *International Journal of Urban and Regional Research*, 33(4), 998–1013.

Fujita, Y. and Shionoya, Y. (eds) (1997) *Kigyo nai Fukushi to Shakai Hosho [Employee Benefits and Social Security]*, Tokyo: Tokyo University Press.

Genda, Y. (2001) *Shigoto no Naka no Aimai na Fuan [The Vague Uneasiness of Work]*, Tokyo: Chuo Korou Shinsha.

Groves, R., Murie, A. and Watson, C. (eds) (2007) *Housing and the New Welfare State: Perspectives from East Asia and Europe*, Aldershot: Ashgate.

Hirayama, Y. (2003) Housing and social inequality in Japan, in M. Izuhara (ed.) *Comparing Social Policies: Exploring New Perspectives in Britain and Japan*, Bristol: Polity Press.

Hirayama, Y. (2007) Reshaping the housing system: home ownership as a catalyst for social transformation, in Y. Hirayama and R. Ronald (eds) *Housing and Social Transition in Japan*, London: Routledge.

Hirayama, Y. (2010) Housing pathway divergence in Japan's insecure economy, *Housing Studies*, 25 (6), 777–797.

Hirayama, Y. and Ronald, R. (eds) (2007) *Housing and Social Transition in Japan*, London: Routledge.

Hirayama, Y. and Izuhara, M. (2008) Women and housing assets in the context of Japan's home-owning democracy, *Journal of Social Policy*, 37(4), 641–660.

Hirayama, Y. and Ronald, R. (2008) Baby-boomers, baby-busters and the lost generation: generational fractures in Japan's homeowner society, *Urban Policy and Research*, 26(3), 325–342.

Iwagami, M. (1999) Niju-dai, sanju-dai mikonsha no oya tono dobekkyo kozo [The research about unmarried people in their twenties and thirties co-residing with own parents in Japan], *Jinko Mondai Kenkyu [Journal of Population Problems]*, 55(4), 1–15.

Izuhara, M. (2005) Residential property, cultural practices and the 'generational contract' in England and Japan, *International Journal of Urban and Regional Research*, 29(2), 341–357.

Kitamura, A. (2001) Seijin mikonsha no rika to oyako kankei [Unmarried adults, home leaving and family relations], *Life Design Report*, 7, 22–45.

Kurz, K. and Blossfeld, H. (eds) (2004) *Home Ownership and Social Inequality in Comparative Perspective*, Stanford, CA: Stanford University Press.

Mandic, S. (2008) Home-leaving and its structural determinants in western and eastern Europe: an exploratory study, *Housing Studies*, 23(4), 615–636.

Ministry of Health, Labour and Welfare (2003) *Kosei Rodo Hakusho [Government White Paper on Health, Labour and Welfare]*, Tokyo: National Printing Bureau.

Ministry of Health, Labour and Welfare (2006) *Rodo Keizai Hakusho [Government White Paper on the Labour Economy]*, Tokyo: National Printing Bureau.

Miura, A. (2005) *Karyu Shakai [Low Class Society]*, Tokyo: Kobunsha.

Miyamoto, M. (2004) *Posuto Seinenki to Oyako Senryaku [Post-Youth Period and Family Strategies]*, Tokyo: Keiso Shobo.

Miyamoto, M., Iwagami, M. and Yamada, M. (1997) *Mikonka Shakai no Oyako Kankei [Family Relations in Unmarried People Society]*, Tokyo: Yuhikaku.

Mulder, C. (2006) Home ownership and family formation, *Journal of Housing and the Built Environment*, 21(3), 281–298.

Nagase, N. (2002) Jakunenso no koyo no hiseikika to kekkon kodo [Marriage timing and the effect of increase in non-standard employment among the youth in Japan], *Jinko Mondai Kenkyu [Journal of Population Problems]*, 58(2), 22–35.

Nagase, N. and Murao, Y. (2005) Shakai hosho ya zeisei tou ha kazoku, kazokukeisei ni eikyo wo ataeruka [Do social security and taxation systems influence family formation?], *Kikan Shakai Hosho Kenkyu* [*Journal of Social Security Research*], 41(2), 137–149.

National Institute of Population and Social Security Research (2001) *Setai nai Tanshinsha ni kansuru Jittai Chosa* [*Survey on Parental Home Dwellers*], Tokyo: National Institute of Population and Social Security Research.

NHK Broadcasting Culture Research Institute (2004) *Gendai Nihonjin no Ishiki Kozo* [*People's Attitudes in Contemporary Japan*], Tokyo: Nihon Hoso Shuppankyoku.

Ohishi, A. (2004) Jakunen shugyo to oya tono doubekyo [Young people's employment and their living arrangements with parents], *Jinko Mondai Kenkyu* [*Journal of Population Problems*], 60(2), 19–31.

Ronald, R. (2008) *The Ideology of Home Ownership: Homeowner Societies and the Role of Housing*, New York: Palgrave Macmillan.

Sato, I. (2007) Welfare regime theories and the Japanese housing system, in Hirayama, Y. and Ronald, R. (eds) *Housing and Social Transition in Japan*, London: Routledge.

Shirahase, S. (2005) *Shoshi Korei Syakai no Mienai Kakusa* [*Invisible Inequalities in Low Fertility, Aged Society*], Tokyo: Tokyo University Press.

Shirahase, S. (ed.) (2006) *Henkasuru Shakai no Fubyodo* [*Changing Social Inequalities*], Tokyo: Tokyo University Press.

Tachibanaki, T. (2006) *Kakusa Shakai* [*Gap Society*], Tokyo: Iwanami Shoten.

Yamada, M. (1999) *Parasaito Shinguru no Jidai* [*The Time of Parasite of Singles*], Tokyo: Chikuma Shobo.

Yamada, M. (2004) *Parasaito Shakai no Yukuei* [*The Fortune of Parasite Society*], Tokyo: Chikuma Shobo.

Yip, N.M., Forrest, R. and La Grange, A. (2007) Cohort trajectories in Hong Kong's housing system: 1981–2001, *Housing Studies*, 22(1), 121–136.

Yokoyama, F. (2002) *Sengo Nihon no Josei Seisaku* [*Public Policy for Women in Postwar Japan*], Tokyo: Keiso Shobo.

Yui, Y. (2004) Daitoshi niokeru shinguru josei no manshon konyu to sono haikei [Condominium purchase by single women in large cities], in Y. Yui, H. Kamiya, Y. Wakabayashi and T. Nakazawa (eds) *Hataraku Josei no Toshi Kukan* [*Urban Space and Working Women*], Tokyo: Kokin Shoten.

10

HOME OWNERSHIP – CONTINUING OR FADING DREAM?

David Thorns

Introduction

Both Australia and New Zealand have seen home ownership as a social and political project that contributed to building strong families and communities and serving as a bulwark against political extremism. The high rates of home ownership achieved are now showing signs of change with significant decline amongst younger cohorts and for those entering housing for the first time. The question is explored as to whether this is a long-run structural and life-course change or a temporary adjustment brought on by current market conditions. This chapter addresses the question of the strength of home ownership sentiment in settler societies drawing primarily on the experiences of New Zealand, but also in the context of comparable developments in Australia.

The chapter is organised in six sections. The first examines the development of home ownership and the emergence of a strong ideology that underpins this tenure as the most desirable and the expectation for all citizens. The second reviews and develops a theoretical position that seeks to combine a macro analysis with one reflecting the differential experience of 'cohorts' that move into and through home ownership at different life stages and at different moments in time. The most recent time periods and the effects of booms and slumps from the 1990s to the present and their impact on home ownership rates are analysed in the next three sections. These show how fluctuations in house prices and values affect both affordability and the growth in value of housing and thus the transfers of wealth through housing from those seeking to enter the market to those who are already owners. One consequence has been to reduce the home ownership rate amongst the younger age cohorts (20–40 years) and those in the lower-income groups creating trapped renters. The final section concludes by raising the question of whether we are seeing a structural change with a long-run decline in home ownership likely or a short-term delay until the market recovers from the present financial and housing crisis, and considering the implication of this for housing policy development

Development of home ownership in settler societies

Home ownership has been a central ambition of New Zealand people. The achievement of this tenure status has been equated with reaching 'adulthood' and becoming a fully functional citizen. From the 1870s onwards the colonial government favoured freehold tenure and the owning by individuals of title to land and housing (Hawke, 1985; Oliver, 1968). The towns and cities of New Zealand, as a settler society, grew as a result of immigration rather than rural to urban movement. Housing policies through to the 1970s have focused on increasing supply, which was seen as deficient, as the urban structure had to be created.

In New Zealand and Australia one of the features that has enabled people to exercise some degree of control over their living spaces is the high level of owner-occupation. The commitment to home owning is deeply ingrained and has become a significant aspect of the culture of both societies. In government policies and in popular ideology, home ownership has been continually presented as virtuous and beneficial. For example, Walter Nash, one of the prominent members and Minister of Finance in New Zealand's first Labour government in the 1930s stated that:

> But I am also a conservative in the sense that I look upon the family as the foundation of the nation. I believe that no nation can prosper or progress where people lack the conditions necessary for a 'home' and 'home life' in the best and fullest meaning of these words. It is by the toil of their hands, that men live, and by the strength of the family that the race will continue.
> (quoted in Winstanley, 2001, p. 63)

The emphasis on 'home' and 'family' as the building blocks of the nation were seen as underpinned by owning property and ones own 'home'. This secured a place where they could establish themselves and then contribute to their local and national communities. It was seen as a bulwark against extremism and potential destabilising doctrines that were prevalent in the 1930s and 1940s on both the right and the left of the political spectrum.

A similar sentiment at the time was expressed by Robert Menzies, the Liberal Prime Minister in Australia, indicating that these sentiments were evident across the political spectrum. He stated that:

> The material home represents the concrete expression of habits of frugality and saving 'for a home of one's own'. Your advanced socialist may rage against private property even whilst they acquire it; but one of the best instincts in us is that which induces us to have one little piece of earth with

> a house and a garden which is ours, to which we can withdraw, in which we can be among friends, into which no stranger may come against our will . . . My home is where my wife and children are; the instinct to be with them is the greatest instinct of civilised man; the instinct to give them a chance in life is a noble instinct, not to make then leaners but lifters.
>
> (quoted in Mitchell, 2000, p.78)

The linking of home ownership with family values, security and commitment to the country and locality was thus a strong sentiment underpinning thinking and policy to enhance and support owner-occupation. Both politicians reflected the essentially patriarchal view of the times with respect to the roles of women and men in both the family and society. In the immediate post-war years both countries encouraged women to return to the home and be wives and mothers after their more extensive participation in the workforce during the war. Thus, marriage, home ownership and family formation were encouraged by state policies. The delay in marriage and childbirth from the war years and the re-emphasis on home and family helped to create the post-war surge and the baby boom generation (post-1945 birth cohort).

In New Zealand this strong home ownership sentiment and government support through housing loan schemes administered by the State Advances Corporation, special saving schemes and the ability to capitalise family benefits (used towards the deposit) enabled home ownership to be achieved by low- and modest-income families. Government loans were directed at first-time homeowners buying new houses through group building schemes, which provided entry-level housing at a low cost that could be afforded with state loans. This form of funding and building encouraged suburban peripheral growth, especially in the 1950s and 1960s (Davidson, 1994). In the late 1970s the New Zealand government removed the requirement for loans for first-time home-owners to be tied to the purchase of a new house. The context for this was less favourable economic growth and outmigration to Australia, which weakened housing demand and reflected the outcome of the slump that occurred after the boom in the early 1970s.

The economic and social reforms of the 1984 Labour government encouraged a move to greater reliance upon targeted benefits, usually through an income supplement, and to increased competition and choice through market provisions (Murphy, 1999; Campbell and Thorns, 2001/2; Thorns, 2000). In respect to housing these policies were resisted through to 1990 when the incoming national government restructured housing assistance to almost total reliance upon a demand-side Accommodation Supplement (AS) through the Housing Restructuring Act 1992. This Act abolished the Housing Corporation and created a new entity, Housing New Zealand, to manage the rental stock, sold off the mortgage portfolio to the Bank of New Zealand, created a more market-based approach to rent setting in public housing and introduced the AS, an income supplement, as the major form of state support available to low-income households (Murphy, 1997; Kemp, 1998). The AS was available to assist both rent payment and purchase but was income tested and the majority of the funding has gone to assist rental payments in the public and private sectors rather than to assist in home purchase (Thorns, 2007).

The raft of supports for owner-occupation put in place in the 1950s and 1960s and the underpinning rhetoric was seen by feminists as being patriarchal, with fewer women than men sharing access to home ownership and the prevailing policies emphasising the 'male' as the breadwinner and owner of the household (Ferguson, 1994; de Bruin and Dupuis, 1995). The growth of first-wave feminism at the end of the 1960s and through the 1970s challenged these assumptions and built a powerful critique of state policies that led to change in the 1980s and a reworking of the underpinning ideology of home ownership. It was still advocated as the 'normal' form of tenure but was less explicitly set within a gendered rationale, and the housing needs of sole parents and single people gained greater attention (Winstanley, 2001).

The ideology underpinning home ownership continues to be strongly held. It still emphasises the way that this form of tenure aids in the creation of stable, secure, thrifty citizens, and reinforces the idea of home ownership as the 'normal' tenure of choice and that not wanting this is somehow a mark of failure. One writer recently commented, 'Owning your home in New Zealand is considered almost a birthright. A New Zealand tradition, a culture of home owning so embedded in the national psyche that it assumes its own momentum' (Ansley, 2001, pp. 18–20).

After extensive consultation in 2003 and 2004, the Labour-led government developed a National Housing Strategy that again asserted the importance of home ownership. For many households, home ownership contributes to positive economic outcomes and associated improvements in health and educational well-being. High home ownership rates have positive effects within communities, and are associated with social capital growth and neighbourhood stability (New Zealand Housing Strategy, 2004, p. 38).

By 2004 there was still the emphasis on family and community building, but in addition there was a more explicit recognition of the importance of home ownership as an enabler of local economic and social development. This reflects the changed nature of the housing market over this 25-year period, characterised by booms and slumps, the increased necessity of dual incomes to 'afford' housing and the possibilities that booms create for substantial capital gains for those in the market and increased problems of affordability for those seeking to enter the market. This has been aided in New Zealand where there is no tax on imputed rents, no capital gains tax except for traders in property and no land transfer tax. Home ownership and second home purchase both as 'holiday' homes and as a form of investment for retirement have been favoured forms of wealth accumulation. Over the last six years this has been marked, and during the latest housing boom it has contributed to the rate of price increases.

The positive sentiment towards home ownership was carried through to the housing strategy document released in 2005, which stated that, 'Government believes that asset ownership is important to enable people to participate fully in society in that it provides families with greater long run security, control and independence' (New Zealand Housing Strategy, 2005, p. 30). We again see here the stress on families and the ability to participate fully that comes with 'roots' in a place. The commitment to a local area that owning brings is seen as valuable for creating a sound social fabric and building social capital.

In the six years from 2001 to 2007, New Zealand experienced one of its longest boom periods. This has seen home ownership rates falling, causing political anxiety and debate as to how the decline can be arrested. The prevailing view is still that this is the tenure system of choice and the continuing ambition of the majority of the population. In April 2008 the then Minister of Housing, Maryan Street, speaking at the Labour Party Conference, stressed the political importance for Labour of home ownership: 'The thing about housing is it's a heartland issue for Labour . . . This is about families, it's about the Kiwi dream, we're not giving up on the Kiwi dream of home ownership' (stuff.co.nz, 2008).

Having shown the enduring importance of home ownership as a social, political and economic objective it is now necessary to turn to the analysis of this conceptually.

Conceptual framework

In the housing research literature, houses are seen as exchange commodities, something we 'use' to provide us with shelter and as a way of creating our sense of identity and ontological security (Dupuis, 1992; Dupuis and Thorns, 1998). Housing has thus both a material quality with an exchange value as a result of the housing stock increasing in capital value and an emotional value carrying meaning (Perkins and Thorns, 2003; Gurney, 1990; Gorman-Murray and Dowling, 2007; Ronald, 2008).

As an exchange commodity, the last 25 years have been significant for reinforcing its exchange value and source of capital appreciation/gain. Many New Zealanders are poor savers and the principal asset that many possess is the house that they own or are buying. In times of rapid growth in capital values there has been a tendency to trade up and/or remortgage and release some of the 'capital' to enhance consumption expenditures. In the latest boom period banks were encouraging of this practice and extensive remortgaging against the capital gain has caused some households to suffer negative equity as values have fallen in the current downturn, by up to 40 per cent in some countries (e.g. parts of the US and UK markets).

High rates of owning have generated considerable speculation about intergenerational wealth accumulation and inheritance, and how that money is used across the generations to enhance social and economic opportunities (Forrest and Murie, 1995; Hamnett, 1999; Hamnett et al., 1991; Badcock and Beer, 2000). In the most recent boom period, house prices rose rapidly, reinforcing the link between home owning and asset accumulation. Rising prices open up further the gap in wealth between owners and renters and across the various segments of the housing market. Housing in 2008 made up 70 per cent of household wealth in New Zealand and was thus by far the most significant source (Government House Prices Unit, 2008).

The impact of the 20 years of house price changes from 1980 to 2001 has been a doubling of net wealth per capita. However, during the latest boom period from 2001 to 2007 this doubled again, showing the significant impact of this boom upon wealth transfers and accumulation. The majority of this transfer is from new entrants, both newly formed households and migrants moving into the market, to existing 'owners' (Arcus and Nana, 2005).

Greater per capita income allows choice as to whether some of this is used for consumption expenditure, or is saved for future use (e.g. in retirement), or is transferred across generations through gifts and inheritance. Such transfers tend to reinforce existing social inequalities and affect life-course opportunities. Macro-economic performance is affected by house price changes and the level of investment in housing and other forms of property. The recent volatility in prices has made monetary policy more complicated for central banks, which at the present time have few levers to control inflation apart from official bank lending rates. In New Zealand this has proved to have limited impact on the housing boom because of the greater use now of fixed two- to three-year mortgages; there is thus a considerable lag effect from bank rate adjustments.

Home ownership though is about more than money. It is also valued as it provides security, social status and the ability to personalise the property and invest it with meaning. Homes are places of memories and artefacts that are linked to the family's/household's story of themselves and their connection with people and place (Perkins and Thorns, 2003; Marcus Cooper, 1995). The stress here is upon the non-material attributes of housing and the connection with identity, security, independence, civic engagement and the building of social capital (Putnam, 2000).

In understanding how attitudes, lifestyles and opportunities change over time it is necessary to examine the structure of housing provision, the macro context and the decision and lifestyle 'choices' that are being made, realising that any set of choices are always constrained ones. The choices we make are always shaped by both the macro policy settings and the individual's and household's housing trajectory. The way that these have been analysed theoretically within the housing literature are through the idea of the housing career and the life course, which direct us to a 'cohort analysis' (Rossi, 1955; Kendig, 1984). The time and stage in the life course are critical mediating variables. However, the notion of housing career is limited and for many it is flawed as it suggests a clear and conscious developmental path, whereas for many life is much more messy (Winstanley et al., 2002; Forrest and Kennett, 1996).

Figure 10.1 provides a way of thinking about the two dimensions of time periods during which the structures of provision have changed through economic

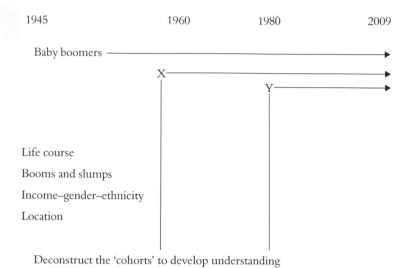

FIGURE 10.1 Cohorts and time frames, 1945–2009.

circumstances, market volatility, affordability shifts, government housing policies and general economic settings. Increasingly, the interrelation of global and local events, from the United Kingdom entry into the European Union in the early 1970s to the subprime[1] failures of the US housing finance and mortgage markets of 2007 and 2008, are significant factors in shaping housing markets. The extent of local/global interconnections in markets has increased as a result of the economic liberalisation of the 1980s and 1990s. This has affected the extent to which individual nation-states can shape their own housing policies and practices. The mortgage collapses and credit crunch beginning in the United States spread quickly around the world causing the destabilisation of the financial system, which has resulted in substantial government bailouts and guarantees to try and stabilise the system and the extent of the recession that has ensued (Stone, 2009).

The housing career that seemed to fit the baby boomer generation was one with a relatively predictable set of expectations. This particular cohort married and had children, and the children then left the family home and they became mortgage-free owners with relatively high spending power taking them through to retirement. In this model the asset accumulation gave rise to speculation about how it might be released, and passed on through inheritance. Areas of research that have been stimulated include those of reverse equity mortgages, inheritance patterns and formation of family trusts.

Understanding home ownership trends and changes requires us to take a long view as it is the experience over the life course that is crucial. So, for example, the recent period of boom conditions has had different consequences depending on how long people have owned, how stable have been their partnerships, how often they have moved and where and when these moves occurred. Viewing these experiences by cohort gives a better understanding of the dynamics of housing change and allows both structural factors and individual trajectories to be analysed.

In New Zealand, those born after 1945, who are part of the baby boom generation, experienced very favourable conditions as they benefited from a high degree of state support to enter home ownership and have generally been assisted by the booms that have occurred subsequently, which have increased the value of their housing stock (Thompson, 1996; Thorns, 1993). Their housing-related wealth has grown and they look to be well placed to either transfer this or consume it in their retirement. Entering their sixties they have very high rates of ownership without debt. However, the next 'generation' entered the market in the late 1970s and through the 1980s at a time when state support was being 'targeted' and rolled back, interest rates on mortgages were rising rapidly, the market was characterised by booms and slumps, purchase required increasingly two incomes and unemployment rose to over 10 per cent.

In the most recent boom period of 2000–2007 it has again been a difficult time to enter the housing market, particularly for first-time homebuyers. The context for this group is one of falling rates and growing affordability problems. The revised housing career model indicates that a more varied set of trajectories is now present which gives rise to the possibility of more tenure changes and much more varied accumulation patterns and much less certainty. This raises questions as to the continuing utility of the idea of the 'housing career' as a model for analysing housing mobility (Winstanley et al., 2003).

Further problems with the 'housing career model' are that it makes little attempt to disaggregate experiences through the life course on the basis of income, gender, ethnicity and locality. Adding these to the mix creates much more complex life-course patterns. In New Zealand, for example, in 2006, home ownership rates varied considerably between the European population (76.4 per cent), the Māori population (42.5 per cent) and Pacific peoples (34.1 per cent).

Asset accumulation and home ownership are significantly lower amongst women than amongst men with the exception of single older women – many of whom are widows and have obtained control of the assets on the death of a spouse. Differentials across the country have also increased over the past two decades as price increases have varied by region, generally being driven by the larger urban centres, especially the Auckland and Wellington urban areas.

In the next section the focus is on the latest period of change spanning booms and slumps, which has seen the rate of home ownership fall steadily from a peak of 73 per cent in 1991.

Booms and slumps, 1991–2009

Figure 10.2 shows the changes that have taken place over the period from 1991 to 2007. There have been two boom periods. The first was in the mid-1990s and the

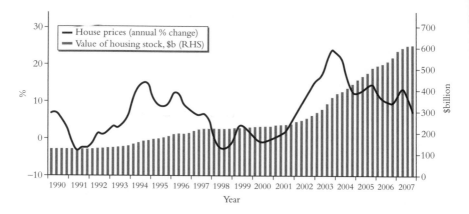

FIGURE 10.2 House price and value shifts, 1990–2007.[2,3]
RHS, Reserve Bank Housing Statistics.
Source: Adapted from http://www.rbnz.govt.nz/keygraphs/index.html.
© Copyright Reserve Bank of New Zealand.

second was from 2001 to 2007. The latter was much stronger and led to substantial increases in housing stock values. Both of these booms were associated with periods of economic growth and fluctuations in mortgage rates. These initially fell from 15 per cent in 1990 to under 8 per cent by 1994 and then rose again during the boom period to over 10 per cent to fall back to just over 6 per cent in 1999–2000 as the market slumped before the most recent boom. During this boom the mortgage rate has risen in response to upward movement in the official cash rate as the Reserve Bank sought to contain inflationary pressure generated by the booming housing market (Figure 10.3). These upward and downward movements have impacted upon housing affordability over this period.

Figure 10.4 shows the other significant relationship that affects affordability – that between wages and housing prices. During the first boom period the rates of wage increases and housing price increases were closer together than in the second period when housing costs increased much faster making housing less affordable. In this period there was a strong growth in house and land prices with real house prices increasing by 80 per cent from 2002 to 2007 (Grimes *et al.*, 2007). These movements resulted in a continuing and widening gap in the house price to household income ratios. The 2008 Report of the House Prices Unit noted that 'a return of house price to household income ratios of close to the historical average of around 3.5 would either require household disposable income to increase by 80% or house prices to fall by over 40%' (Government House Prices Unit, 2008, p. 60). However, neither of these trends appears likely to happen so any improvements in affordability are likely to be gradual and thus a dramatic turnaround in the home ownership rate is unlikely.

A further factor driving up housing cost was that of land prices. Rising concern about city growth and the increased attention to the carbon imprint of cities led to the formation of a government urban strategy that emphasised

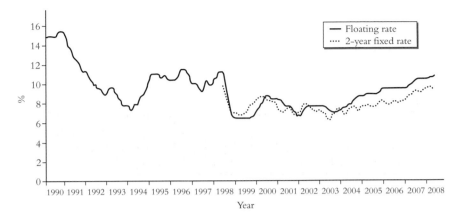

FIGURE 10.3 Mortgage interest rates, 1990–2008.
Source: Adapted from http://www.rbnz.govt.nz/keygraphs/index.html.
© Copyright Reserve Bank of New Zealand.

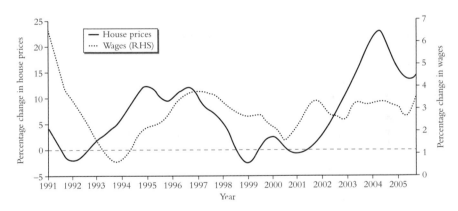

FIGURE 10.4 House prices and wages, 1991–2005.
RHS, Reserve Bank Housing Statistics.
Source: Adapted from DTZ New Zealand (2007, p. 144).

sustainability. Limiting urban growth and creating more compact urban form has gained support. In the Auckland urban region, New Zealand's largest, this has resulted in a plan to limit growth and encourage intensification with a consequent flow-on effect on land values (Grimes *et al.*, 2007). This increases the land cost proportion of housing and has led to the development lobby arguing for less restrictions to lower the cost of land and ease the affordability problem. Although this may solve one problem it does not address the infrastructure costs associated with continued peripheral growth. However, with a change to a centre right government in November 2008 there are moves to change the Resource Management Act and lessen the focus on sustainability and reduce compliance costs, which are seen to increase land and housing costs.

Affordability of home ownership

One of the key issues here is how to measure affordability. One major survey used by the development lobby is that of the *Demographia Index* (http://www. demographia.com/dbr-ix.htm), which compares the United Kingdom, the United States, Ireland, Canada, Australia and New Zealand. The metric that is used is the ratio of median household income to median house prices. Housing on this basis is unaffordable when the cost is greater than three times the median income. The most recent data for New Zealand and Australia placed both among the most unaffordable countries surveyed with ratios of housing costs to median household income of 6.3. The method used has limitations in that it relies on median prices and aggregate sales data and does not sufficiently differentiate by household type or region, both of which, along with ethnicity, are crucial in New Zealand for assessing affordability. A commonly used metric for government policy discussion is the proportion of income used for housing costs (buying or renting). Here the measure used is generally 30 per cent of household income with greater than this indicating housing stress and likely to attract government income subsidy (Accommodation Supplement in New Zealand; see Thorns, 2007).

In boom times an alternative measure that may be more useful is the cost of access to housing. This shows that during boom conditions costs rise dramatically for those seeking to enter housing as interest rates tend to rise as central banks try and restrain inflation, more 'deposit' money is required and rents may also increase reducing capacity to save. One outcome of the financial crisis has been lower interest rates and higher deposit to value ratios required by banks to issue a loan. These have moved from the 5 per cent level to nearer 20 per cent. Such changes impact most on those trying to enter the ownership market as they now have to save for a larger deposit with falling interest rates. Further, the debates around affordability tend to focus on the current situation rather than take a longer-term view tracking the experience of the household/family over time. This crucially disguises the cohort and time effects that shape household experiences.

As we showed earlier, it is the life course that shapes housing opportunities more than the current market conditions for the majority of homeowners. For example, New Zealand Ministry of Social Development data in the 2008 Social Report (Figure 10.5) show that the increasing proportion of household income going to housing over the period 1988–2007 fluctuated, reflecting the booms and slumps that occurred in the overall housing market (New Zealand Ministry of Social Development, 2008). Further, the data in Table 10.1 show the impact of the increasing costs on the younger age groups, with the greatest outgoings to income for those between 24 and 44 years and those under 18 years in 2007.

Statistics New Zealand data show that, for the majority of households, affordability, expressed as the percentage of income spent on housing, improved from the late 1990s.[4] These figures include those who owned before this time.

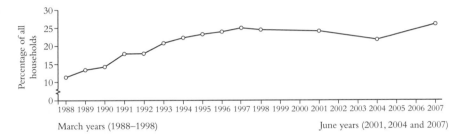

March years (1988–1998)   June years (2001, 2004 and 2007)

FIGURE 10.5 Changing affordability rates over time, 1988–2007: proportion of households with housing cost outgoings-to-income ratio greater than 30 per cent.
Source: Adapted from Ministry of Social Development (2008).

TABLE 10.1 Proportion of population with more than 30 per cent of outgoings on housing costs

	1988	1993	1998	2001	2004	2007
Total population	10.6	20.6	24.9	24.1	21.3	26.0
Population aged 15 years and over	9.9	19.0	21.9	20.9	19.7	23.6
Males aged 15 years and over	10.3	18.8	21.0	19.9	20.0	22.2
Females aged 15 years and over	9.5	19.3	22.7	21.9	19.5	25.1
Age groups						
Under 18 years	11.9	25.6	33.1	31.8	26.4	31.7
18–24 years	12.4	24.6	26.3	28.6	28.4	28.9
25–44 years	14.7	26.3	31.1	28.3	25.0	32.8
45–64 years	5.0	12.3	13.8	15.6	15.2	19.0
65 years and over	3.2	4.0	7.1	7.1	5.8	9.1

Source: Derived from Statistics New Zealand's Household Economic Survey (1988–2007), by the Ministry of Social Development (http://www.socialreport.msd.govt.nz/economic-standard-living/housing-affordability.html).
Note: Data are for March in years 1988, 1993 and 1998 and June in years 2001, 2004 and 2007.

For this group of owners housing expenditure fell as their household incomes improved during a time of sustained economic growth and high employment. These data show that there is a need to be careful with the interpretation of aggregate data and a need to focus on cohort effects over time to reflect both macro-structural changes and life-stage trajectories.

As noted previously there are significant ethnic differences in affordability and access to home ownership. Figure 10.6 provides data which show that Māori, Pacific and other ethnic groups expend a greater proportion of their income than Europeans on their housing costs. For households with at least one Māori member, the proportion of households expending more that 30 per cent

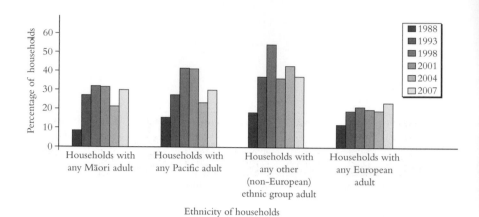

FIGURE 10.6 Housing cost to income ratios greater than 30 per cent by ethnicity.
Source: Adapted from Ministry of Social Development (http://www.socialreport.msd.govt.nz/economic-standard-living/housing-affordability.html).

of income on house costs rose from 8 per cent in 1988 to 36 per cent in 1997, then fell to 21 per cent in 2004 before rising again during the boom years to 31 per cent. For Pacific households, by 1997 the rate was 48 per cent, falling back to 23 per cent before rising to 30 per cent in 2007.

Owner-occupation rates and changes in tenure patterns

Figure 10.7 shows the rates of home ownership for selected societies for the period from 1970 to 2003.[5] This indicates that New Zealand, Australia, Ireland and the United States were amongst the leading home-owning countries in 1970. The New Zealand rate subsequently peaked at 73 per cent in 1991 and has since begun to fall. This is the only country in this group that shows this particular trend. For all of the others growth continued through until 2003. The growth period now seems to have ended as evidence mounts of housing stress and housing market decline as a result of the failures in the US subprime mortgage market. Weakening growth in the UK and Australian markets has also had consequential impacts on lower-income groups and people trying to access the market for the first time.

In New Zealand the rate has continued to fall from 1991 and in 2001 it reached 65.8 per cent and is predicted to reach 61.3 per cent by 2016. The pattern of decline is not even across the country, with a faster rate of decline in the Auckland region, where the rate in 2001 was 64.8 per cent. This is predicted to fall to 58 per cent by 2016 (DTZ New Zealand, 2005, 2007). Complicating the picture somewhat is the fact that in 2006 family trust ownership was identified, which previously would have been hidden within the owner-occupation category. This form of ownership represented 12 per cent of all tenure in 2006,

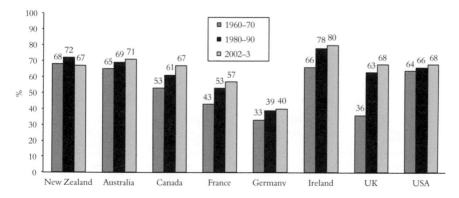

FIGURE 10.7   Home ownership rates: selected countries.
Source: Author's calculations. Statistics New Zealand; Australian Bureau of Statistics (ABS) Census of Population and Housing; Maclennan, D. (2008) *Focusing on Housing Systems and Modernising Housing Policies*, Wellington: Centre for Housing Research Aotearoa New Zealand (CHRANZ).

showing how family trust ownership has grown in popularity as a way of protecting the family asset base accumulated, mostly, from house ownership.

Property purchase for investment purposes was boosted by the popularity of this form of investment among baby boomers with spare cash. Financial capacity for this cohort resulted from the move into the 'cash rich' stage of the life course, with most baby boomers having discharged the mortgage on their family home. One consequence of this was that rents rose more slowly than the cost of owning, so did not become as unaffordable as buying a house. This opened up further the gap between the costs of renting and the costs of buying and contributed to the decline in home ownership over this period. A further factor affecting the cost of new housing was that the market concentrated upon the middle- to upper-income levels. With the average size of households falling but average floor area and number of bedrooms increasing, the demand for housing space from middle- to upper-income dual-earning households was a factor driving up the price of new housing (Statistics New Zealand, 2007a,b). In the latest boom, building focused on meeting the needs of those upgrading housing rather than on low-cost starter homes for first-time buyers.

Aggregate-level data are not the most revealing; rather, what are crucially changing are home ownership propensities, which are neither uniform across age groups, nor uniform for different household types with both the same and different levels of income (Yates, 2007). The structuring of tenure thus needs to be disaggregated so that cohort effects are clearer. One significant cohort effect that has been the subject of attention is the movement of the baby boom generation, with its high home ownership rates, into retirement. Important research questions here focus on accumulation through the life course of housing wealth and the impact of this on retirement years, wealth distributions and

intergenerational equity and transfers and release through reverse equity mortgages (Forrest and Murie, 1995; Hamnett *et al.*, 1991; Venti and Wise, 1987). If
the rising cohort has a falling rate of home ownership there may be fewer buyers
for houses when the older generation would like to trade down and release
equity and move into retirement accommodation, such as retirement villages
or supported care. This could seriously affect their wealth expectations in the
retirement years (Burke, 2007; Davey *et al.*, 2004).

A decline in home ownership rates is now being observed in a number of
home-owning countries, including Japan, Australia and New Zealand, in the
rising cohort of younger people (Hirayama and Ronald, 2008; Burke, 2007;
Morrison, 2008; Yates, 2007). In New Zealand rates have declined unevenly
across the age groups, with the impact being felt most by those in the 25–29
and 30–34 age groups. Between 1986 and 2006 home ownership rates fell
17.9 per cent in the 25–29 age group and 17.7 per cent in the 30–34 age group
(Government House Prices Unit, 2008). The next largest falls were in the 35–39
group (15.5 per cent) and the 40–44 age group (12.2 per cent). The time to
acquire home ownership for these younger age groups is thus lengthening, with
consequences for when they are likely to be mortgage free. Such trends produce
quite a different profile of wealth acquisition from that of those who entered
home ownership in their early twenties. In the period between the census of
2001 and 2006 the only group to increase their rate of home ownership was the
over 75 age group (New Zealand Ministry of Social Development, 2008).

The current projections suggest that the number of owner-occupier households in older age groups will increase and those in the under 40 age group are
likely to decline by 17 per cent by 2016 (DTZ New Zealand, 2005). Younger
households have been particularly affected as the cost of entering the housing
market has risen, with increases of 39–60 per cent from 2000 to 2005 (Grimes
et al., 2007), and increases of 88–131 per cent from 1996 to 2005 being sustained
in the Auckland regional market. These changes may represent a lagged or permanent structural change. However, further research will be required to answer
this question adequately (Morrison, 2008).

Australian data show a similar pattern of decline in age-specific home ownership rates for younger households. From 1976 to 2001 there was an 11 per cent
decline in home ownership rates amongst the 25–29 age group, from 54 per cent
to 43 per cent. A 10 per cent decline was observed for the 30–34 group, from 67
per cent to 57 per cent, and a 6 per cent fall for the 34–39 group (Yates, 2007).
As in New Zealand it was the baby boomer generation that benefited most from
home ownership, and there is growing concern that the current rising generation will not be able to make their way into home ownership given the high cost
of entry. Further, the implications of a concentration of land and housing accumulation for overall levels of inequality, wealth distributions, transfers across
generations and investment in the economy have significant distributional
consequences and reinforce existing patterns of social inequality. Some specific
factors that created upward pressure in Australia included changes to the capital

tax regime and the introduction of the First Home Owner grants to compensate for the introduction of a goods and services tax in 2000. Boom conditions in the early 2000s dramatically increased the house price-to-income ratio in Australia as in New Zealand, making housing for many aspiring owners unaffordable.

New Zealand has significant differences in home ownership rates by ethnicity. In 1986 the European rate was 76.4 per cent and by 2006 this had declined to 70.5 per cent. However, for the Māori population the rates were 49.2 per cent and 42.5 per cent respectively, and for Pacific peoples the fall was from 44.4 per cent to 34.1 per cent. So a similar trend has occurred across all major ethnic groups but starting from a lower base. A declining rate further opens up the gap between those owning across the major ethnic groups that comprise the New Zealand population. The cost of entering appears to be the most crucial factor across all groups as this has been rising steeply during the latest boom period, up by 60 per cent from 2000 to 2005 and up by 131 per cent over the ten years from 1996 to 2005.

In recent New Zealand research one identified outcome of these changes is the emergence of an intermediate market defined as working households unable to purchase a dwelling at the lower quartile house price under standard bank lending criteria. The relative size of the intermediate housing market (IHM) is a measure of housing affordability for first-time buyers (DTZ New Zealand, 2007, 2008). This group falls outside state assistance but has too low an income and accumulation potential to access the prohibitive home ownership market. The size of the intermediate market provides an indicative measure of the number of households being left behind by the housing market as they can no longer afford to buy a dwelling. The data show that the size of this market fell from 1996 to 2001, largely because of a 3.3 per cent fall in interest rates, but then increased by 239 per cent between 2001 and 2006 because of a combination of higher house prices, up 72 per cent, and a steady increase in interest rates (DTZ New Zealand, 2007, 2008). The IHM numbers then increased considerably from 72,300 to 187,000 between 2001 and 2006. Of this total, 36 per cent were in Auckland. The IHM is concentrated in single and two-parent households in which there are two or fewer income sources and the reference person is under 40 and in a lower-income occupation. The size of this sector of the market is predicted to grow considerably up until 2016 as the recent boom and emerging downturn in the economy and housing market take effect. By 2016 the total numbers could be between 165,100 and 282,332 depending on whether an assumption of low or high nominal house price growth is made (DTZ New Zealand, 2008).

Structural change or short-term adjustment: dilemmas for policy development

The cooling of the boom and the downturn in prices has been as dramatic as the rise. The failure of the subprime mortgage market in the United States and the string of failures of financial companies and institutions taking place across housing markets globally have led to a housing slump. In New Zealand over the past two years there has been a string of failures of finance and investment companies, leaving many investors with frozen funds or facing substantial investment losses. Many of the failures have been in the consumption sector and in hire purchase on goods and motor vehicles, but this has now flowed through into the housing sector. People who over-committed themselves on the assumption that house prices were going to keep rising are now being forced to sell at a loss. House prices during the 2007 to mid-2009 downturn in New Zealand appear to have fallen by around 10 per cent less than the 20 per cent predicted, with signs of a market starting to increase again by September 2009. This has created concern in the Reserve Bank that the 'kiwi's love affair with housing' has not been dimmed by the falling market during the downturn but is reappearing again and deflecting investment into housing rather than other areas of the economy. The Real Estate Institute of New Zealand has calculated that housing prices have more than tripled since 1992, with an average rate of return of 11.8 per cent, whereas shares have returned an average of 7 per cent but suffered a much greater decline than housing in the latest slump. The 'over-zealous housing investment' has created renewed policy interest in capital gains and land speculation taxes, but as yet no changes have been proposed to the current system, which does not include a tax on capital gains from housing transactions.

Predictions are difficult in the growing climate of financial uncertainty and in the wake of financial institution failure in the United States and United Kingdom, and, moreover, demand for greater world financial reform and regulation to prevent a repeat of the current market failures. Financial failures and the decline in confidence in the banking system persist and have a global impact. The effects of these failures and the decline in confidence, because of the increasingly interconnected world of global finance, are being felt in the Australian and New Zealand housing market. This will affect the money available for loans through the banking system and the cost and also impact upon the house-building industry, with a decline in building activity and permits already becoming apparent. This in turn is leading to speculation that there will be a future housing shortage that will feed through into rising prices. Interest rates are likely to continue to be higher than official bank rates because of the cost of money that local banks have to borrow on the global market. So although house prices have fallen, it is difficult to estimate the likely effect on affordability and whether home ownership rates will again rise or continue to decline as greater numbers can no longer afford to enter this sector of the market.

This raises questions about what is the key driver of the changes that are showing in the home ownership rates. Are we seeing a structural shift created by global economic changes and the booms and slumps of housing markets, or is it the result of cohort life-course changes? Such changes are part structural and part related to life cycle choices and career mobility, which for some now involves transnational migration. Or is it simply a case of deferment until conditions once again become more favourable? A further factor in the deferment argument in New Zealand and Australia is the impact of the repayment of student loans, as these have to be repaid once the person with the loan enters the workforce.

With respect to New Zealand government polices, there has been an expansion of the public rental stock,[6] but this still accounts for only 5.5 per cent of all housing. The demand-side assistance is still the most significant housing support programme linked with the tax credit system of working for families. These do provide income support and thus contribute to reducing housing costs. For those seeking to enter the home ownership market, credit is likely to become harder to secure in the wake of the credit crunch and higher initial deposits will be required by a more nervous banking system.[7] Consequently, the possibility for low-income households to save enough to move into home ownership will further decline, creating a growing pool of people for whom rental will be a long-term option. Building an adequate pool of private rental stock for this sector will be a major challenge. Government initiatives to address the deposit gap have included welcome home loans, trialling equity share schemes in some of the most expensive locations and introducing a 'kiwi saver' that enables a proportion of the saving, after a defined period, to be used towards a deposit (Thorns, 2009). The extent of the fall in house prices and mortgage costs and the path of wage growth are critical in determining whether this will be sufficient to enable a tenure move by the lowest income households and those making up the growing 'intermediate' housing market.

Each of the possible future scenarios would have different outcomes. The dilemma for public policy is that because so much uncertainty exists it is difficult to work out the 'best' options. One thing is clear: the 'experiment' with using monetary policy by the central banks as the only lever to control inflation within a national context appears to have failed to avert instability in the housing market or to dampen down price surges (PricewaterhouseCoopers, 2009).

The New Zealand Housing Strategy, which was the guide for government policy settings, and which is now under review with the change to the New Zealand government, had embraced the need to link housing and broader economic policy and so had begun a move to investigate ways of trying to create more low cost housing for purchase and rent. These included the Housing Affordability legislation, introduced into Parliament at the end of 2007 and passed into law in 2008,[8] that seeks to encourage local councils to take initiatives around mixed-use development and include some component of 'affordable housing' in new developments. The Labour-led government at that time embarked on new development projects on land released from other public use and community renewal of areas of older stock and run-down facilities. This greater degree of intervention marks a further shift from the policies pursued during the 1990s, which were largely reliant on market mechanisms. Many of these initiatives are in danger of being overwhelmed by rapidly changing market conditions, as the effects of the global financial crisis bite and resulting from the more neo-liberal orientation of the present National Party-led administration.

Significant questions arise over the long-run viability of home ownership under the changed conditions of the post-boom credit squeeze and subsequent policy responses to the declining rate of home ownership. Political and public sentiment in New Zealand still supports home ownership as the preferred form of tenure for both social and economic reasons. However, its attainment may now be shaped even more by intergenerational inequalities and transfers, and broader global and local economic and social policy settings, as much as by housing-focused policies. Policies relating to tax, economic development, sustainability, labour markets and income support are as significant in ensuring that housing is affordable and that people can exercise choices as to their tenure preferences as specific housing policies. Working towards whole-of-government solutions requires greater integration across public policies to meet the needs of an increasingly diverse population. Further analysis needs to combine a macro-structural analysis with one that enables an understanding of the cohort experiences and life-course changes that are taking place. Without such a combination our understanding will at best be only partial and policy making will be limited.

References

Ansley, B. (2001) Home truths, *New Zealand Listener*, 20 January, 18–23.
Arcus, M. and Nana, G. (2005) *Intergenerational and Interfamilial Transfers of Wealth*, Wellington: Centre for Housing Research Aotearoa New Zealand.
Badcock, B. and Beer, A. (2000) *Home Truths: Property Ownership and Housing Wealth in Australia*, Carlton, Victoria: Melbourne University Press.
Burke, T. (2007) *Experiencing the Housing Affordability Problem: Blocked Aspirations, Trade-offs and Financial Hardships*, Research Paper No. 9, Melbourne: Australian Housing and Urban Research Institute.
Campbell, S. and Thorns, D.C. (2001/2) Changes to New Zealand housing policy at the beginning and end of the 1990s, *Housing Finance Review*, 11–17, York: Joseph Rowntree Foundation.
Davey, J., de Joux, V., Nana, G. and Arcus, M. (June 2004) *Accommodation Options for Older People in Aotearoa/New Zealand*, New Zealand Institute for Research on Ageing, Wellington: Centre for Housing Research Aotearoa New Zealand.
Davidson, A. (1994) *A Home of One's Own; Housing Policy in Sweden and New Zealand, from the 1840s to the 1990s*, Stockholm: Almqvist and Wiksell.
de Bruin, A. and Dupuis, A. (1995) *The Implications of Housing Policy for Women in Non-Nuclear Families*, paper presented at the Eighteenth Conference of the NZ Geographical Society, University of Canterbury, Christchurch.
Dupuis, A. (1992) Financial gains from owner occupation. The New Zealand case 1970–1988, *Housing Studies*, 7(1), 27–44.
Dupuis, A. and Thorns, D.C. (1998) Home ownership and the search for ontological security, *Sociological Review*, 46(1), 24–47.
DTZ New Zealand (2005) *Housing Tenure Aspirations and Attainment*, Wellington: Centre for Housing Research Aotearoa New Zealand.

DTZ New Zealand (2007) *The Future of Home Ownership and the Role of the Private Rental Market in the Auckland Region*, Wellington: Centre for Housing Research Aotearoa New Zealand.

DTZ New Zealand (2008) *The Intermediate Housing Market in New Zealand*, Wellington: Centre for Housing Research Aotearoa New Zealand.

Ferguson, G. (1994) *Building the New Zealand Dream*, Palmerston North: Dunmore Press.

Forrest, R. and Murie, A. (eds) (1995) *Housing and Family Wealth in Comparative Perspective*, London: Routledge.

Forrest, R. and Kennett, T. (1996) Coping strategies, housing careers and households with negative equity, *Journal of Social Policy*, 25(3), 369–394.

Gorman-Murray, A. and Dowling, R. (eds) (2007) Home, *M/C Journal*, 10(4). Online. Available at http://journal.media-culture.org.au/0708/01-editorial.php (accessed 23 April 2008).

Government House Prices Unit (2008) *Final Report of House Prices Unit: House Price Increases and Housing in New Zealand*, Wellington: Department of Prime Minister and Cabinet.

Grimes, A., Aitken, A., Mitchell, I. and Smith, V. (2007) *Housing Supply in the Auckland Region*, Wellington: Centre for Housing Research Aotearoa New Zealand.

Gurney, C. (1990) *The Meaning of Home in the Decade of Owner Occupation: Towards an Experiential Perspective*, Working Paper 88, Bristol: School of Advanced Urban Studies, University of Bristol.

Hamnett, C. (1999) *Winners and Losers: Home Ownership in Modern Britain*, London: University College London Press.

Hamnett, C., Hamer, M. and Williams, P. (1991) *Safe as Houses, Housing Inheritance in Britain*, London: Paul Chapman.

Hawke, G. (1985) *The Making of New Zealand*, Cambridge: Cambridge University Press.

Hirayama, Y. and Ronald, R. (2008) Baby boomers, baby busters and the lost generation: generational fractures in Japan's homeowner society, *Urban Policy and Research*, 26(3), 325–342.

Holland, K. (2008) America in turmoil as credit crisis firms its grip, *Christchurch Press*, 22 September, A7.

Kemp, P. (1998) *Review of Housing Allowances*, Wellington: Ministry of Housing.

Kendig, H. (1984) Housing careers, life-cycle and residential mobility: implications for the housing market, *Urban Studies*, 21(3), 271–283.

Marcus Cooper, C. (1995) *House as a Mirror of Self*, Berkeley, CA: Conari Press.

Ministry of Social Development (2008) *Social Report*, Wellington: Ministry of Social Development.

Mitchell, G. (2000) The industry time forgot, in P. Troy (ed.) *A History of European Housing in Australia*, Cambridge: Cambridge University Press.

Morrison, P. (2008) *On the Falling Rate of Home Ownership*, Wellington: Centre for Housing Research Aotearoa New Zealand.

Murphy, L. (1997) New Zealand's housing reforms and Accommodation Supplement experience, *Urban Policy and Research*, 15(4), 269–278.

Murphy, L. (1999) Housing policy, in J. Boston, P. Dalziel and S. St John (eds) *Redesigning the Welfare State in New Zealand*, Auckland: Oxford University Press.

New Zealand Housing Strategy (2004) *Building the Future: Towards a New Zealand Housing Strategy (Draft for Discussion)*, Wellington: HNZC.

New Zealand Housing Strategy (2005) *Building the Future: The New Zealand Housing Strategy*, Wellington: HNZC.

New Zealand Ministry of Social Development (2008) Ministry of Social Development 2008 social report. Online. Available at http://www.msd.govt.nz/about-msd-and-our-work/newsroom/factsheets/social-report/

Oliver, W.H (1968) *The Story of New Zealand*, London: Faber and Faber.

Perkins, H. and Thorns, D.C (2003) The making of home in a global world, in R. Forrest and J. Lee (ed.) *Housing and Social Change: East–West Perspectives*, London: Routledge.

PricewaterhouseCoopers (2009) *New Zealand Monetary Policy and the Residential Housing Market – a Scoping Study*, Wellington: Centre for Housing Research Aotearoa New Zealand.

Putnam R.D. (2000) *Bowling Alone: The Collapse and Revival of American Community*, New York: Simon & Schuster.

Rossi, P. (1955) *Why Families Move*, Glencoe, IL: Free Press.

Statistics New Zealand (2007a) *QuickStats About Housing, 2006 Census*, Wellington: Statistics New Zealand.

Statistics New Zealand (2007b) *QuickStats About Population and Dwellings*, Wellington: Statistics New Zealand.

Stone, M.E. (2009) *Housing and the Financial Crisis*, paper presented at the Australasian Housing Researchers Conference, Sydney, August.

stuff.co.nz (2008) Affordable housing heating up as election issue. Online. Available at http://www.stuff.co.nz/363194/Affordable-housing-heating-up-as-election-issue (accessed April 2009).

Thompson, D. (1996) *Selfish Generations? How Welfare States Grow Old*, Cambridge: White Horse Press.

Thorns, D.C. (1993) Tenure and wealth accumulation: implications for housing policy, in P. Koopman-Boyden (ed.) *New Zealand's Ageing Society*, Wellington: Daphne Brasell Associates Press.

Thorns, D.C. (2000) Housing policy in the 1990s: New Zealand a decade of change, *Housing Studies*, 15(1), 129–138.

Thorns, D.C. (2007) The New Zealand experience of housing allowances, in P. Kemp (ed.) *Housing Allowances in Comparative Perspective*, Bristol: Policy Press.

Thorns, D.C. (2009) Housing booms and changes to housing affordability: the policy challenge, *Journal of Asian Public Policy*, 2(2), 171–189.

Venti, S. and Wise, D. (1987) *Aging, Moving, and Housing Wealth*, Cambridge, MA: National Bureau of Economic Research.

Winstanley, A. (2001) *Housing, Home and Women's Identities*, PhD thesis, University of Canterbury.

Winstanley, A., Thorns, D.C. and Perkins, H. (2002) Creating home: exploring residential mobility, *Housing Studies*, 17(6), 813–832.

Yates, J. (2007) *Affordability and Access to Home Ownership, Past, Present and Future?*, Research Report No. 10, Melbourne: Australian Housing and Urban Institute.

NOTES

1 Beyond home ownership

1 Although home ownership is the minority tenure overall, most middle-aged and elderly people own their homes and many better-off urban renters own residential property elsewhere and let it out on a commercial basis (see Helbrecht and Geilenkeuser, 2010).

2 Such as mortgage interest tax relief, although it is rarely explicitly designated as a subsidy. In the Netherlands, for example, this facility for homeowners currently costs the government more than €14 billion a year compared with a housing allowance bill, for low-income renters, of between €2 billion and €3 billion.

3 More than 2.5 million US homes were foreclosed between December 2007 and October 2010.

4 In the United Kingdom, Sweden, Denmark and Austria almost one in five households is still housed in social rental housing (and one in three in the Netherlands). Germany and Switzerland are notable exceptions as housing needs have been met by measures applied in the private rental sector.

5 It is further suggested that in contexts in which home ownership dominates there is likely to be greater resistance to the high taxes necessary to support generous public welfare programmes, with homeowners already pressed by mortgage repayment costs. Voters may also be inclined to back those governments that support conditions for private capital accumulation via the housing market (Watson, 2009).

6 HomeBuy is the common term used for the various shared ownership and affordable housing schemes in the United Kingdom.

7 A particularly good example is the Thatcher government, which was actually spending more on housing subsidies (specifically in the form of housing benefits for low-income renters) ten years after right to buy, and more on public welfare spending overall.

8 For example, Support for Mortgage Interest (SMI) in the United Kingdom and the Housing Rescue Plan in the United States. In total, $75 billion of the Obama administration economic rescue package is directed to housing and supporting households in arrears (see *Washington Post*, 2009).

9 This term demographically denotes the post-war surge in births, but also culturally denotes a less traditionally minded group with shared experiences of the post-war and contemporary world.

10 Denmark, Norway, Sweden, Finland and Iceland.

3 The housing pillar of the Mediterranean welfare regime

1 Countries considered are Greece, Italy, Portugal and Spain. 'Post-socialist' Southern European countries and France are not discussed here for simplicity of analysis. In the former case, detailed discussion would be required on the two economic and political transitions experienced in these countries during the twentieth century (see Mandic, Chapter 4, this volume). As regards France, characteristics common to other Continental European countries – low home ownership rate, a large social housing sector and a highly professionalized housing development industry – interact with features common to Mediterranean countries, such as the role of informal practices and family support in the social production of home ownership. The French housing system can thus be considered a kind of mixed model combining features shared by both groups of countries.

2 Also for settlement by immigrants.

3 Under Italian law it is possible to ask for an end-of-lease eviction without any specific cause being necessary apart from expiry of the lease. This form of eviction was widely used when strict rent regulations were in force (1978–93) as a way to evade rent control by threatening current tenants with non-renewal of the lease if they refused to pay more than the rent fixed by the law and/or as a way to find new, more accommodating tenants.

4 More recent trends concerning workers in house building and labourers in agriculture are at least partially due to changes in the composition of these groups, given that house building and agriculture are two of the main sectors in which foreign immigrants work. However, it is unlikely that this significantly affects the findings for the period 1951–91, because foreign immigration into Italy has almost entirely taken place in the past two decades.

5 A third important factor was the movement by investors of their assets from the financial market to real estate during the crisis that followed the September 2001 terrorist attack in New York.

6 http://www.bancaditalia.it/statistiche/indcamp/bls (accessed 25 August 2011).

4 Home ownership in post-socialist countries

1 The European Quality of Life Survey, 2003 was carried out in the 15 EU member states before May 2004 (EU15), the ten acceding countries becoming new member states in May 2004, and the three candidate countries (Bulgaria, Romania and Turkey). The questionnaire covered a number of life domains, such as working conditions, housing and family, and other domains, and provided fully cross-nationally comparable information. The population interviewed was adults aged 18 years and over who were residents in the 28 countries in 2003. A multi-stage stratified random sampling procedure was used with 1,000 interviews conducted in the larger countries and 500 in the smaller ones. Data were collected by face-to-face interview. Weighting variables were produced according to age, gender and region within the country.

5 Home ownership and Nordic housing policies in 'retrenchment'

1 The results of this project were published in 2006 in a Swedish-language book titled *Varför så olika? Nordisk bostadspolitik i jämförande historiskt ljus* [*Why so Different? Nordic Housing Policies in Comparative Historical Light*] (Bengtsson (ed.), Annaniassen, Jensen, Ruonavaara and Sveinsson, 2006).

2 Editor and project leader.

3 This chapter written by Karlberg and Victorin is for the same comparative study from which Lujanen's statement of the common foundation of Nordic housing policies is taken.

4 This distinction between market and social or non-market home ownership is analytically distinct from the difference between direct and indirect forms of owner-occupation. Both indirect and direct forms can be market or social housing.

7 Home ownership as public policy in the United States

1 According to Decker (1992), the ethical doctrine of the "American Dream" emerged as a symptom of loss and identity confusion during the Great Depression.
2 However, this did not pertain to all white men. Catholics, Jews, Quakers, and others were excluded. In 1792 New Hampshire was the first state to abolish the rule requiring property ownership, but it took another 64 years for the last of the states, North Carolina, to follow.
3 A rural home ownership program (Section 502) was authorized in the Housing Act of 1949. In addition, two small-scale urban-focused federal programs preceded the Section 235 program. In 1965 a program was created to enable public housing tenants to purchase their units and in 1966 Section 221(h) provided low-income households with the opportunity to buy previously substandard houses from non-profit sponsors after they had been purchased and rehabilitated by these entities (U.S. Commission on Civil Rights, 1971, p. 4).
4 Reflecting on the 1990s, the Millennial Housing Commission (2002) noted that "the number of lower-income home owners increased by about 2.5 million, African-American owners by about 1.2 million, and Hispanic owners by about 1.2 million" from 1994 to 2000 (p. 21).
5 Only 11 percent of the 5.4 million units that receive direct federal housing assistance are owner-occupied. The Section 502 Rural Homeownership Program comprises the great majority of these households (547,622). The now-defunct Section 235 program still assists 31,176 households (Millennial Housing Commission, 2002, pp. 95, 111–112).
6 Of those earning less than 80 percent of area median income, about 42 percent are homeowners; among those earning greater than 80 percent of median income, 78 percent are homeowners (calculated from National Low Income Housing Coalition, 2001). Three-quarters of all white households own their own homes, compared with 48.4 percent of black households and 47.4 percent of Hispanic households (Joint Center for Housing Studies, 2004, p. 35).
7 The federal HOME program (a block grant program for housing) also has included extra funding for down-payment assistance. More generally, both the HOME and Housing Choice Voucher programs allow funds to be used for home ownership; however, these programs provide only modest subsidies.
8 George W. Bush, Proclamation 8263, National Homeownership Month, 2008, May 29.
9 A similar tax credit had been proposed by the Millennial Housing Commission. It justified this approach with the observation that: "The advantage of the home ownership tax credit over direct subsidy programs is that it devolves authority to states and relies on private-sector partners to deliver allocated resources" (Millennial Housing Commission, 2002, p. 31).
10 Although promoting home ownership opportunities for women has not been a traditional goal of home ownership programs, foreclosures stemming from subprime loans appear to be having a disproportionately negative impact on this population (Leland, 2008).
11 There are now only two of the big five investment firms still in business: Morgan Stanley and Goldman Sachs. However, both are being converted to bank holding companies, effectively ending the era of the large Wall Street investment firms.
12 A new financial reform law was enacted on July 21, 2010, the Dodd–Frank Wall Street Reform and Consumer Protection Act.

8 Home ownership risk and responsibility before and after the U.S. mortgage crisis

1 GSEs made loan purchases in two ways: either for securitization for their own port-folios or as investments in residential mortgage-backed securities (RMBS) originated by investment firms. Of the former, the majority of loan purchases were prime mort-gages (perhaps around 85 percent). GSEs did, however, purchase subprime loans through RMBS issued by Wall Street investment houses, which often were rated, unrealistically, AAA. Such RMBS could be counted toward GSEs' affordable housing targets. Notwithstanding affordable housing goals, as these higher-risk RMBS paid higher returns than other RMBS, and given the considerable pressure on GSEs to realize profits, the GSEs were attracted to these investments in their own right. In 2007, Freddie Mac offered to stop making investments in subprime RMBS. Shortly thereafter, both GSEs were ordered to stop. This information is based on private email communications from Dan Immergluck, July 1 and 9, 2009 (cited with permission).
2 Stone (1986) predicted a similar scenario even earlier.
3 For additional information on the federal responses, see http://www.recovery.gov/, http://www.ustreas.gov/press/releases/tg33.htm and Congressional Oversight Panel (2009).
4 A new financial reform law was enacted on July 21, 2010, the Dodd–Frank Wall Street Reform and Consumer Protection Act. Although it remains to be seen whether the changes contained in this legislation will adequately address the range of problems identified during the mortgage crisis, early reports were discouraging. With intense opposition to the law by Republican members of Congress, guidelines for imple-mentation were slow in coming and President Obama's first choice to head the new consumer protection agency, Elizabeth Warren, appeared unlikely to be confirmed by the Congress.
5 This takes into account future changes in interest rates that may occur on adjustable or variable rate loans.
6 The recommendations in the text were written prior to the enactment of the Dodd–Frank Wall Street Reform and Consumer Protection Act. As stated in note 4, this law attempted to address many of the problems associated with the mortgage crisis and includes: increased government oversight for "systemically important" financial institutions; an overhaul of the rules governing the marketing of derivatives; the creation of a new Consumer Financial Protection Bureau; instituting new capital requirements for banks; and requiring mortgage originators, such as mortgage com-panies, to retain some of the risk after the loan is sold.

10 Home ownership – continuing or fading dream?

1 The subprime mortgage market was an innovation of the late twentieth century whereby home loans were issued to people who would not previously have qualified because of poor credit history, inability to make a down payment or low income. An extreme example is 'ninja' loans issued to borrowers with no income, no job and no assets (Holland, 2008).
2 Explanations of how dwelling values are calculated by Quotable Value Ltd (QV), the way the QV house price index is derived, how the Reserve Bank of New Zealand compiles the long-run housing stock series and house price data may all be found, respectively, at the following websites: http://www.rbnz.govt.nz/keygraphs/1697998.html; http://www.rbnz.govt.nz/keygraphs/1697975.html; and http://www.rbnz.govt.nz/keygraphs/1689413.html.
3 The house price index for each quarter is released in the fourth month following that quarter. The dwelling value estimates are disseminated with a similar lag. The 'housing stock' value (excluding chattels) illustrated includes all private sector resi-dential dwellings – detached houses, flats and apartments, 'lifestyle blocks' (with a

dwelling), detached houses converted to flats and 'home and income' properties – more than 1,450,000 as of December 2005. Farm and publicly owned dwellings are not included. Although changes in the imputed price of existing dwellings drive most of the increase in the housing stock value, the annual amount spent on *new* dwellings (including land) in 2007 is estimated by the Bank to have exceeded $15 billion.

4 Statistics New Zealand data presented to the Select Committee on Affordable housing in 2007. See http://www.parliament.nz/en-NZ/PB/SC/MakeSub/0/7/9/07969b38 02794267b7bc7e256abe6037.htm.

5 These countries were selected as data were available at the three dates chosen to show trends over the 1960–2003 period.

6 The current holding is 69,000 rental units, which is 80 per cent of all social housing – and 5.5 per cent of the total housing stock; however, the National Party-led government that came to power in November 2008 announced a plan in September 2009 to reintroduce selling state houses to tenants to give them an opportunity to achieve ownership.

7 Suggestions in the media are that there are up to 130,000 people exposed to negative equity.

8 The Affordable Housing: Enabling Territorial Authorities Act 2008 gives territorial authorities new enabling powers to require developers to include affordable housing in their developments, make payments towards the cost of providing affordable housing elsewhere or provide land for the construction of affordable housing.

INDEX